WORKING TOWARDS EQUITY

Disability Rights Activism and Employment in Late Twentieth-Century Canada

In *Working towards Equity*, Dustin Galer argues that paid work significantly shaped the experience of disability during the late twentieth century. By investigating and analysing archival records, personal collections, government publications, and a series of interviews, Galer demonstrates how demands for greater access to gainful employment from disabled people stimulated the development of a new discourse of disability in Canada.

Family advocates helped people living in institutions move out into the community as rehabilitation professionals played an increasingly critical role in the lives of working-age adults with disabilities. Meanwhile, civil rights activists crafted a new consumer-led vision of social and economic integration. Employment was, and remains, a central component in disabled peoples' efforts to become productive, autonomous, and financially secure members of Canadian society. *Working towards Equity* offers new in-depth analysis on rights activism as it relates to employment, sheltered workshops, deinstitutionalization, and labour markets in the contemporary context in Canada.

DUSTIN GALER received his PhD in history from the University of Toronto. He is the founder of MyHistorian (www.myhistorian.ca) where he works as a personal historian.

T0260474

Working towards Equity

Disability Rights Activism and Employment in Late Twentieth-Century Canada

DUSTIN GALER

UNIVERSITY OF TORONTO PRESS
Toronto Buffalo London

© University of Toronto Press 2018
Toronto Buffalo London
utorontopress.com

ISBN 978-1-4875-0131-0 (cloth)   ISBN 978-1-4875-2130-1 (paper)

Library and Archives Canada Cataloguing in Publication

Galer, Dustin, 1983–, author
Working towards equity: disability rights activism and employment in late
twentieth-century Canada/Dustin Galer.

Includes bibliographical references and index.
ISBN 978-1-4875-0131-0 (hardcover)   ISBN 978-1-4875-2130-1 (softcover)

1. People with disabilities – Civil rights – Canada – History – 20th century.
2. People with disabilities – Legal status, laws, etc. – Canada – History –
20th century.   3. People with disabilities – Employment – Canada – History –
20th century.   I. Title.

HV1559.C3G36 2018   362.40971   C2017-907099-1

This book has been published with the help of a grant from the Federation
for the Humanities and Social Sciences, through the Awards to Scholarly
Publications Program, using funds provided by the Social Sciences
and Humanities Research Council of Canada.

University of Toronto Press acknowledges the financial assistance to
its publishing program of the Canada Council for the Arts and the Ontario
Arts Council, an agency of the Government of Ontario.

Canada Council   Conseil des Arts
for the Arts   du Canada

Funded by the   Financé par le
Government   gouvernement
of Canada   du Canada

ONTARIO ARTS COUNCIL
CONSEIL DES ARTS DE L'ONTARIO
an Ontario government agency
un organisme du gouvernement de l'Ontario

To my family

Contents

Illustrations

Acknowledgments

I wish to extend my appreciation to an array of people who helped make this project possible. Ian Radforth was an exceptional mentor for this project and I thank him sincerely for his support and guidance. Thanks also to Geoffrey Reaume, Dan Bender, Ravi Malhotra, Len Husband, and the anonymous reviewers, whose critical commentary and supportive feedback strengthened the final product.

I would like to thank all the interview participants for taking the time to share their work experiences, thoughts, and beliefs with me. Your personal narratives illuminated new avenues of inquiry and greatly deepened my understanding of living with disability that is not necessarily stored and secured in an archive. I appreciate the generosity of Rob McInnes, Gary Annable, and Joanne Smith for entrusting me with the temporary care of their personal collections of documents and multimedia. Thanks are also due to the many archivists and privacy officials at Library and Archives Canada, Archives of Ontario, Archives of Manitoba, and Toronto Archives for helping me navigate the process of locating and accessing restricted records.

Thank you to my friends and family for commenting on various aspects of my research and, most important, allowing me to bounce around new ideas. I owe an insurmountable debt of gratitude to my parental units, Wayne and Sheri, for their unwavering support. Thanks also to my partner, Andreas Vatiliotou. His love, patience, and dedication were matched by his writing and editorial skills, which he gave generously in times of need at various stages of the project. You motivate me to think more critically, to write more clearly, and to learn how to put things in perspective. Thanks are due in particular to my sister,

whose trials and successes turned me on to the study of disability issues. Azure-Lee, you have enriched the lives of those around you and
become a constant teacher in mine.

Abbreviations

ACCD	American Coalition of Citizens with Disabilities
ADA	Americans with Disabilities Act
AMEIPH	Association multiethnique pour l'intégration des personnes handicapées
AODA	Accessibility for Ontarians with Disabilities Act
ARCH	Advocacy Resource Centre for the Handicapped
BIDS	Business Industrial Development Strategies
BOOST	Blind Organization of Ontario with Self-Help Tactics
CACL	Canadian Association for Community Living
CAP	Canada Assistance Plan
CARP	Canadian Association of Rehabilitation Personnel
CCC	Canadian Chamber of Commerce
CCD	Council of Canadians with Disabilities
CCHA	Canadian Council on Hospital Accreditation
CCRW	Canadian Council on Rehabilitation and Work
CDW	Centre for Disability and Work
CEC	Canada Employment Centre
CEEPD	Coalition on Employment Equity for Persons with Disabilities
CEIC	Canada Employment and Immigration Commission
CILT	Centre for Independent Living Toronto
CIWA	Canadian Injured Workers Alliance
CLC	Canadian Labour Congress
CLFDB	Canadian Labour Force Development Board
CMHA	Canadian Mental Health Association
CNIB	Canadian National Institute for the Blind
COPOH	Coalition of Provincial Organizations of the Handicapped

COTA	Community Occupational Therapy Association
CPP-D	Canada Pension Plan for the Disabled
CRCD	Canadian Rehabilitation Council for the Disabled
CUBSM	Canadian Union of Blind and Sighted Merchants
CUPE	Canadian Union of Public Employees
DARE	Daycare, Assessment, Rehabilitative Education
DASM	Developing Alternative Service Models
DAWN	DisAbled Women's Network
DNHW	Department of National Health and Welfare
DPEE	Disabled Persons for Employment Equity
DPPP	Disabled Persons Participation Program
DPU	Disabled Persons Unit
DRDP	Declaration on the Rights of Disabled Persons
DSA	Developmental Services Act
DVA	Department of Veterans Affairs
EEA	Employment Equity Act
EEC	Employment Equity Commission
EEO	Equal Opportunity Employment
EOP	Equal Opportunity Plan
ERDCO	Ethno-Racial Disabled Persons Coalition of Ontario
HALS	Health and Activity Limitation Survey
HEP	Handicapped Employment Program
HRDC	Human Resources Development Canada
HRSDC	Human Resources and Skills Development Canada
ICIDH	International Classification of Impairments, Disabilities and Handicaps
IL	Independent Living
IWC	Injured Workers' Consultants
IYDP	International Year of Disabled Persons
JAN	Job Accommodation Network
LPH	Lakeshore Psychiatric Hospital
MAMR	Metro [Toronto] Association for the Mentally Retarded
MCSS	Ministry of Community and Social Services
MORE	Mobilize Organize Represent and Educate
MPP	Member of Provincial Parliament
NAND	National Aboriginal Network on Disability
NDP	National Democratic Party
NUPGE	National Union of Public and General Employees
OACDI	Ontario Advisory Council for Disability Issues
OACPH	Ontario Advisory Council for the Physically Handicapped

ODA	Ontarians with Disabilities Act
ODP	Office for Disabled Persons
OFL	Ontario Federation of Labour
OFPH	Ontario Federation for the Physically Handicapped
OHRC	Ontario Human Rights Code
OMOD	Ontario March of Dimes
OPS	Ontario Public Service
OPSEU	Ontario Public Service Employees Union
PALS	Activity Limitation Survey
PC	Progressive Conservative
PCEH	President's Committee on the Employment of the Handicapped
PSAC	Public Service Alliance of Canada
PUSH	People United for Self-Help
PVA	Paralyzed Veterans Association
STEP	Supported Training and Employment Program
TCG	Training Coordinating Group for Persons with Disabilities
TASH	Technical Aids and Systems for the Handicapped
TILAC	Toronto Independent Living Advisory Committee
UHGO	United Handicapped Groups of Ontario
UIW	Union of Injured Workers
UN	United Nations
VRDP	Vocational Rehabilitation for Disabled Persons [Act]
VRS	Vocational Rehabilitation Services
VRSA	Vocational Rehabilitation Services Act
WHO	World Health Organization

WORKING TOWARDS EQUITY

Disability Rights Activism and Employment
in Late Twentieth-Century Canada

Introduction

The lived experience of disability in Canada during the late twentieth century revolved around work. Widespread unemployment and poverty among people with disabilities from the 1960s to the early 2000s were considered by disabled people, their allies, and governments to be the main obstacle to full social integration. Many working-age Canadians with disabilities existed in a perpetually liminal state during this period, as they were neither fully integrated nor completely outside the labour market. Disability activists and advocates of all stripes found that public declarations in support of disability issues had failed to produce significant measurable change in the overall labour market participation of disabled people. Some people with disabilities in Canada were captivated by contemporary civil rights movements involving other disenfranchised groups and sought to develop their own rights movement dedicated to achieving full participation in society. Indeed, a renewed perspective of disability, which departed from the long-standing acceptance of a largely negative ontology of disabled people, represented a compelling result of this period.[1] But was greater public awareness of barriers faced by disabled people enough to sustain concerted action on the part of employers and policymakers? Disability rights activists joined family advocates and rehabilitation professionals in transforming the field of employment for people with disabilities, while repeated awareness campaigns, new ideologies, and legislative protections de-emphasized a disability master status that dogged many Canadians with disabilities who were simply trying to live and work.[2]

Multiple disability movements, each with its own ideological position, political alliances, and socio-economic influences, emerged during this period and achieved varying levels of success. Predominantly middle-class parents of disabled children were among the first to challenge the institutionalized segregation of people with physical disabilities, intellectual disabilities, and mental health issues that had persisted since the construction of centralized residential institutions in the nineteenth century. Confronted with systemic barriers to the successful reintegration of their clientele, groups of rehabilitation professionals also formed a movement that built alliances with family advocates – and initially against disability rights activists – to establish and defend community-based service agencies in order to promote and facilitate disabled peoples' greater participation in the life of local communities. By the 1970s disabled people increasingly resisted the perceived paternalism of parent-based organizations and medical authorities, forming their own rights movement guided by a social model of disability.

Voices within these movements often clashed, given the varied background of advocates and activists and their influence on policymakers and the public. Rather than focusing on the differences separating these movements, however, this book sees disability advocacy and activism as part of a combined push to develop greater rights and opportunities for people with disabilities in the labour market and the broader community. This approach enables us to look beyond the parameters of a single ideology, group, or organization to perceive broader changes shaping the lived experience and public presentation of disability in the labour market. Indeed, certain government bureaus, some employers, labour leaders, and even ordinary individuals qualify as legitimate sites of disability rights activism. As this book demonstrates, public outrage regarding both the neglect and poor treatment of people with disabilities and the transformative possibilities of employment constructed bridges between disabled people and their varied allies. Struggles and alliances between disabled people and their advocates shaped the broader discourse of disability, which in turn influenced the actions of policymakers. Waves of awareness (and forgetfulness) about disability issues produced new changes in social attitudes and policy. While there were strongly contested ideas of the capabilities of disabled people for paid work during this period, there was also a shared desire for greater inclusion in its many definitions.

From the early 1960s to the turn of the twenty-first century people with disabilities and their allies endeavoured to reconstruct the social, political, and economic environment that sidelined many disabled people. The struggles of disabled people to secure certain rights and opportunities elicited several dilemmas. Should disability rights activists press for mandatory affirmative action and hiring quotas in order to force employers to comply with their emancipatory objectives? Was subtle reinforcement through hiring campaigns the way to go? Alternatively, could activists and disabled workers ride a wave of unprecedented awareness during the early 1980s that would carry them to new shores of economic prosperity? A lack of consensus on these and other long-term strategic issues was complicated by few enforceable political commitments with a life beyond the next election or business cycle. Successive policy and statistical reports throughout these four decades demonstrate a disturbing pattern of similar conclusions regarding chronic poverty and unemployment in the disability community coupled with a recurring set of similar recommendations for improvement. This book seeks to untangle rhetoric from reality regarding conceptual and strategic responses to the economic problem of disability during this period. Positioning various manifestations of disability activism alongside the activities of decision makers in the sphere of the labour market reveals new insights about the labour history of people with disabilities while filling substantive gaps in the historiography of disability and work in Canada.

What did economic liminality and exclusion from the labour market look like for most people with disabilities in Canada and how did small groups of disability activists and their allies politicize these struggles? Written as a social history of the disability community within the framework of critical disability studies, this book documents the histories of working and unemployed disabled people in Canada while situating these accounts in a wider context of social, political, and economic developments. Disability history shares social history's methodology of writing history from the "bottom-up," concerned primarily with the liberation of disabled characters and subjects from invisibility in the historiographical record. As Douglas Baynton famously remarked, "Disability is everywhere in history, once you begin looking for it, but conspicuously absent in the histories we write."[3] Baynton's observation – which has become something of a mantra for disability historians – suggests that our knowledge of disabled people as historical subjects and disability as an analytical category for historical inquiry is seriously lacking, presenting an enticing challenge to all historians to be more attentive to disability in the historical record.

Disability history operates from the perspective that disability is a social category of existence that can be incorporated into the historian's analytical toolbox alongside categories such as race, class, and gender.

In doing so, important questions are raised that warrant thoughtful consideration: Is disability a stable enough identity with which to draw historically contiguous lines between different eras? How can we equate physical impairment and mental health in the same category when each has its own particular history and subcategorization that define the lived experience of disability? In the past such concerns have perpetuated the scholarly disambiguation of disability and of disabled people within academic and medical discourse while preventing historians and other scholars from taking a more holistic approach to the study of disability. In her case for "another 'Other'" in a well-cited survey review piece on disability history, Catherine Kudlick demonstrates the power and possibilities for approaching disability as a social category, reminding us that "disability cuts across all races, classes, genders, nationalities, and generations because it can potentially happen to anyone at any time; an accident, a degenerative disease of the limbs, eyes, ears, or nervous system, can instantly transport someone into a new category of existence."[4] As many disability activists argue, we all are simply "temporarily able-bodied" (TAB) and disability likely seeps into other social categories, destabilizing personal identity and public social status.[5]

Labour has profoundly shaped the experience of health and impairment, particularly among middle- and working-class subjects, where the exchange of labour for wages is a defining feature of life in capitalist societies. Similar to disabled people, working bodies have also been conceived, classified, and subjugated as cultural constructs in industrial capitalist societies by a strictly utilitarian evaluation of physical and mental abilities.[6] Disability studies scholars employed a historical materialist approach in order to demonstrate how the birth of industrialization and rise of the working class was a key historical moment associated with the economic dislocation of disabled people.[7] Cultural ideals supporting judgment of physical and moral capabilities were heightened by the introduction of industrial capitalism, since workers were forced to compete more directly with each other for wages in an industrialized labour market. This economic system tended to marginalize people with disabilities who were unable to compete effectively with "able-bodied" workers, while casting unemployed disabled people as a social and economic "problem" and burden on others.[8] The "logic of capitalism" thus asserted itself in the classification and oppression of people whose bodies betrayed them in search and exchange of labour for wages.

This book examines the emergence during the 1970s of resistance to the "logical" systemic exclusion of disabled people from the labour market. It describes a national story with a particular emphasis on developments in the province of Ontario and city of Toronto, owing to the jurisdictional nature of the sources analysed and the relatively limited historiographical corpus upon which to build. Provincial governments were responsible for vocational rehabilitation, healthcare, and other social programming that often determined the employability of disabled people. Yet many of the key accomplishments of disability activists during the late twentieth century involved *national* coalitions of provincial organizations. The leading disability rights organization during this period, the Coalition of Provincial Organizations of the Handicapped (COPOH), was founded as an assembly of regional groups representing every province across the country, each defined by local politics. Key developments on the national stage were often determined by these provincial bodies and grass-roots organizing at the local level. This book also incorporates the oral narratives of people with disabilities whose diverse lived experiences of disability and individual work histories warranted a geographically scaled-down approach in order to improve comparability between research participants. Toronto does stand apart from other cities during this period, given its position as Canada's largest city, the seat of the largest provincial government, and an engine of national economic growth in the second half of the twentieth century. Toronto was also recognized in the national Federation of Canadian Municipalities as a pioneer and national leader in the introduction of progressive public sector employment practices. The city also helped popularize the implementation of physical accessibility measures such as curb cuts and ramps. By no means the definitive assessment of the relationship between disability activism and work in Canada, *Working towards Equity* presents an entry into uncharted historiographical terrain that will hopefully generate future studies in this area.

The temporal focus of this book allows for the examination of multiple generations of disabled peoples' working experiences in relation to an evolving context of disability activism and legislative reform. Conditions that gave rise to the introduction of unprecedented human rights protections in the early 1960s were not initially conducive to the promotion of disability rights. In the early 1960s pioneering human rights legislation, including the Canadian Bill of Rights and the Ontario Human Rights Code, were introduced as early measures to comprehensively address issues of discrimination through human rights legislation. However, both the Code and the Bill of Rights were seriously limited in that they did not include disability as a protected category and there was no serious attempt by a disability movement to press for such protections. At that time an evolving social movement of parents' groups worked to reconfigure popular beliefs about the limited capabilities of disabled people. But parent activists did not engage in an identity politics of disability, nor did they promote a movement seeking human and civil rights protections to enable disabled people to resist sources of segregation. The rise of organized disability rights activism during the late 1970s and early 1980s transformed the political landscape of disability, including the introduction and revision of provincial and federal human rights legislation. For the next quarter-century disability rights activists guided by a social model of disability struggled against political indifference and competing ideologies among disability advocates in order to dismantle barriers to full social and economic participation. By the turn of the twenty-first century an entirely different set of social, political, and cultural conditions surrounded the introduction of controversial disability rights legislation, including the Accessibility for Ontarians with Disabilities Act (AODA) with its goal of achieving "accessibility for Ontarians with disabilities with respect to goods, services, facilities, accommodation, employment, buildings, structures and premises on or before January 1, 2025." Yet the AODA, as well as other complaint-based legislation, attracted significant debate concerning the lack of enforcement, scaled-down target outcomes, and proposed efficacy when many of the same prejudices and troubling employment statistics persisted in the disability community.

As this book demonstrates, the political impact of temporally overlapping disability movements contributed to the redefinition of disability in the late twentieth century, even when those movements worked in conflict with one another. To date, the history of disability issues and policy reform has been largely autobiographical, penned by activists, sociologists, and former bureaucrats often discussing developments in which they were directly involved. Prior to the emergence of disability history and critical disability studies in Canada during the 1990s, disability movements were largely studied by political scientists and individual activists recounting experiences and observations drawn from their involvement in various disability organizations. Disability activists, many of whom went on to successful careers in the legal profession, education, and the public sector, have produced much of the existing literature on the evolution of the disability rights movement in Canada. Much of this historiography focuses on the central role disability organizations have played in the advancement of human rights and anti-discrimination legislation.[9]

Organizations of and for people with disabilities represented a consolidating force in the local and international disability community, but they are only part of the story. Christine Kelly argues against a simplistic description of "the" disability movement in Canada, proposing contemporary examples where disability activism existed outside the confines of organizations "of" and "for" people with disabilities.[10] There were legitimate examples of alternative forms of disability activism, including individual struggles against systemic barriers. Kelly raises valid criticisms of "the" disability rights movement, including the traditional perspective that there is a single, unified movement. Indeed, one of the central arguments in this manuscript is the existence of multiple, overlapping movements (parents, rehabilitation, consumer, independent living, labour) that used different approaches to advance disability rights. According to this approach, the boundaries of social movement activism include seemingly benign endeavours such as an individual's determination to succeed in the workplace against all odds. Analysis of the documented activities of disability organizations alongside individual narratives of people with disabilities reveals new lines of inquiry into the written record. As such, this manuscript unpacks "the" disability rights movement, noting that "circles of awareness" are often created around disabled individuals as they struggle and succeed in life. These circles have the effect of contributing to broader efforts to secure and protect disability rights and deserve to be studied as such.

There has been growing interest in the relationship between disability and work, both in Canadian scholarship and abroad, though much of it has been ahistorical. Disability studies scholars have examined the relationships between disability and work, focusing on various aspects of the cultural construction of a "burden narrative" and its impact on people with disabilities.[11] *Working towards Equity* builds on this body of scholarship by revisiting key political developments as they relate to the progression of a new social and economic paradigm of disability not based on the concept of burden. Rather than conceptualizing the evolution of disability movements as a series of incremental and progressive developments, this book finds repeated waves of public and political awareness that produced a halting and uneven approach to the advancement of disability rights. A lack of consistent attention to disability issues in the public discourse and political sphere during the late twentieth century in Canada meant disability activists from a variety of backgrounds were continually regrouping to find new ways to promote their agendas. This book also seeks to examine the porous boundaries of "the" disability movement by highlighting the interaction and tension between multiple movements, institutions, and individuals. In line with a social historical approach to the study of social movements, it highlights the role of ordinary people with disabilities whose contributions to macro-level cultural and political developments were no less vital than that of disability organizations.

Post-census surveys indicated a consistent pattern of high unemployment rates averaging around 50 per cent that confirmed other studies and reports indicating employers' reluctance to hire disabled people. In 1981 Statistics Canada began documenting these high unemployment rates by collecting data on the employment of disabled people through the Work History Survey. Although the Survey was replaced in 1986 by the Labour Market Activity Survey, which was replaced in 1993 by the Survey of Labour and Income Dynamics, it continued to show similar data on unemployment.[12] These post-census surveys revealed characteristics about jobs held and changes in labour market status among survey participants that confirmed findings by the above government reports. The labour surveys complemented findings from the Health and Activity Limitation Surveys (HALS) conducted in 1986 and 1991 and replaced in 2001 with the Participation and Activity Limitation Survey (PALS), which outlined limitations in workforce participation as a result of health-related issues.[13] The HALS and PALS consistently indicated that people with disabilities were approximately half as likely to be employed as non-disabled people and that the workforce non-participation rate (i.e., people who had stopped looking for work) among disabled people was twice as high as that of their non-disabled peers.[14]

Statistical indices of unemployment in the disability community confirmed that awareness and hiring campaigns failed to change employer hiring practices during this period. Numerous studies since the 1960s have documented the prevalence of unemployment and poverty among disabled Canadians. Sociologists and political scientists have repeatedly pointed to high unemployment rates that contribute to disproportionate levels of poverty among people with disabilities across Canada.[15] Such studies indicate that disabled Canadians are nearly twice as likely to live below the poverty line and rely on the social security system for income support. Most of the total income of poor people with disabilities has derived from various kinds of government transfers.[16] When disabled people do find employment, they have tended to earn less money and have been concentrated in entry-level and low-wage jobs.[17] Recent statistics for 2009 indicate that average annual incomes among working-age poor disabled people were highest in Alberta ($11,482) and lowest in Nova Scotia ($8,565).[18] It was estimated in 1993 that only 7.6 per cent of working disabled people made over $30,000 compared with 15.1 per cent of non-disabled workers. Total employment of people with disabilities from the late 1980s to early 2000s averaged between 40 and 50 per cent, with a high of 51.3 per cent in 2006 and low of 40.3 per cent in 1986.[19] Disabled women in particular have been at an even higher risk of living in poverty. While disability doubles the chances of living in poverty, young disabled women are nearly twice as likely as disabled men to receive social assistance and three times more likely than non-disabled young women.[20] The Canadian Council on Social Development reported in 2000 that the poverty rate among disabled women was a staggering 40 per cent compared with 8 per cent among non-disabled women. Disabled women were more likely to live alone, experience hunger, rely on income support, and experience longer periods of unemployment. When they did find jobs, disabled women were often concentrated in the lowest-paid unskilled jobs.[21] Unpacking these statistics and the historical developments that gave rise to them constitutes a major objective of this book.

Working towards Equity significantly contributes to Canadian labour history by making the case that disability rights activism in the late twentieth century revolved around labour issues and constituted a labour-oriented social movement. The Canadian disability rights movement was motivated by a broad vision of social inclusion and independent living, while it promoted concrete measures to ensure disabled people secured paid employment. As a result, disability activism during this period constituted a labour movement of sorts by virtue of its focus on reforming the economic system to actively involve working and unemployed people with disabilities. An in-depth examination of the archival record reveals the ways in which disability activists contributed to the development of new labour policies, vocational programs, and employment conferences, as well as organized labour's responses to social justice and social movement activism. This perspective of disability activism as a manifestation of labour-oriented social movements contributes to the general labour historiography of the period and enables us to consider the cultural processes and economic aspirations behind disability rights activism in Canada.

A discussion regarding the use of identifying language in this book is in order. Debate surrounding "politically correct" language in which to identify people with disabilities has been shaped by various political, ethical, cultural, and other paradigms. Participants in these debates often take diametrically opposed positions and leave little room for constructive discussion. Where one assertion argues that the term "disabled" underlines social oppression,[22] another asserts "disabled persons" confirms the reality of disability and the possibility of impairment as a positive factor in one's life.[23] Others note that "disability" was originally an employment term referring to declarative work limitations such that people were "disabled" only insofar as they were unable to work or deemed unemployable.[24] Although "persons" or "people with disabilities" became part of the common legal and political parlance by the 1990s, it was previously held that the World Health Organization's distinction between "impairment," "handicap," and "disability," initially outlined in the 1980 International Classification of Impairments, Disabilities, and Handicaps (ICIDH) entailed a more accurate assessment of the nature of interdependency between biomedical sources of impairment, physical experiences of these impairments, and social or environmental influences.[25]

By the 1970s disability activists in Canada were arguing that the term "handicapped" was a loaded term used by professionals and that social processes, in effect, "handicap" people when in fact an individual was "a person with a disability."[26] In a 1983 paper the COPOH argued that "A disability is a physical reality whereas a handicap is a social or environmental consequence of a disability" and that, when the terms are used interchangeably, the social location of limitations is obscured.[27] However, critics of the "person-first approach" argue that "people with disabilities" implies that "disability is the property of the individual and not of society," that the phrase "conveniently sidesteps the consequences of institutional discrimination," that it represents "an explicit denial of a political or 'disabled identity,'"[28] and that "those who refer to 'people with disabilities' are thus adopting the 'medical model' and must be re-educated or repudiated."[29]

Disability language reflects the logic of the time period in which it was used and must be documented as such in the historiography. Irina Metzler argues that it is important to use terminology from the time period being studied, particularly in a cultural history, as it reveals part of the references to disability.[30] Yet the lack of objective standard criteria for determining who is disabled not only frustrates the historian's task of tracking change over time, but also complicates a balance between historically appropriate yet politically sensitive terminology.[31]

Insofar as these linguistic and representational debates are not engaged, they are also not directly refuted. It is conceded that there is historical and emancipatory importance attached to constructive debate regarding the use of linguistic markers to connect individual experiences with sociocultural conceptualizations of disability. But I leave this to other arenas of discussion. As a result, terms such as "disabled people" and "people with disabilities," which are widely used within and outside the disability community, are used here interchangeably and non-dogmatically, while care is taken throughout to situate other terms such as "handicapped" and "crippled" within their particular historical contexts.

This book incorporates a range of published sources, oral narratives from interview participants, and archival documents. The records of the Council of Canadians with Disabilities held at the Archives of Manitoba complemented records at Library and Archives Canada, the Archives of Ontario, the City of Toronto Archives, and private collections. Numerous government and non-profit publications were also secured from libraries across Canada. These sources tell only part of the story about relationships between disability and work. It became necessary to go beyond written records of disability organizations, government bureaucracies, and service agencies in order to uncover the unwritten histories of work experiences. Inspired by American disability activist James Charlton's call for "nothing about us without us," this book involves the collection of oral narratives from people with disabilities whose memories of work help refine an analysis of historical events and accounts provided by archival records.[32] Charlton appealed for academic work that not only reflects the experiences of people with disabilities but actively involves them as participants in the research process.

Participants in the research for this book were recruited through advertisements for individuals with disabilities with current or former work experiences during the research time frame. Such advertisements were placed in disability forums and newsletters, were passed on through word of mouth and personal and professional contacts, and the non-probability "snowball method" of population sampling also was used.[33] Individuals were selected based on the agreement that the bulk of their work experiences occurred in the Toronto area, in order to provide a scaled-down geographical scope in which to cross-analyse the historical experiences of participants and afford exploratory insights into a cross-disability assortment of individuals with experiences of acquired and/or congenital physical, sensory, and intellectual disabilities and mental health issues. Study participants included the narratives of individuals living with one or more experiences of visual impairment or blindness, hearing impairment, D/deafness, cerebral palsy, multiple sclerosis, polio and post-polio syndrome, muscular dystrophy, scoliosis, spinal cord injuries, fibromyalgia, brain injury, attention deficit hyperactivity disorder, learning disabilities, chronic depression, schizophrenia, autism disorder, other mental health issues, and a number of concurrent conditions. Eleven male and nineteen female participants ranged in age from twenty-six to seventy-three, with an average age of fifty-three years old. The average age of participants entering the workforce was seventeen, the youngest being eleven years old and the eldest being twenty-nine years old. Approximately 50 per cent of participants had entered the workforce before 1980 and another 30 per cent entered between 1980 and 1984, indicating that the participant population was weighted comparatively in favour of the eldest generation followed by middle-aged workers. Of the seven participants who were retired or had stopped working at the time of the interview most had retired after the year 2000 at an average age of fifty-five. The vast majority (93 per cent) of participants identified as "white," "Caucasian," "European," or "Anglo Saxon."

Chapters are organized thematically, although chapters 2 through 4 reflect the chronological emergence of three different streams of disability activism during this period. Chapter 1 introduces us to individuals with disabilities and considers the impact of disability activism on the ideological construction of work and labour market experiences. The chapter reflects upon the ideological importance of work in identity politics and in the construction of individual self-identities. Drawing on findings from interviews with thirty people with disabilities in Toronto, this chapter demonstrates how many people with disabilities in Canada constructed their identity primarily through work and paid employment and not necessarily in the sphere of identity politics. While collective and individual identity formation appeared to be at odds, they in fact found resolution in the shared individual and collective pursuit of economic integration.

Chapter 2 introduces us to the emergence of disability activism in the mid-twentieth century and its conceptual roots in past social reform movements of the late nineteenth and twentieth centuries. Families of people with disabilities spearheaded debates about the capabilities of their children and adult relatives to live outside residential hospitals and back rooms of family homes. Inspired by medical breakthroughs and new philosophies of community living, local groups such as the Woodlands Parents' Group in British Columbia and the Parents' Council for the Retarded based in Toronto involved parents of children with physical and intellectual disabilities forging a national social movement to usher disabled children away from a life of segregation. Organized advocacy by concerned parents and family members of people with disabilities represented an important first step in the pursuit of full citizenship for people with disabilities. Family advocates established the groundwork for the development of a new discourse of disability that challenged the status quo while providing concrete measures for the realization of these goals.

Chapter 3 examines the evolution of the rehabilitation industry and the role played by service agencies. Community living created an unprecedented demand for a range of community-based rehabilitation and social services, as disabled people and their families held greater expectations for participation in mainstream opportunities. However, people with disabilities accessing these services often found their path to integration blocked by physical and social barriers, prompting rehabilitation professionals to address broader social issues conventionally outside the scope of their therapeutic activities. Rehabilitation organizations, including the Canadian Rehabilitation Council for the Disabled and Canadian Council of Rehabilitation Workshops, initiated massive awareness campaigns, becoming disability advocates who promoted their unique vision of disability to a wider audience. These organizations advocated a proto-social model of disability that underscored the limitations and restrictions of impairment while noting the significant barriers caused by social attitudes and conventional responses to disability. While this approach worked towards dismantling barriers to integration, it also served to promote the interests of the rehabilitation industry, given that awareness campaigns also constituted advertisements for the expansion of rehabilitation services. As such, public and political endorsements of rehabilitation had a tendency to insulate rehabilitation professionals from a developing movement of disability rights activists promoting self-help consumer philosophies and a social constructivist model of disability.

In contrast to the collaborative relationship established between family advocates and rehabilitation professionals, chapter 4 examines the emergence of disability rights groups of youthful disabled people in the early 1970s. Inspired by other civil rights movements and a culture of anti-authoritarianism, people with disabilities, led mainly by wheelchair users such as Beryl Potter at Scarborough Action Awareness and blind activists such as David Lepofsky and John Rae, forged a new social movement to challenge physical and attitudinal barriers in the workplace and the larger community. Groups of disillusioned youth resisted what they perceived as a highly hegemonic rehabilitation industry, citing their rights as citizens and consumers of rehabilitation services. Disability rights activists asserted their own brand of identity politics in the creation of organizations such as People United for Self-Help and forged new coalitions within the disability community, including the Coalition of Provincial Organizations of the Handicapped, which carved out self-determined paths to social and economic integration.

Sheltered workshops demonstrate one area in which different conceptual models of disability were brought into stark contrast. Chapter 5 demonstrates how sheltered workshops took on new forms and political symbolism during the 1970s. Originally designed as a way for people with physical disabilities to (re)enter the paid workforce, workshops run by the Salvation Army and Canadian National Institute for the Blind increasingly focused on servicing deinstitutionalized people with intellectual disabilities and mental health issues as part of an under-resourced response to the deinstitutionalization movement in Canada. While initially divided by their adherence to different models of disability, family advocates, rehabilitation professionals, and disability rights activists tentatively reconciled their differences in combined protest to the sheltered workshop system and its role in the lives of disabled people in the community.

The final three chapters examine responses to disability activism by major policymakers and players in the labour market. Chapter 6 assesses the influence disability activism had on the policies, practices, and attitudes of private and public sector employers. Employer attitudes were consistently identified by activists, policymakers, and specialized employment agencies, such as The World of One in Seven, as critical factors that prevented disabled people from enjoying full citizenship. While some employers and business associations publicly declared their support for disability issues, these pronouncements were ultimately undermined by widespread reluctance to actually recruit disabled people. Employers' actions were shaped by a core set of prejudicial attitudes that positioned disabled people as potential risks to business operations, effectively blocking a platform of promotional activities and economic incentives to hire disabled people. Public sector employers stood apart from the larger private sector by presenting themselves as models of progressive and equitable employment practices. The introduction of new computer technologies in the 1980s led many disability rights activists and business leaders to believe that the incorporation of technology in the workplace would "level the playing field" upon which disabled and able-bodied people competed for employment. However, this expectation proved unfounded, as many employers continued to outwardly voice their support for disabled people while failing to take steps to actually employ disabled workers.

Chapter 7 takes a closer look at the role of the state in terms of its relationship to disability rights activism and responses in the sphere of labour policy. During the late 1970s and early 1980s political authorities at the federal, provincial, and municipal levels engaged disability rights activists in order to formulate official responses to a series of international developments in the arena of disability rights. Governments established formal relations with the disability community through advisory councils, such as the Ontario Advisory Council for the Physically Handicapped, and specialized bureaus, including the Handicapped Employment Program, in order to promote the employment and employability of people with disabilities. These new bureaus and committees functioned as centres of activism within the state apparatus, which helped to promote policy development that was favourable to the social model of disability while facilitating greater access to the labour market. However, this collaborative relationship suffered in response to a "common sense revolution" in provincial and federal politics that, ultimately, radically undermined public sector support of disability activism as the state steadily reduced its involvement in the labour market.

Chapter 8 considers the labour movement's response to disability activism. Disability rights activists and government bureaus reached out to organized labour in order to endorse their platform of social and economic reform. Special coalition-building projects, including the *Together for Social Change* partnership between the National Union of Public and General Employees and the Coalition of Provincial Organizations of the

Handicapped, fostered new relations between disparate social movements. While labour leaders reacted favourably, the situation was very different on the ground. Many union leaders and rank-and-file members remained sceptical about the impact that disability rights, including the new Charter of Rights and Freedoms, might have on collective agreements, and unions were caught between opposing forces within the labour movement, which frustrated the acceptance of a new social model of disability. As a result, the incorporation of disability rights clauses in collective agreements happened slowly, as did meaningful collaboration between disability and labour organizations.

Work was a central feature in the lives of people with disabilities in Canada during the late twentieth century. As disability activists in multiple social movements worked to transform the public discourse on disability, people with disabilities lived and worked through a period of intense contrasts. New cultural, political, and economic developments transformed the playing field upon which disabled people competed with others for economic opportunities. But this was a playing field scarred by open pitfalls and unseen barriers that continually frustrated individual and collective attempts at meaningful change. A sense of optimism rose, faded, and grew again with each awareness campaign, policy development, and technological innovation. The introduction of new legal protections also brought new sources of resistance. Many physical and attitudinal barriers remained intact, while unfamiliar ones arose suddenly. Despite decades of change, many aspects of disabled peoples' troubled relationship with the world of work remained disturbingly static. Remarkable examples of creativity and flexibility emerged within the disability community during this period in the pursuit of work, reminding us not only of the human capacity for resilience and adaptation against all odds, but also the existence of a shared social responsibility for building an inclusive society.

Chapter One

Disability Activism, Work, and Identity

I am a person with dreams and ambitions
And I have a song to be sung
I am determined that when it is over
I will have only begun
To show to the world my potential
To show to the world what I've done
I am a child of the universe too
Out of every seven I'm one

. . .

I need so much more than just sheltered employment
I need less than pity and tears
I need your respect and I need your compassion
Lend me your eyes and your ears
Then see me and touch me and feel as I feel
Hear what I say can't you see I am real

. . .

So look beyond what I am not
And you will see just what I am
I'm a woman, I'm a child, I'm a man.[1]

The appeal to "look beyond" disability in order to appreciate the true nature of one's humanity, as suggested in the above excerpt from Canada's official song for the 1981 International Year of Disabled Persons, was intended to encourage the reassignment of socially constructed disabled identities into more inclusive categories. Disability and identity were particularly entwined in the sphere of employment where "able-bodied" working bodies were often separated from disabled non-working bodies. People with disabilities during the late twentieth century often were unable to develop their identity through work because of physical and social barriers that prevented meaningful participation in the labour market. A dissociative relationship between paid work and identity existed for many people with disabilities, exempting them from mainstream expectations to work, making them unable to fully incorporate labour into the process of identity development.[2] Yet many people with disabilities in Canada during the late twentieth century did not exempt *themselves* from the conventional cultural expectation to work. Disabled people generally shared the mainstream ethos that participation in the competitive workforce constituted a primary feature of their identity, and they undertook opportunities to develop themselves through paid employment. Narratives of Canadians with disabilities whose working-life histories traversed the 1960s to the 2000s reflected a desire to be productive, autonomous, and independent individuals, whose participation in the competitive workforce constituted a primary feature of their identity. Despite barriers to labour-market participation, many individuals with disabilities rejected the notion that they constituted a burden on others, pointing to skills and capabilities that made them employable and empowered them to resist potent forces of social and economic exclusion.

This chapter explores the role of work within the historical praxis of identity formation among people with disabilities in Toronto during a period in which disability activism in Canada created a highly charged political identity of disability. The first section discusses relevant theoretical constructions of work and identity, including the evolution of processes that ascribed a collective or politicized identity to disabled people within the context of employment. The final section deconstructs selected oral history narratives of people with disabilities interviewed as part of this study in order to analyse how and why personal identities were constituted around work during this period.

Upon reflection about how his work experiences from the 1960s affected his self-development, interview participant "Robert" responded that work was inextricably linked to the projection and internalization of his identity. Robert explained, "The first question that most of us ask (I try not to) is, 'What do you do for a living?' We identify ourselves by what we do for a living. It was very difficult to answer the question because we take on the broader attitude of society which identifies us by what we do in paid employment. That's how we identify ourselves."[3] As Robert suggested, the ubiquitous question "What do you do?" during initial social encounters signified an attempt to resolve the complexity of individual identity through a determination of employment status.[4] Other characteristics and social markers aside, the underlying question suggested "Who are you?" which ascribed social identity and value to an individual while situating them within certain sociopolitical and economic structures. The question reflected a particularly utilitarian perspective of identity formation that emerged from one's employment position or engagement within the paid labour market. The allegorical respondent is forced to self-reflexively consider "Who am I?" by relating to others through experiences of paid work. While the conflation of identity with occupational status was not necessarily a universal experience, it did underscore the importance placed on work in the process of identity formation. Without work as an element in their history, individuals were seen (or saw themselves) as lacking the means to develop a "working identity" based upon the valuation of productivity and independence sought within this figurative line of questioning.

The conceptualization of work during the late twentieth century in Canada assumed a central position in the development of personal and social identity. Work identities were often created and reinforced through social interaction, so that people describing their work to others identified themselves as subjects within various work roles. Work was part of a multifaceted process of self-identity formation in which personal identity emerged from biographical aspects of an individual's work history.[5] Yet self-discovery also emerged from interrelated associations between the self, identity, and work roles, situating identity formation and self-actualization firmly within the terrain of labour market participation.[6] Work provided intrinsic meaning to individuals as well as an outward representation to others such that the *pursuit* of work partly reflected a search for identity. Self-identity also involved a process of self-objectification or reflexive self-consciousness whereby people perceived themselves as others saw them.[7] People with disabilities in particular possessed fluid identities and did not necessarily see themselves as disabled, since self-identity emerged from a constantly evolving process of self-discovery that defied fixed or essential categories imposed on them by a disability "master status."[8]

Disability was stigmatized in the labour market as many factors often stacked up against other sources of social prejudice surrounding disabled people, such as hiring practices that were shaped by an employer's calculation of a worker's potential profitability minus costs of training and compensation.[9] The social construction and categorization of people with disabilities incorporated multiple interpretations of disability, including the approaches of employers and unions that informed interactions with the economy and broader labour market. Disability highlighted tension surrounding formulations of the "working body" and an uncompromising ethic of individualism that underpinned industrial and post-industrial capitalism.[10] Although labour market status was fundamental to the process of self-definition in capitalist societies, bodily or mental differences and limitations prevented many disabled people from becoming employed.

Disability historian Paul Longmore asserts that the precarious relationship between identity formation and work status during the twentieth century reflected the predominance of a particularly individualist ethos in Western society that marginalized disabled people.[11] For many people with acquired disabilities, self-identity was firmly anchored to employment status such that the interruption of employment or modification of work roles due to ill health or impairment often led to the unhinging of a sense of self. The body and self are not identical and tension exists between the two regardless of when disability presents itself in the life cycle or the nature of interference with typical social roles.[12] As a result, the assignment of a disability identity to people with acquired or congenital disabilities forced individuals to reconcile their internalized sense of selves with the outward projection of a socially constructed self.[13] For interview participants in this study, functional abilities were expressed and internalized through employment status and mitigated a "loss of self" when work activities were reintroduced following the onset of various symptoms, demonstrating the extent to which self-identity was closely structured around work and health.[14]

The development of "working identities" during this period requires a close analysis of actual people with disabilities regarding the ways in which work shaped their identity. Oral narratives of study participants suggested the existence of tension between individuals with disabilities who constructed their identities through the pursuit of work versus the collective project of disability activists and their allies to improve labour market opportunity structures for an imagined "cross-disability community." Without necessarily rejecting the validity of a politicized disability identity, most participants articulated their identity within the context of evolving labour market roles. Regardless of whether an individual or a politicized identity was claimed, analysis of participant narratives regarding work experiences and attitudes towards paid employment revealed that the pursuit of personal autonomy and independence was fully compatible and in fact reinforced the emancipatory goals of disability activists. Individuals with disabilities sought not simply to shrug off an identity defined by burden, but to claim an identity marked by self-fulfilment. Within the world of paid work, tension and compatibility coexisted between disability activism and individuals with disabilities who expressed the value of employment in personal terms while ostensibly developing their identity through work roles.

Participants were asked to convey various aspects of their work histories, career trajectories, and attitudes towards work within the context of an evolving disability rights movement in Canada. They shared many common responses, experiences, and perceptions of work that crossed generations, socio-economic background, gender, race, and type of disability. When cross-referenced with individual work trajectories and developments affecting disabled Canadians since the 1960s, participants' responses to questions about how work and a disability identity interacted demonstrated the importance employment played in their lives. In particular, participants were encouraged to consider why work was important to them and how they felt employment affected the evolution of their identity within the context of a changing disability rights landscape. Given that participants had been selected on the basis of an active or former work history, the general consensus was that work formed a primary feature of their aspirational and actual identities, shaping the experience of disability in addition to the influence of ideologically charged political group identities. In her study on the influence of disability rights on the employment of Americans with disabilities, Karen Hirsch found that while disability rights activism fostered the development of a cross-disability identity, "Many disabled workers have employment experiences that show why passing – denying or hiding the disability as much as possible – is still the best choice when a career and a respectable income are important goals."[15]

In confirmation of Hirsch's assertion about selective identification with a politicized identity, participants in the present study did not deny the accuracy of collective experiences of chronic unemployment and poverty among disabled people as well as political solutions proposed by disability activists. However, collective struggles were largely conceptualized within the context of an individual struggle to contribute to the economy, achieve independence, and participate in mainstream society. Most participants acknowledged the existence and influence of various barriers to labour market participation in their own lives, but they articulated these barriers as obstacles to individual employment objectives without necessarily relating to these experiences to hurdles faced by the wider disability community. While participants shared the overarching aim of disability rights activism to assert the citizenship of disabled people, work experiences were envisioned as an outgrowth of individual characteristics and circumstances that constituted one's "working identity." Analysis of participant narratives revealed individual "working identities" that only secondarily interacted with socially constructed barriers in the labour market as envisioned by disability rights activism. As a result, a certain confluence existed in the minds of participants between individual and politicized identity projects from the 1960s focused on overcoming the historical associations between disability and the concept of "burden" that promoted the exclusion and liminality of a wider disability community.

The following section provides key findings from semi-structured, in-depth oral interviews conducted with thirty people with disabilities in Toronto and other locations in southern Ontario regarding individual engagement with the labour market. Three generations of work experiences from the 1960s to the early 2000s were condensed into three pairs of selected participants arranged chronologically in order to reveal significant insights regarding the impact of a changing disability rights movement on individual identities in a major Canadian city. Despite varying levels of engagement with an evolving discourse of disability rights during the late twentieth century, interview participants in each generation constructed their identity explicitly around work roles and values that emerged from their employment experiences. The following pairs of interview participants demonstrate how self-identities were created through individual biographies, work experiences, and selective engagement with an evolving discourse of disability rights.[16]

William and Grace

Reared during a period in which political activism around disability issues belonged more to the experience of their able-bodied parents than to that of their disabled peers, "William" and "Grace," though differentiated by experiences of paralysis and visual impairment, respectively, shared an understanding that work was a central constitutive element in the formation of personal identity. While people with disabilities had not yet affirmatively developed an alternative model of disability during the 1960s in Toronto, parents forged an initial path towards the pursuit of social and economic inclusion that included political activism and the projection of such ideologies upon their children.[17] Both William and Grace grew up in working-class households and entered the workforce at an early age – William as a farm labourer and Grace shining shoes – when they first responded to the encouragement of family and caregivers to view work as part of a natural trajectory of personal development. Despite William's growing up "able-bodied" and acquiring a spinal cord injury at age sixteen and Grace's having lost most of her eyesight by age five, both cited the importance of work as something that superseded the variable experience of disability. William noted, "I had the sense that I had to work as everybody else did, as my parents did. The idea of sitting in my parent's house with my hand out was really repugnant to me ... My family were independent workers. It was a matter of personal pride really."[18] Grace similarly found, "All those really early jobs I had were low pay but it helped build a work ethic. Also, I was just expected to work. I was from a very poor family and my parents frowned on welfare and any form of it. So it was: 'Get off your butt and do something, kid.'"[19] For William and Grace the importance of work was communicated to them during their formative years by parents and elders as a primary mechanism through which intrinsic meaning and personal identity were cultivated.

Work provided William and Grace with an opportunity to construct an identity separate from disability in the absence of a political framework in which to develop an empowered disability identity that emerged from within the disability community. Their personal identities firmly anchored to strong work ethics and labour market status, both interview participants believed that, despite the availability of supposed economic security through acceptance of welfare benefits, such acceptance represented the "easy road," which did not address the desire for self-development and fulfilment through continuous and progressive participation in the workforce. Having grown up surrounded by visually impaired peers and adults, Grace perceived a choice between a life of subsistence on welfare or one of paid work: "When I finished school I was younger than other students so I was too young to go on the Blind Person's Allowance. So I was never on a government pension like that. I know some kids were as soon as they turned eighteen ... But work has always been important to me. What we do is who we are, eh?"[20] William similarly interpreted the "work-or-welfare" dilemma as a test of his work ethic, fearful that dependency would compromise his identity as an independent wage earner. He recalled, "After I went away [...] to university I never went back home to live. I missed quite a lot of meals in the early days but still didn't go back. I just kept at it until I got a job and could support myself. I had no sense that it was because of my disability."[21]

Rehabilitation influenced the formation of William's and Grace's personal identities in different ways. Given that William's injury occurred during his adolescent years, he described the intensive two-year rehabilitation program as an event or obstacle followed by the resumption of a normal life cycle. A retrospective assessment of his peers in the program confirmed to William that his focus on developing a work-based identity insulated him from the negative influence that was seen to emerge from typical experiences of paralysis. He observed, "I know one person who went through Lyndhurst with me in 1960–61; the rest are dead. Dead from personal neglect and alcohol and drugs. It's a difficult thing for some people to get over. A large portion become quite angry, have bad attitudes."[22] For Grace, however, rehabilitation was more loosely defined, given that she attended a separate school for the blind from a very young age and found employment with the Canadian National Institute for the Blind, cultivating her work identity, experience, and professional networks around others in the blind community. Yet despite employment within the arena of services for her peers with visual impairments, Grace's focus on self-development through work did not dissuade her from taking progressively more responsible positions that took her outside the blind community.

Despite their similar values and experience finding upward advancement in professional and managerial positions, William and Grace adopted dissimilar attitudes towards identification with an emerging politicized identity as members of an imagined disability community. William rejected the notion that his visible mobility impairment defined him in any meaningful way, particularly within the context of the work. He eschewed participation in equity groups who "met and discussed their problems" and believed such people were generally "incompetent or hiding behind their disability to get things they shouldn't get." William asserted, "I didn't want any part of that. I just did my job and applied and got this job and got that job."[23] He even found that employment equity provisions introduced during the 1980s and 1990s represented "reverse discrimination," arguing that such legislation directly threatened his hard-won identity as an experienced professional.[24] William recounted one experience that led him to reassert his identity during an application for a job promotion: "They actually put in a policy whereby anybody with an ethnic singularity or a disability automatically had ten points given to them in the interview, which I found really insulting. In fact, one time I applied for a high-profile project job which would have lasted about a year. I won the competition. I asked the HR guy what the second person's score was. He wouldn't tell me; said it was private. I asked if I won by more than ten points. He said no. So I rejected the job."[25]

In contrast to William, but similarly protective of an identity shaped by work experience and competence, Grace expressed more confidence in the potential for legal rights and disability activism to promote, rather than negate, positive disability identities. Rather than undermining her accomplishments, Grace described the introduction of legal rights for disabled workers since the 1970s as a matter of creating awareness of issues affecting disabled people and equalizing the playing field in the labour market. She explained, "Initially when I was hired as a consultant I had to fight to get on as a permanent employee. I had to fight for that even though I was doing the same job as other non-disabled people ... But that was the mid-'70s and when we got to 1981, which was the IYDP, a lot of work was done around that time and a lot of things changed; much for the better."[26] Grace found that during the 1970s there was limited access to accommodations or assistive devices in her public sector policy analysis work, forcing her to supply her own devices or practice forms of self-limitation. By the 1980s, however, she found that growing awareness of disability issues simultaneously resulted in positive changes to public policy that only served to enhance her ability and confidence in her work.

Nathan and Michael

"Nathan's" adolescent working years during the 1970s found him labelling paint cans, stocking shelves at a grocery store, assembling products on assembly lines, and bartending – all while relishing the individual freedom of hitchhiking across the country. Because he left home and school at age sixteen, paid work was not only a matter of survival for Nathan, but a key feature in his bid for assertion of a working masculinity. He argued, "Men worked. Men are obliged to work ... While I took little or no satisfaction or fulfilment from the work tasks, the income was important. In my family and in my social circle everyone worked and men worked for money and they began working at what some would consider being an early age. So emulating those around me and wishing to be a man, I had to work."[27] As a qualified mechanic by the early 1980s, Nathan appeared to have secured his personal identity goals through employment status.

The pursuit of identity through work, however, exacerbated the effects of Nathan's mental health issues, which included bipolar spectrum disorder, anxiety, attention deficit hyperactivity disorder, and depression. Despite the advent of legal rights and heightened public awareness of disability issues during the 1980s, Nathan refused to disclose his mental health issues to employers or co-workers, confident that accommodations would not be forthcoming and in anticipation of losing job security. Instead, Nathan believed that he was obliged to conceal his mental health issues, given the liberal individualism characteristic of mainstream employment that forced disabled workers to self-manage their limitations in socially inaccessible workplaces. He explained, "Having been in many, many workplaces, I have an understanding of what is required of the task, the demands. I self-limit. Any place I go where I don't believe I could cope, I don't apply for the job."[28] In addition to mental health issues, Nathan sustained a workplace injury in the 1990s that resulted in chronic musculoskeletal disorders, which forced him to abandon his career as a mechanic when his employer refused to accommodate him. Although Nathan eventually found employment in the legal profession, his experience of an abrupt dislocation of work identity caused him to distrust the capacity of legal rights to protect him in employment, further distancing him from identification with a disability. He concluded, "I have experience of how people deal in the workforce, how people interact and deal with individuals with disabilities. How employers don't want to accommodate … My research and personal experience tells me that the vast majority of workplaces do not accommodate individuals with disabilities."[29]

In contrast to Nathan, but careful to avoid acceptance of a disability identity, "Michael" discovered an empowered identity and self-realization through the assertion of his mental health issues within the context of employment and an evolving disability rights framework. Michael used "person-first" terminology to identify himself as "a person with experience of schizophrenia" in order to simultaneously demarcate the pathology of mental health status from the complexity of his individuality. He explained, "It's a generational thing. The Schizophrenia Society of Ontario was called, not that long ago, Ontario Friends of Schizophrenics. It's just mainly 'the label defines you.' It was comfortable for a certain generation to define it that way."[30] Similar to Nathan and William, Michael referred to the influence of his family upbringing as the root of a desire to develop his personal identity through work. He asserted, "I come from a middle-class family where my parents worked hard and my sister has been successful. I come from this ethic of 'work hard.'"[31] Unlike Nathan, however, Michael described work not as providing confirmation of his masculinity, but rather as part of a search for self-fulfilment of deeply rooted personal values. He declared, "It's part of my identity because I'm a giving person. I was raised to be generous ... I find that I want to contribute and I find that's what I'm doing."[32]

Both Nathan and Michael found that disability shaped the trajectory of their employment history and altered their sense of self. While Nathan's physical injuries prompted a sudden career change despite hidden ongoing experience of mental health issues, Michael's career in "information science" was transformed by a period of hospitalization during the early 1990s in which he sought treatment for his mental health issues. Unlike William, who perceived his physical rehabilitation in the early 1960s as a singular event, Michael found that acute medical intervention in his life began a relatively prolonged process of recovery and increased self-awareness about the relationship between his mental health issues and work that eventually led him back to the workforce on completely new terms. Although driven by a set of "work ethics" similar to that of Nathan, William, and Grace, Michael did not find his personal values were compromised by acceptance of welfare benefits. Instead, he preferred to view such benefits as the means by which he could selectively engage the labour market in work that was both rewarding and accommodating for his needs and abilities. He recalled, "I did make the point with somebody who was helping me with my personal experience speech, and we were coming to the part where I was talking about the past. I said that I had difficulty with finding work. Her suggestion was, 'You weren't able to work.' I said, 'No, I had difficulty working.'"[33]

Michael crafted his own path towards reintegration in the workforce by securing employment in non-profit organizations that operated within a consumer-survivor, peer-support context and were particularly flexible, supportive, and understanding about the need to provide certain accommodations. In contrast to Nathan, who felt his job security would be jeopardized by claiming an identity and set of needs marked by mental health issues, Michael felt comfortable disclosing his mental health issues up front in working environments in order to establish working terms that were acceptable to both himself and his employer. As Nathan found, "I feel my biggest obstacle I have to overcome is my inability to identify as a person who needs accommodation ... Dealing with most of my colleagues, I have the impression that it's not the place that would not be accommodating to my particular type of disability. My physical disabilities they have no problems with. I can get assistive technology; if I was in a wheelchair they could widen the doors or whatever. My mental illness – that's another thing. My experiences are such that I cannot declare as a person with a mental illness without risking my employment."[34]

Mary and Danielle

"Mary" and "Danielle" entered the workforce during the mid- to late 1980s amid the development of legal rights for women and people with disabilities entrenched in the Charter of Rights and Freedoms and unprecedented wave of public awareness about disability issues. Unlike the situation of their peer Grace, who entered the workforce during the early 1960s, social activism during the 1970s and early 1980s cultivated empowered identities for women with disabilities in the wider public sphere. Similar to Grace's upbringing, Mary grew up with a visual impairment in a separate school where she was educated apart from her able-bodied peers and subjected to a different set of expectations about her capabilities and potential. While Mary and Grace shared similar family-based reassurances of their ability to construct identities through work, Mary entered the workforce during a period in which important developments in rights, benefits, and technology transformed access to employment opportunities for people with visual impairments. Widespread transition to new computerized work stations transformed many Canadian workplaces, while emerging assistive technologies for blind computer users promised to allow people with visual impairments to compete on a level playing field with their sighted colleagues.[35]

As work environments were progressively reshaped by the "computer revolution" Mary rejected her family's encouragement to pursue a university education, instead opting to obtain a college diploma that made her qualified to work in the growing technology sector. She recalled her enthusiasm, "When I started working, I was 23 and really excited. I thought, 'Oh boy, I'm going to bring home a pay cheque, I'm contributing to a company, and helping people.'"[36] Proud of her status as the first blind customer service representative in her large national company, Mary also understood that she benefited from the interface of employment equity regulations that governed her workplace, the relatively new government subsidization of assistive devices, and the increased availability of new accessible technologies that enabled her to use the company's computer systems.[37] The intersection of these circumstances with Mary's ambition to succeed in the labour market enabled her to manoeuvre herself into various management positions within the company. Although trained separately as a result of the need to understand how the accessible system worked, Mary worked alongside her able-bodied colleagues and attended training sessions with her peers. For Mary, visual impairment did not appear to inhibit the development of a working identity, nor did she feel the need to assert her legal rights or a disability identity.

In contrast to Mary, Danielle grew up able-bodied and found that following the onset of a physical disability, legal rights meant to protect disabled people from discrimination in the workplace failed to provide a suitable remedy. As a professional working woman during the late 1980s with a self-described "Type A personality," Danielle excelled in her field of administrative and financial services, where she developed a reputation as a dynamic and highly effective professional. Despite her success, Danielle found herself locked in a perpetual struggle with undisclosed mental health issues. She explained, "I was living with major depression all of that time but pretty functional. I was always the employee that had the most sick-time. I always lost one or two days a month to depression. None of my employers were ever very tolerant of that. Of course, back then one didn't necessarily talk about staying home from work because you were depressed."[38] Danielle believed that a general lack of awareness and respect for mental health issues meant that it was her reputation as an effective professional that insulated her from major reprisals from her employers. By the early 1990s Danielle was diagnosed with multiple sclerosis following an extended period of uncertainty in which she was on sick leave to secure a diagnosis for her undetermined illness. When her employer engaged in a series of actions that concluded in wrongful dismissal, Danielle reluctantly filed a human rights complaint, alleging her employer had discriminated against her on the basis of disability. She recalled, "It was the most horrific experience. With a chronic illness or disability and you have an employer who doesn't support you, you start feeling guilty for being sick. I was devastated."[39] An ensuing protracted legal struggle ended with minimal compensation for the loss of her job, coupled with an eroded sense of self. She explained, "When I lost my job, not only did I lose my job, I lost a career. I lost who I was. The energy and emotional fortitude it takes to rediscover or recreate a self-image; that took me … I had no self-image for eight years."[40] Although Danielle had sought accommodations for her developing health issues in order that she could continue to maintain her self-identity as a competent and capable professional, the discriminatory actions of her employer forced her to engage legal rights and a politicized identity that she had not set out to acquire.

By the time Danielle's legal struggle with her employer had concluded in the late 1990s, Mary similarly had discovered that the constellation of factors that had enabled her to nurture her self-identity through advancement in her company quickly eroded when her employer suddenly switched to an inaccessible computer system. The introduction of graphic user interfaces in the early 1990s brought about by the popularization of the Microsoft Windows operating systems replaced standard text-based DOS (Disk Operating System) computer systems.[41] As disability activist David Lepofsky argued at the time, "The Windows operating system was premised on the assumption that users could see the technology they have introduced … People who are victims of the current practices of the mainstream computer industry need to use the legal mechanisms they have available to them now to bring claims."[42] It is also not clear that computer programming training programs initiated by IBM in the early 1970s and 1980s continued to be effective in the rapid evolution of computer technology in the workplace.[43] Mary similarly argued, "I was more equal in 1987 back in the DOS and 'dumb terminal' days than I am now because back then it was easier to make something accessible because the original was simpler … The screen reading technology just can't keep up."[44] While Mary avoided availing herself of a disability identity, having constructed her identity primarily around work during a period in which early computer technology created a welcoming work environment, her employer's decision to adopt a new inaccessible operating system thrust Mary into the same position as other blind employees. She recalled, "The company decided they needed a new computer system and they ignored the needs of their blind employees. Basically the bottom line was they didn't care enough to expend time and money to find an application that would work for everyone."[44] As an experienced employee with qualifications now inaccessible to her job profile, Mary was effectively made redundant and transferred to various "make-work" projects before eventually deciding to resign. Similar to Danielle's situation, the process of developing a working identity followed by forced disengagement resulted in a devastating effect on Mary's self-identity. Mary concluded, "It became very demoralizing. Employment has the possibility of being a really good thing and a really bad thing at the same time depending on how it goes and what your employer is like."[45]

As activists in identity politics and as workers, people with disabilities sought to cultivate working identities in the late twentieth century. Despite the existence of social barriers to labour market participation, disabled people did not exempt themselves from the mainstream expectation to contribute to the economy and the cultural imperative to develop one's self-identity through the pursuit of paid work. However, the risks of associating identity development with employment status were augmented by the reality that many people with disabilities experienced poverty and underemployment during this period. The liberal individualism that motivated these expectations and imperatives convinced many people with disabilities that work was a necessary component of full citizenship, despite the prevalence of "disabling" social attitudes and physical environments. As a nascent disability rights movement promoted a cross-disability identity and worked to erect a political framework in which to support this identity, many people with disabilities constructed individual identities apart from the disability community.

These narratives of Canadians with disabilities stretching from the 1960s to the present demonstrate the extent to which employment was a central component in the process of individual and collective identity formation. Analysis of participants' oral narratives reveal a general ambition to be productive, autonomous, and financially independent in opposition to conventional notions that disabled people were burdensome. Participants rejected the stereotypical association of disability with the concept of "burden," instead pointing to skills and intrinsic resources that enabled them to resist forces of social and economic exclusion. Realization of certain employment goals thus were seen by participants as a primary mechanism for achieving the conventional mainstream value of independence through paid work. Multiple generations of disabled people internalized predominant values of paid employment as a key aspect of personal identity formation, making them indistinguishable from their "able-bodied" peers in this respect.

Immersed in a society that placed a heavy emphasis on the importance of work, many people with disabilities identified with the liberal individualism of the mainstream and sought to distance themselves from the "burden" ethos through individual effort and achievement.

As will be demonstrated in the following chapters, disability rights activists and their allies sought to harness this motivation to escape obscurity to a larger political platform. Through attempts to introduce new labour market opportunities and promote a politicized identity with shared experiences of oppression, activists and allies sought to overturn the long-standing cultural exemption of people with disabilities from paid work. Where disability politics reflected the dynamic interplay of a relatively few people with disabilities, it also lent wider expression to the prioritization of work at an individual level. A reciprocal relationship thus existed in which employment was situated at the centre of both individual and collective efforts to replace long-standing stereotypes of disability as a social or public burden with empowered, productive, "working" identities of people with disabilities.

Chapter Two

Family Advocacy and the Struggle for Economic Integration

I think it's partly parents saying, "No, I don't want to put my child in an institution," or "Why should this child be in this school and my other children that
school?" It's people who are caring for people with disabilities saying, "Why
are they being separated?" ... It never occurred to me that I wouldn't be going
to school with the kids on my street. I don't know how much my parents had
to fight for that.[1]

All those really early jobs I had were low pay but it helped build a work ethic.
Also, I was just expected to work. I was from a very poor family and my parents frowned on welfare and any form of it. So it was, "Get off your butt and
do something kid!" It was expectations on the part of my parents that I had the
opportunity to do these things.[2]

Parents and families of people with disabilities formed the vanguard
of a developing movement in Canada during the 1960s that challenged
long-standing attitudes and practices concerning disabled people. Family
advocates sought to transform exclusionary institutional arrangements
and social responses to disability by promoting disabled people's capacity to participate in the community. Primarily middle-class parents
of disabled children forged informal gendered networks of grass-
roots activism, giving rise to a social movement intent on addressing
the lack of community services that perpetuated the segregation of
their children. Parents' groups created formal advocacy organizations
and service agencies that broke down physical and social barriers
separating disabled people from the rest of society. As modern-day
reformers seeking a new and more inclusive ideology of disability,
family advocates engineered work opportunities for disabled people

and fostered the development of community-based services at a time when there were few alternatives to total institutions. By the mid-1970s parent-based disability organizations increasingly clashed with disability rights activists. A rising tide of disability rights activism blamed overprotective parents for their unwillingness to relinquish control to disabled consumers. Local parents' groups built a formidable network of community agencies, but did not fundamentally question the prevailing political economy structured around "able-bodied" standards of employability and the construction of disabled people as members of the "deserving" poor.

This chapter explores the evolution of family advocacy during the 1960s and 1970s in Canada and its role in the development of a new discourse around disability and work. The first section documents the legacy of twentieth century social reform movements and the core role of family advocates in the movement to deinstitutionalize people with disabilities in the context of community living philosophies. The final section examines the development of the voluntary sector as a source of employment and the upsurge of a reactionary movement of activists who challenged disability organizations to include people with disabilities as equal partners in the pursuit of social and economic integration.

In the post-war period services and advocacy support for disabled people in Canada were developed and controlled increasingly by charitable non-profit agencies run by local, provincial, and national parents' groups. As medical and pharmacological advancements improved the health of Canadians, optimism about medical breakthroughs engulfed the public consciousness of disability. Fundraising campaigns conducted across North America to find a polio vaccine epitomized the harnessing of local charitable efforts to a wider project to conquer disability through the concerted support of improvements in medical science.[3] In 1951 the Canadian Foundation for Poliomyelitis, later renamed the Ontario March of Dimes after the popular "Marching Mothers" campaigns in the United States, featured mothers of children with polio, who canvassed local neighbourhoods to raise funds (even if "Just a Dime") for poliomyelitis vaccine research. The marches engaged concerned, predominantly middle-class parents in the frenzied response to the polio epidemic that afflicted a generation of baby boomers still in pre-adolescence. The first marches in Canada were held in Toronto during the 1950s, led in 1957 by the "Chief Marching Mother" of a son with polio, (later distinguished politician) Ellen Fairclough, herself a symbol of the prominence of activist parents. The development of a

1 "Marching Mothers" in Toronto with donation bags in hand, led during the 1950s by "Chief Marching Mother" Ellen Fairclough (at right), to raise funds for the medical research that led to the development of the polio vaccine. The popular campaign, which also raised public awareness about people living with polio, led to the creation of the Ontario March of Dimes (after the fundraising slogan "Just a Dime") as a major service organization for people with disabilities in Canada.[4] Public domain.

vaccine for poliomyelitis by Dr Jonas Salk in 1955 confirmed the success of these fundraising campaigns by concerned parents who turned their attention to expanding the activities of the Ontario March of Dimes.[5] The organization rapidly broadened its advocacy efforts to support new medical research while providing services and supplying assistive devices to people with physical disabilities regardless of the nature of their impairments.

Family-driven organizations such as the Ontario March of Dimes complemented the work of other organizations in Canada dedicated to particular populations of disabled people, including the Muscular Dystrophy Association, Canadian National Institute for the Blind, Canadian Paraplegic Association, and War Amps. These groups collectively established networks of services and a pattern of disability advocacy

on behalf of disabled people, defying generations of logic that excluded disabled people from mainstream society. These charitable organizations addressed the social and economic "problem" of disability
through a combination of specialized services, medical research, public
advocacy, and political lobbying. Charities were increasingly recognized as engines of greater disability awareness, blurring the boundaries between service agency and advocacy association as they acquired
influence over policies affecting disabled people. Charitable organizations cultivated widespread appeal by tapping into deep-seated anxiet-
ies and moral obligations towards the less fortunate. Charities inserted
themselves into a dependent relationship with disabled people, channelling long-standing perceptions about the dependence of people
with disabilities upon charitable social assistance.[6] With the realities of
supporting dependent disabled people increasingly cast as a public social issue rather than a private family burden, family-driven charitable
associations played an important role in cultivating responses to the
social and economic "problem" of disability in the community.

  For most of the twentieth century working- and middle-class parents and families were forced to relinquish their disabled children and
adult relatives into the care of residential hospitals or face the daunting
alternative of raising them at home without supports within socially
and physically inaccessible communities. Within the culture of rever-
ence for medical authority of the time the medicalization of disabled
people framed disability as a complex phenomenon that required expert intervention and management by trained professionals. As historian Paul Longmore explains, "Because disease and disability seem so
self-evidently matters of biology, rather than sociology or public policy,
the disadvantaging social and economic consequences endured by
sick or disabled individuals are perceived as 'natural,' the inevitable
social outcomes of biological 'facts.'"[7] As a result, many families believed they lacked the resources and knowledge to effectively care for
disabled people in the community, which led them to accept doctors'
recommendations for institutionalization as a definitive assessment
of a relative's needs and abilities. In her oral history of children with
physical disabilities who lived at Bloorview Hospital in Toronto between 1960 and 1989 Tracy Odell, an ex-resident, notes that one-third
of study participants were placed in institutions because of medical
needs that families believed could not be treated at home. Yet these
same people, Odell observes, had "difficulty remembering the value
or relevance" of the therapy they received while living at the hospital.

Odell suggests that residential hospitals during this time represented convenient depositories for non-normative children rather than places where intensive medical management was both appropriate and necessary.[8] Nevertheless, widespread faith in medical institutions as centres of healing and recovery committed generations of people to long-term residential care during this period.

However, the mid-twentieth century polio epidemic triggered a series of events that unexpectedly transformed a generation of white, middle-class parents and families into a powerful group of social reformers. Children who survived the poliomyelitis disease often experienced a form of infantile paralysis that typically presented families with their first exposure to disability and a multitude of previously unseen systemic barriers. Iron-lung respirators, crutches, and reliance on wheelchairs for mobility, which accompanied the disease, suddenly became a reality for many families, who were forced to recalibrate their expectations around ability and health. Although some families placed recovering children in long-term care hospitals, many parents, especially those espousing middle-class ethics, were driven by a new set of expectations about the possibilities of social integration that insisted their children participate fully in the community.

Middle-class parents capable of investing economic resources and a high degree of energy in the recovery and rehabilitation of disabled children often found these experiences "accidentally" transformed them into advocates fighting for disability rights. As Melanie Panitch notes, "activist parents whose struggle at an individual level for their own son or daughter launched national organizations."[9] Of course, not all parents and family shared this new-found optimism about the capabilities of disabled people or had the resources to engage in advocacy efforts. Others openly rejected the notion that disabled people, particularly those with intellectual disabilities, could care for themselves. Nevertheless, the polio epidemic in Canada did give rise to a critical mass of concerned parents determined to find space for their children in the community.

Six interview participants for the present study began their working lives during the 1950s and 1960s, mostly as teenagers and young adults, because their families simply expected them to work or their working-class background required them to contribute to the family economy. Most participants experienced some form of institution-based treatment or rehabilitation for visual impairment, spinal cord injury, poliomyelitis, or fibromyalgia. Yet nearly all participants maintained that institutional education or treatment did not fundamentally disrupt their personal goal of finding paid work or pursuing a career. Half of the participants found their way into a booming public sector as civil servants at all levels of government, while the remainder found jobs in the private and non-profit sectors. Despite growing up with the belief that paid work was a natural part of the life cycle, participants in this eldest generation faced long-standing negative stereotypes about disability among employers and the broader public that were manifested in the pervasive inaccessibility of local communities and workplaces. Nevertheless, participants confronted sets of barriers with the determination to forge careers for themselves, maximizing their abilities and downplaying the needs that accompanied their disabilities.

Growing up during the 1940s and 1950s, interview participant "Sofia" learned that surviving the polio virus as a young child and the resulting scoliosis and mobility impairment that required her to use arm crutches and a wheelchair did not exempt her from personal and family expectations to find paid employment. "Sofia" described herself as belonging to a unique cohort of polio survivors who collectively entered young adulthood together with greater expectations of labour market participation. She found that if "you could do the job you got the job," but this assumption was partly related to the widespread awareness of polio, which may have created a conditional level of acceptance among employers. While she understood that significant attitudinal and architectural barriers existed in the community and most workplaces, she managed to find a job at age nineteen working for a major retailer in Toronto in their telephone catalogue department. Although employment options during the 1950s and 1960s were already highly circumscribed for women, Sofia quit her retail job to attend a local business college and took various jobs in the non-profit sector before becoming a teacher and librarian. At one school where she worked the principal advised her, "I don't care how you do the job as long as you do it" – an ideology of work that Sofia in fact shared. While some informal accommodations were made, such as exemption from outside duties during recess, she was expected to access and move about the school on her own. Sofia described how most schools where she worked in Toronto during the 1960s were inaccessible and children in wheelchairs would have to be carried up and down the stairs. Despite her mobility impairment and not wishing to be treated differently from others, Sofia was often made to work in second-floor classrooms – a situation that required her to take her lunch breaks in her classroom in order to avoid the physical energy and pain of joining her colleagues in the downstairs lunchroom.[10]

"William," also born in the early 1940s, grew up as an able-bodied boy working in the summer as a farm labourer until, at age sixteen, he sustained a spinal cord injury in a diving accident. He spent the next two years in Lyndhurst Rehabilitation Hospital in midtown Toronto, where he regained partial use of his arms and hands. Back at home and two years behind his peers academically, he quickly finished high school before moving on to pursue a university education. As a student in downtown Toronto, William confronted a widespread lack of accessible sidewalks and transportation as well as limited housing options; he was assisted by social workers at Lyndhurst, who helped bridge the gap between rehabilitation and community living. However, upon graduating in the mid-1960s, William went into the workforce, surviving on jobs below his competency level while attending countless interviews and receiving few callbacks. William described physical and attitudinal barriers as compounding issues that likely prevented him from landing a job. "Finding somebody who would hire me and then [working] in a building I could get into in the first place was not an easy thing." Unwilling to pursue a job that was literally inaccessible, he restricted his applications to workplaces in accessible buildings and eventually landed a job with the provincial government, where he held a series of progressively responsible managerial positions.[11]

During the 1960s many parents and families of people with developmental disabilities increasingly questioned the quality of care and rationale for lifelong institutionalization. Although many families accepted conventional medical opinion that many disabled people were safer and less of a burden in residential institutions, reports on the poor state of residential hospitals shook the confidence of many parents who were increasingly reluctant to relinquish their children into the total care of medical authorities. At the urging of influential parent activists Gerald and Betty Anglin in Toronto, well-known Canadian author Pierre Berton (then a journalist for the *Toronto Star*) conducted an investigation in 1959 of the Orillia Hospital School for the Mentally Retarded. The Anglins, who had removed their son Mark from the residential wing of the Orillia Hospital, led Berton on a tour of the facility in order to illustrate the concerns held by many parents that Ontario's institutions for people with developmental disabilities were often substandard and contradicted the notion that disabled people enjoyed better care in such environments than in the community.[12] Berton's subsequent article based on his observations ignited a firestorm of controversy around the state of residential institutions in Ontario and fuelled a wider movement in Canada focused on radical reform of care for people with disabilities living in institutions.[13] Berton's exposé built upon similar media-led investigations in the United States, such as Geraldo Rivera's award-winning investigative documentary on Willowbrook State School on Staten Island in New York City, which exemplified the conditions that led to the advancement of individual and organized advocacy by parents across North America.[14]

Inspired by a growing movement in the United States to deinstitutionalize disabled people, parents' groups in Canada coalesced around local closures of residential institutions, separate schools, and other segregated facilities. A movement spearheaded by loosely structured ad hoc coalitions of parents and families of disabled people emerged during the 1950s and 1960s focused on steering people out of segregation and into the community. The development of local parents' groups often originated with informal discussions in kitchens and living rooms of middle-class homes and quickly spilled out into local neighbourhoods and entire cities, providing the basis for the establishment of provincial and national parent-based advocacy associations.[15] A letter published in the *Toronto Star* in September 1948, for example, called for more resources to help parents keep their disabled children at home. The letter led to a meeting at the Carlton Street United Church (now St Luke's United) in Toronto and the subsequent founding of the Parents' Council for Retarded Children (now Community Living Toronto), which also served as the national headquarters for the Canadian Association for Retarded Children (now Canadian Association for Community Living).[16] Similarly, the Ontario Federation for the Physically Handicapped (OFPH) was established following a letter that was circulated in 1971 to clients and families at various service agencies inviting them to a discussion of common problems affecting people with physical disabilities. Eleven respondents quickly ballooned to a meeting of 150 people in July 1971 at Jesse Ketchum School in midtown Toronto open to "all who are concerned about the physically handicapped."[17] Such local groups fed into a larger movement focused on replacing segregated care with a constellation of need-specific services as family advocates demanded more opportunities for their children and adult relatives with physical and developmental disabilities than a life of segregation.

The leadership of many parents' groups that emerged during this period were typically white, middle-class, and urban dwelling. From the original clusters of Marching Mothers to the families that gathered at Jesse Ketchum School to found the Parents' Council for Retarded Children, concerned parents quickly mustered the resources to confront conventional medical thinking and construct an entire system of community services. These developments were made possible by the significant political influence and organizing capacity of closely connected middle-class families. As a result, the voices of poor, immigrant, and Aboriginal people were not represented among early parents' groups, whose singular vision did not necessarily account for ethnocultural and socio-economic differences. For example, early efforts to deinstitutionalize children with disabilities did not address the forced institutionalization and sterilization of hundreds of Aboriginal children in residential schools across the country, including children at the Provincial Training School for Mental Defectives in Red Deer, Alberta. Whereas many disabled children of predominantly white, middle-class parents benefited from involved advocacy on their behalf, many disabled Aboriginal children, particularly in Alberta, were sterilized in conformity with provincial sexual sterilization legislation. Since influential parents' groups were not composed of immigrant and ethnocultural minorities, little attention was paid to the ways in which disabled people within these ethnocultural communities were marginalized.

Oral narratives of interview participants growing up during this period reflected the important role of parents in the cultivation of personal identities. Interviewees declared that, in the absence of expectations in the broader public sphere of their capability for productive work, parents and families provided a stimulus to engage in the labour market. Most participants found that relationships with their parents had a profoundly empowering influence on their confronting social and physical barriers to economic participation. Forced to advocate for access to mainstream opportunities, parents instilled traditional work ethics in their children despite their physical or mental disabilities. Study participants whose parental relationships dated from the 1960s and earlier revealed that parents had a great deal of influence in the cultivation of individual values around work and integration. A strong work ethic, motivation, and self-confidence in their capabilities often stemmed from the social dynamics of family environments. "Michael," born in 1966 and living with mental health issues, argues that his family convinced him that work was a necessary component of personal development and community integration. Michael notes, "I come from a middle-class family where my parents worked hard and my sister has been successful. I come from this ethic of 'work hard.'"[18]

Social conditioning within participants' family environments emphasized the importance of work and functionality despite the perceived limitations of individual impairments. Most participants agreed that stable family support provided the means to cultivate personal identities based around capability, including sloughing off stereotypes linking disability with dependency. "Grace," who acquired infantile glaucoma and lives with visual impairments, states, "I was from a very poor family and my parents frowned on welfare and any form of it. So it was, 'Get off your butt and do something, kid!'"[19] Similarly, "William," also born in 1942 and who sustained a spinal cord injury at age sixteen, asserts, "I had the sense that I had to work as everybody else did, as my parents did. The idea of sitting in my parents' house with my hand out was really repugnant to me. After I went away to Toronto to university I never went back home to live."[20] Parental expectations around work, such as those expressed by interview participants, regardless of physical or mental impairments, imprinted utilitarian values but also challenged predominant expectations that enabled individual people with disabilities to resist conventional attitudes around disability.

Although there were many paths that led parents and families of disabled people to become vocal advocates promoting a progressive vision that focused on capabilities rather than deficits, parent activism entailed relating individual struggles to larger issues. Melanie Panitch argues that the term "parents' movement" obscures the reality that it was primarily mothers who became activists, even though it was mainly men who formed the leadership of emergent advocacy organizations.[21] The March of Dimes, for example, was firmly rooted in the organizing work of mothers, whose activism revolved around forging networks of like-minded women. Panitch observes that these mothers were "accidental activists" in that they were spurred to activism not necessarily by second-wave feminist goals, but rather from a sense of "gendered obligation" reminiscent of an older generation of middle-class, maternal feminists.[22] Parents were increasingly confident that a segregated model of care was ultimately damaging to the educational, occupational, and psychological potential of disabled people and that such supports should be deinstitutionalized in order for them to successfully live in the community. This advocacy and its associated struggles were important to the construction of a common platform with other families. Panitch concludes, "Faced with constantly having to present an alternative view of their child to the world, [mothers] became more confident and outgoing in what they knew – and more aware of what the authorities did not."[23]

Personal and emotional inspiration formed the basis of family advocacy, but it also occasionally contrasted sharply with the collective goals of advocacy groups and professionals. The Oscar-nominated film *Lorenzo's Oil* epitomized these dynamics within parent-driven organizations, as one couple (played by Susan Sarandon and Nick Nolte) struggled to raise their child Francesco at home, despite his complex medical needs.[24] Faced with an inflexible system of medical trials and a deferential parents' group, Francesco's parents rejected the collective vision of the other parents and forged their own path towards community living. In her celebrated family autobiography, *Four Walls of My Freedom*, Canadian author Donna Thomson explains the psychology underpinning parent caregiving and activism. Thomson asserts, "The wellbeing of children and their parents is so deeply interconnected that usually parents cannot separate the two. Certainly, I couldn't. In the case of children with disabilities, this extreme closeness lasts much, much longer into adulthood."[25]

Families of people living in institutions during the 1960s increasingly believed that existing residential treatment of disabled people inadequately served the goal of improving the skills and abilities necessary for reintegration in society. The Woodlands Parents' Group, for example, established in Vancouver in 1968, produced a powerful documentary called *Thursday's Child*, which showcased widespread opposition to institutionalization among family advocates in Canada. As part of the national response to the groundbreaking investigation of the Orillia Hospital, the documentary presented the horrified reactions of parents who criticized the state of Canadian residential institutions. The film featured unattended patients wandering sterile hallways or compulsively rocking in chairs, surrounded by incessant crying and screaming.[26] Government officials initially denied the film's producers access to certain units for "the severely retarded" but eventually relented, reserving the right to deem any audio or video unacceptable for use. The Woodlands film echoed earlier exposés of residential institutions such as the infamous Willowbrook investigation in New York and the landmark film *Hurry Tomorrow*, which documented life in a locked psychiatric hospital ward in Los Angeles, both of which sparked a major investigation of the state of care for psychiatric patients across North America.[27]

The Woodlands Parents' Group reported that, after a three-month "settling-in" period parents had difficulty recognizing their skinnier, shaven-head, and heavily medicated children. Reportedly, parents also were made to feel unwelcome or treated with token civility by professionals and others involved in the care of children and were told that, if they considered themselves experts, they should take their children home and care for them on their own.[28] Many parents felt they were forced to make an "intolerable trade off" between inadequate community supports or "placing our children in a traumatic environment in which they would be neglected and abused."[29] Parents felt pitied, not respected, and were "prevented from exercising any meaningful influence in [their] handicapped children's lives," while being "branded as 'over-emotional'" if they expressed anything beyond complete deference to medical authorities.[30]

Many parents were outraged and inspired to develop alternatives to institutional care. By the 1960s family advocates and others within the deinstitutionalization movement argued that community supports and services should replace residential institutions in order to promote the social and economic integration of disabled people. Parents' groups argued that medical authorities often inappropriately shuffled more people with disabilities into residential institutions than was necessary. Parents' groups pointed out that this situation arose partly from the lack of community-based services that discouraged parents from raising their children at home. Parents also argued that these conditions inhibited institutionalized disabled peoples' potential to develop necessary skills and competencies to function in the community. For many families community living did not necessarily mean total independence from medical care, but rather meant a step away from "total care" institutions that segregated disabled people from the broader community.

However, deinstitutionalization was not a straightforward matter. It involved the replacement of institutional care with a complex matrix of community-based medical, social, rehabilitation, and family services. For people with intellectual disabilities and mental health issues, deinstitutionalization involved downloading responsibility to local general hospitals, whose psychiatric wards quickly expanded to handle the spike in demand.[31] But hospital wards were often ill-equipped to handle the influx of new patients and many were simply discharged into the community with minimal supports. People with "severe" physical disabilities also experienced a degree of "re-hospitalization" because of the lack of attendant care programming available to them in their own homes.[32] The Canadian documentary series *Moving On*, for example, included an episode that focused on the experiences of ex-patients following the closure of psychiatric institutions. The episode revolved around healthcare initiatives and the narratives of people with disabilities who were concerned with both the diversion of funds to support institutions and the result of "re-institutionalization" for many people with mental health issues. The story revealed that many people discharged from residential hospitals during the 1970s faced communities not equipped to meet their needs and were later re-hospitalized into acute care wards or lived in extreme poverty and/or homelessness. One woman featured in the episode noted, "If somebody can live in the community, get a job, pay for their own way then I think society is better off than that person being locked in an institution."[33]

The activism of concerned middle-class parents provided service organizations with the fundraising capacity and public recognition to develop into effective lobby groups seeking improvement to public services. Parent-driven organizations cultivated funding relationships with political authorities and built public credibility to become increasingly significant sources of services alongside an evolving welfare state. Parent networking also remained an important feature in the establishment and promotion of charitable services that made community living a reality, and parents of disabled children and adults often sat on the boards of major charitable service organizations, providing support and direction to the development of new and existing services.[34] Non-profit charitable organizations accrued extensive experience during the 1960s and 1970s in helping families of disabled children and adults find social and economic integration through in-house programming and promotional campaigns targeting prejudicial attitudes towards the disabled. The Easter Seals of Ontario, for example, ran a Parent Delegate program during this period that was "rooted in the wisdom of generations of mothers," in which nurses would befriend new parents and connect them with relevant services, support, and advice.[35] Such disability organizations carved out a key position in the non-profit social service system that developed in the post-war period by acting as centres of expertise, research, and advocacy.

The expansion of the non-profit service system for disabled people was also due in large part to the widespread practice of servicing as well as employing clients as unpaid volunteers. Service agencies that employed disabled clients increasingly came into conflict with parents who shared differing priorities than an increasingly organized and professional network of social workers and rehabilitation professionals. For example, Goodwill Industries in Toronto reported that, as more disabled people were referred to their organization at a younger age during the 1970s, there was increasing opportunity for conflict with parents, who sometimes disagreed with operational issues.[36] Goodwill noted in 1981 that 30 per cent of referrals were terminated at the end of an eight-week assessment, likely in part because of parents' influence around access to services. Government officials with Ontario's Handicapped Employment Program (HEP) concluded that "home environments affect successful employment rates," particularly when it came to the nature of interactions with a developing infrastructure of disability-related services in the community.

Many voluntary organizations were set up to deal with a particular type of disability, and their services typically were structured to address the needs of that specific group. As a result, service agencies during this period were fractured by a myriad of impairment-specific "causes" aligned with different medical categories of disability. This approach tended to focus on the immediate concerns facing particular pathologies of disability rather than cultivating a broader identity or engaging a larger constituency of disabled people. Parents of children and adults living with various types of "mental retardation" drove the deinstitutionalization movement and also were responsible for establishing local agencies to address the problems of social and economic integration facing this specific group of people with intellectual disabilities.[37] As a result, services for people with intellectual or developmental impairments proliferated, while people with mental health issues and other disabilities did not necessarily enjoy the same expansion in a safety net of community agencies following rapid deinstitutionalization.[38] As silos of disability advocacy developed in this manner, there was also little conversation or collaboration among them, despite the fact that they collectively constituted the disability movement at the time. Each type of disability or category of impairment had its own medical experts, social advocates, and issues and generally lacked the framework in which to pursue a unified agenda that benefited all people with disabilities or in which to address the shared problems of employment, housing, education, and transportation.

Non-profit charities sought to improve opportunities for disabled people to live and work in the community, but did so without necessarily attempting to reconfigure the predominant view of disability as an individual medical problem. Disability-specific advocacy restricted communication between disability organizations and prevented the development of a collective disability identity, since the medical and social needs of different groups of disabled people were addressed variably by different groups of advocates. Disability studies scholar Tom Shakespeare has argued in support of a revised social model of disability that legitimates the realities of impairment beyond socially constructed barriers. Shakespeare notes, "Voluntary organisations and charitable relations will continue to be necessary, both on the road towards a more equal society, but also even after equality has been achieved. This is because disabled people and their families will continue to have complex needs, and voluntary organisations will often be the best way to support those needs."[39] Family advocates prioritized fundraising for scientific research and development as it related to improvements in diagnosis, treatment, rehabilitation, and assistive technology for people with specific disabilities. Significant advancements in medical science and assistive technology tied research fundraising initiatives to disability awareness campaigns that shaped a particular image of disabled people. While these initiatives were necessary for the funding of medical advancements and development of service agencies that initially enabled community living, such measures ultimately reinforced the notion of disability as a complex individual problem requiring medical intervention.

People with disabilities increasingly observed that fundraising initiatives largely reflected a charitable approach to disability. Disability activist Susan Peters observes that fundraisers, such as the Jerry Lewis Muscular Dystrophy Association Telethon, reflected a paternalist approach to disability in its showcasing of unfortunate representations of disabled adults and children as marketing tools.[40] The telethon, poignantly broadcast each Labour Day weekend in Canada during celebrations of the achievements of working people, infantilized disabled people, who were referred to as "Jerry's Kids" regardless of their age.[41] The American (Labor Day) telethon was widely viewed in Canada, and Canadians typically donated approximately 10 per cent of the telethon's total multi-million dollar revenue.[42] Barbara Turnbull similarly found that fundraising initiatives turned her into the subject of charity. Turnbull sustained a spinal cord injury from a gunshot wound while working at a Brampton, Ontario, convenience store and was subsequently the subject of intense media coverage.[43] Turnbull recounted one instance where she was in a restaurant with her mother following a period of rehabilitation when a woman walked up to them, confirmed Barbara's identity, and said she wanted to donate to the Barbara Turnbull Fund. The woman then exclaimed, "You never *really* know if the money goes where it's intended," and she leaned down, kissed Barbara on the head, and left $100 on the table.[44] Turnbull recalled that this direct encounter with "fundraising" left her "feeling greatly embarrassed and like, well, like a charity case."[45]

Landmark recognition of disability rights came in the early 1970s with the United Nations (UN) Declaration on the Rights of Mentally Retarded Persons in 1971 and subsequent Declaration on the Rights of Disabled Persons in 1975, which guaranteed equal civil and human rights protections as well as the economic and social security necessary for a decent standard of living.[46] The declarations were due in large part to multinational movements of parent advocates, who struggled to recalibrate the experience of disability and represented the culmination of decades of parent activism focused on building a framework dedicated to securing the rights and protections of disabled people. The UN referenced the pivotal role of families of disabled persons in the entrenchment and protection of these rights as equal participants in the pursuit of community integration. The 1982 UN World Programme of Action Concerning Disabled Persons similarly recognized the critical role of families in the rehabilitation and integration of disabled people. The UN again noted that "in helping disabled persons, every effort should be made to keep their families together, to enable them to live in their own communities and to support family and community groups who are working with this objective."[47] Parents' groups worked to bring about the goals set out in these international commitments, helping transform the political discourse around disability in Canada. Parent-driven organizations recognized the importance of enshrining their particular vision of disability in the legislative framework of the country.

While family advocates sought to reorient expectations around disabled people and energized the voluntary sector to improve resources for disabled people to live and function in the community, they did not necessarily prioritize the development of a new model of disability. Family advocacy in fact constituted a form of consumer activism as parents used their position as proxy consumers of services used by their disabled children and relatives to push for systemic improvements that better reflected their particular vision of disability. As the Woodlands Parents' Group learned, "Parents of people with handicaps sometimes make the mistake of creating too sharp a distinction between human

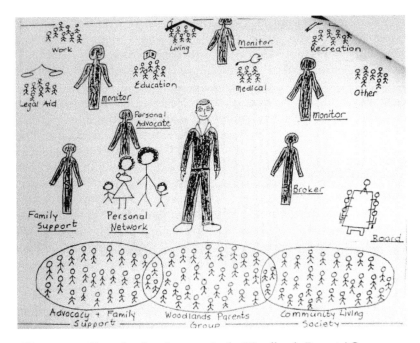

2 Illustration of how family advocates in the Woodlands Parents' Group perceived their supportive role regarding individuals with intellectual disabilities living in the community. Among other issues the working lives of children and adults associated with the group were seen to require monitoring by family and personal networks that ensured individuals were fully supported by families, personal advocates, brokers, and independent monitors to access work, education, housing, medical services, recreation, legal aid, and other services in the community.[48] © Woodlands Parents' Group, 1984. Reproduced with permission.

values and practical systems, and professionals seem particularly prone to this form of myopia."[49] Service agencies and clubs, parents' groups, and other advocacy associations that acted on behalf of disabled people conveyed the message that increased funding for rehabilitation technology, services, and community-based supports would satisfy the needs of disabled people. The predominant approach taken by parent-driven organizations was largely focused on the pragmatic issues involved in improvement of disabled people's ability to function in the community rather than reconfiguring the social and economic fabric of society to improve its inclusivity.

Disability rights activists increasingly observed that, while families were often a springboard to community integration, they could also have a disempowering effect on disabled people; they argued that responses to disability by family advocates often occurred within the paradigm of the patriarchal family unit that projected utilitarian social roles upon people with disabilities. In a documentary televised in 1982 in Canada called *The Disability Myth*, Tracy Carpenter, a former resident at Bloorview Hospital during the 1960s, recalled that she always had strong family support whenever she resisted institutional control over her life.[50] But Carpenter observed that her particular family situation was largely an anomaly in that many of her peers lived in families that presented barriers to their full social and economic participation in the community. Parents were often indicted by disability rights activists for being overprotective, particularly in their role as advocates. The Ontario March of Dimes, for example, lamented that many people with disabilities were "simply not employable" largely because they had grown up with low expectations of their capabilities in segregated schools and had overprotective parents who did not stimulate their development.[51] A prime example of such family dynamics was televised on CTV Network in 1979 in the popular Canadian series *The Littlest Hobo*, in which a father blocked his disabled son, Chris, from participating in a Frisbee competition when Chris's support worker (played by a young Mike Myers) intervenes:

DAD: Did you really think you could compete against these other boys?

CHRIS: I can try!

DAD: I'm sorry son, I can't let you.

CHRIS: Why not?

DAD: Because you might hurt yourself.

CHRIS: Damn it ...

SUPPORT WORKER: How could you do that to him?

DAD: Would you rather see him humiliate himself in a contest with some normal kids? I have to protect him.

SUPPORT WORKER: You're not protecting him, Mr Martin. You're protecting yourself.[52]

As people with disabilities sought greater control over their lives, parents were increasingly seen to embody a position of overprotectiveness and a barrier to full participation. The patriarchal family was often conceptualized as a microcosm of broader relational processes that exerted power over loosely defined subjugated populations, such as the relationship between people with disabilities, parents, and service agencies.[53] As community living generally entailed heavy reliance on service networks controlled in part by professionals and family associations, disability rights activists argued that the approach of parent-driven organizations often resembled the patriarchal family by reinforcing the status quo disempowerment of disabled people.[54] For most of the twentieth century the public face of disability spoke with many and varied voices, the majority of which did not belong to people with disabilities. Individual parents and groups comprised a dynamic set of family advocates who represented the condition, needs, and goals of disabled people to a wider audience. Advocates reflected different power bases that collaborated and clashed in the promotion and protection of people with disabilities.

Disability activists were unlike ethnic or racial minorities but similar to the gay rights movement in that they "cannot rely on their families or those around them to develop their identity."[55] As the discourse of disability community participation increasingly shifted towards the pursuit of disability rights and independent living during the 1960s and early 1970s, family advocates were forced to grapple with the emergence of new disability rights activist organizations that challenged their influence in the disability community. These new voices of activism highlighted the fact that despite laying the foundations for community living, individual parents and organized parents' groups had failed to fashion a collective disability identity that could effectively challenge the political economic discourse of disability. The development of a minority identity among disabled people was both profoundly empowering and shocking to a public that had encountered other civil rights movements but never among disabled people. Different conceptualizations of autonomy thus often resulted in tension between children and parents, creating situations where the full realization of independence for many people with disabilities was effectively blocked by family advocates.[56]

One area of concern for disability rights activists revolved around the reliance of parent-driven organizations on charitable funds. The Canadian disability rights movement challenged the charitable approach to disability on the basis that it promoted negative stereotypes of disability, robbed people of their rightful access to work opportunities, and counteracted attempts to secure social and economic equality.[57] Fundraising initiatives provided disability service agencies with regular opportunities to promote awareness of their disabled constituencies while highlighting the organization's agenda. For a growing movement of disability rights activists, however, the continuation of charitable methods to raise awareness and funds for services were seen as being delivered as a matter of privilege rather than a right that conflicted with a developing discourse around disability rights that sought to move away from the long-standing charitable approach to disability.

Disability rights activists also argued that parents and family organizations contributed to negative attitudes by failing to challenge the association of disability with dependency and the "deserving" poor. In his autobiography, *Daddy Bent-Legs*, Canadian author Neil Matheson, who lives with cerebral palsy, commented on the relationship between his parents and his personal experience of disability that motivated him to activism. He notes, "As parents, my mom and dad may have a good second-hand knowledge and understanding of what it is like to be disabled, but they could never hope to give an accurate firsthand account of anything. Not without living it, as I have."[58] Family advocates and service agencies were increasingly seen by disability rights activists as being responsible for reinforcing the view that disability was a social, economic and political "problem" to be "solved" through research funding, and improved assistive technologies.[59]

From the mid-twentieth century, family advocates established the conditions necessary for the redefinition of disability in Canada. Local family groups and gendered networks of middle-class mothers envisioned new models of care based in the community rather than accepting the status quo of segregated systems of care. These parents worked to create inclusive social and physical environments that supported disabled people. As contemporary examples of older patterns of middle-class social reform, parents and families of disabled people argued that disabled people were capable of living with their families or in group homes if provided with the proper supports. Community living entailed the destruction of an existing system of segregated institutionalized care that had long prevented people with disabilities from seeking social and economic integration. As parents' groups channelled their energies into charitable service organizations, a powerful network of advocacy organizations mobilized to promote resources to the full participation of disabled people in society.

However, a unique dilemma arose with the advent of disability rights activism by the mid-1970s, which challenged families' control over services and the messaging of disability issues to a wider audience. Groups of disabled people emerged during this period, presenting their own vision of rights and integration. As we will see, these new disability activists saw family advocates, charitable and religious organizations, and rehabilitation agencies as barriers to the realization of disabled peoples' civil rights. In the language of identity politics, disability rights activism promised to translate the "good intentions" of others into a practicable platform of legal, cultural, and economic advancement.[60] As the representative voice of disability rights activists during the 1970s in Canada, the Coalition of Provincial Organizations of the Handicapped thus worked towards "strengthening the organizational efforts of the handicapped community in Canada" in order to help disabled people free themselves from dependency-based relationships with family and charitable organizations.[61] Nevertheless, families of people with disabilities remained a fundamental element in the pursuit of social and economic integration and helped to establish a platform for the realization of economic integration.

Chapter Three

Rehabilitation, Awareness Campaigns, and the Pursuit of Employability

Many of the handicapped we have encountered seem to have the attitude that only a handicapped person knows what's good for a handicapped person … While we believe that the handicapped can add a new dimension to the thinking of traditional service delivery systems, being handicapped does not necessarily make one an instant expert. Many responsible disabled persons have become extremely knowledgeable in the field of rehabilitation. Many of these people also have a constituency to whom they are responsible. Thus, a person with a handicap who has developed a good background in rehabilitation, who has the ear of other handicapped, and who has the ability to provide the system with insights which they themselves might not have, can be a valuable person. On the other hand, there are many professionals who are not handicapped, have good rapport with their clients, and are objective enough to realize the deficiencies and short-comings of the system, who are just as valuable to the purpose of promoting change for the better.[1]

During the 1970s and 1980s, people with disabilities became more visible in local communities across Canada, in large part owing to the work of rehabilitation professionals and the proliferation of community-based disability organizations. The "work of disability" encompassed a wide range of professions and vocations dedicated to assisting people with acquired and congenital disabilities to contend with poverty and unemployment by developing individual physical, mental, social, and vocational preparedness for participation in the formal and informal economy. Rehabilitation, particularly in preparation for competitive employment, entailed an extensive and prolonged journey through various training regimens designed to help disabled minds and bodies approximate normative standards of ability. Associations of rehabilitation personnel also shaped the public image of disability and tended to use the social capital they enjoyed as part of the medical complex to enhance their middle-class professional credibility. People with disabilities were regularly featured in awareness campaigns sponsored by rehabilitation organizations designed to highlight their employability while underscoring the importance of the rehabilitation industry as the conduit to disabled peoples' social integration. While rehabilitation certainly played an important role in challenging the status quo exclusion of disabled people from the workforce and broader society, rehabilitation practices and philosophies were increasingly contested in the context of an emerging disability rights movement in Canada. Service agencies and professional associations were initially reluctant to share their advocacy platform with disability activists whom they viewed, not as collaborators, but as clients. Eventually, professional-led organizations and service agencies were forced to acknowledge this collaborative position in the shared pursuit of social and economic participation for all disabled people.

This chapter examines the contested role of rehabilitation in the lives of Canadians with disabilities during a period in which an emerging disability rights movement transformed the political economy of disability. The first section documents the growth of the rehabilitation industry in Canada as increasing numbers of disabled people sought greater participation in mainstream society. Next, we examine the quasi-medical nature and process of rehabilitation practices in relation to the emergence of public awareness campaigns conducted on behalf of the disability community. Finally, we analyse the evolving relationship between professional associations, service agencies, and disability rights activists as disabled people attempted to assert their rights to forge a new collaborative politics of rehabilitation.

The contemporary rehabilitation system in Canada originated largely in the development of supports and services to reintegrate injured veterans into the social and economic fabric of Canadian society. The aftermath of both the First and the Second World Wars and outbreaks of disease such as the mid-twentieth-century polio epidemic enhanced the public's trust in medical authorities while highlighting the importance of the rehabilitation industry. Thousands of veterans with amputations, visual impairments, and other physical and mental disabilities returned to inaccessible homes, workplaces, and public spaces.[2] Many of these injured veterans faced a life of poverty and unemployment common among other disabled people. Although many Canadians with disabilities were excluded from workforce participation, the economic dislocation of injured veterans was considered particularly morally unacceptable to most politicians and the wider Canadian public. As a result, a variety of initiatives specifically targeting injured veterans were introduced in the post-war period to promote reintegration into the paid workforce. The 1951 National Conference on the Rehabilitation of the Physically Disabled, for example, occurred in response to the growing needs of decommissioned injured veterans. The conference provided a watershed moment that led to the creation of a federal coordinator for vocational rehabilitation programming and new cost-sharing agreements with the provinces in an effort to rapidly expand the rehabilitation system to meet the needs of a growing disabled population.[3] Federal-provincial cost-sharing in the area of vocational rehabilitation for veterans set the stage for the rapid development of the rehabilitation industry.

Eager to re-establish themselves as independent wage-earners, veterans formed associations and service organizations to promote awareness of disability and to secure resources designed to improve access to rehabilitation services. Facing the chronic unemployment and poverty seen in the larger disability community, injured veterans organized themselves into lobby groups and established networks of service agencies that stimulated the development of the broader rehabilitation system.[4] Organizations such as War Amps, founded in 1920 by Great War veterans, were established on the principle of fraternalism (or brotherly social support), helping fellow injured veterans acquire prosthetics, vocational training, and other rehabilitation services at a time when few other options existed.[5] Similarly, Sir Arthur Pearson's Association of the War-Blinded and the National Council of Veterans' Associations formed a national lobbying force that pushed for improvements in pensions, legislation, and therapeutic services.[6] In the post-war and interwar periods, such veterans' organizations pressured federal and provincial governments to increase their direct involvement in rehabilitation programs for both disabled veterans and civilians.

Other people with disabilities, however, increasingly complained about the development of a two-tiered rehabilitation system that favoured veterans over civilians. Veterans were among the first to acquire new accessible technologies and rehabilitation facilities, which permitted greater access than civilians had to jobs and other benefits.[7] War-wounded veterans existed within a moral economy separate from other people with disabilities, as it was generally held that their injuries were the result of patriotic sacrifice, qualifying them for extra support.[8] Many veterans reconstructed their living spaces with Department of Veterans Affairs (DVA) funding or found new lodging in buildings with elevators, yet other disabled people, such as civilians receiving workers' compensation, had limited access to such funds.[9] "Civilian" disabled people argued that all people with disabilities needed equal access to work supports and rehabilitation services regardless of the origin of their impairments.[10] For example, a landmark study conducted in the mid-1970s by Cyril Greenland included approximately 2,000 participants across the country and found that basic services provided by the Canadian National Institute for the Blind (CNIB) "compared poorly" with those available to war-blinded veterans.[11] Other studies similarly found that distinctions between veterans and civilians actually inhibited the development of better services for all people with disabilities and prevented the cultivation of a shared political activist agenda.[12]

As wartime coordination agreements between federal and provincial governments expired, people with disabilities enjoyed greater access to rehabilitation services that were critical to labour market integration. The volume of war veterans returning to Canadian communities and the unique social dynamics that surrounded them actually stimulated the development of treatment and rehabilitation facilities for all people with disabilities.[13] Veterans with physical disabilities pushed for the rapid expansion of community-based physical and occupational therapies as well as the other disability-related programs, services, and supports that formed the rehabilitation industry.

In order to facilitate the development of the rehabilitation industry, wartime Orders in Council were replaced in 1961 with the Vocational Rehabilitation of Disabled Persons Act (VRDP), providing federal-provincial cost sharing provisions that enabled the rapid expansion of rehabilitation and job training for all disabled people.[14] Under the VRDP all the necessary costs of rehabilitation programs were covered, including assessment fees, counselling, books, tools, restorative services, vocational and job training, equipment, aids, and other allowances, which were paid through vocational rehabilitation services rather than being deducted from disability pensions or requiring clients to pay out of pocket.[15] Owing to the introduction of the VRDP, rehabilitation services were made available to many disabled people, who could acquire work skills and abilities that would promote greater participation in social and economic life. However, despite the overall growth in re-habilitation services, many civilians continued to deal with congenital and acquired disabilities on their own or through private insurance.[16]

Across North America vocational rehabilitation was the first type of service made available to both veterans and civilians with disabilities.[17] In the United States, for example, President Harry Truman established the President's Committee on the Employment of the Handicapped (PCEH) in 1949 to address increased demand for vocational rehabilita-tion services by disabled veterans and the wider disability community.[18] Canadian veterans similarly pursued initiatives to develop vocational programs for fellow disabled veterans, such as War Amps, which es-tablished a well-regarded key tag recovery service that provided em-ployment to veterans with amputations who were unable to find paid work in mainstream settings.[19] The CNIB also ran a growing catering and concessional stand business that was staffed by clients with visual impairments as part of the upswing in vocational rehabilitation pro-gramming.[20] The venture, named "Caterplan," began as a single lunch counter in Ottawa in 1928 and ballooned into a highly successful busi-ness by the 1960s, with annual sales reportedly in excess of $30 million in over 550 locations across Canada.[21]

"Robert," an interview participant in the present study, who worked in CNIB's Caterplan during the 1960s, recalled, "I worked weekends at the CNIB ... every weekend throughout my high school and univer-sity days. It's relevant because it is very difficult to get part-time and summer employment for a blind or low-vision person. But back in the 1960s and certainly even earlier than that, if you wanted to work you always got a job."[22] Robert got his first job in 1960 at age thirteen, work-ing weekends and summers at the counter at one of the CNIB's con-fectionary stands. Unable to find a job elsewhere because of his visual impairment, Robert knew he could get some extra money and work experience through the CNIB's Caterplan business, but he soon learned he had an aptitude as a manager. This discovery was buoyed by the understanding that other opportunities for advancement within the organization at the services and administrative levels existed – oppor-tunities that he understands existed for only a short time at the CNIB during the 1960s and early 1970s for his age cohort. Determined to be-come a working professional and confident of his competitive ability to access information through various assistive devices, Robert earned a university degree and returned to the CNIB as a supervisor while he worked his way into upper management.

Other interview participants "Dan" and "Grace" similarly found that summer employment at Caterplan during the late 1950s and 1960s was crucial to their success in obtaining full-time employment with the CNIB and eventual work as successful public servants in various levels of government.[23] However, the disability rights group Blind Organization of Ontario with Self-Help Tactics (BOOST) argued at the time that Caterplan, whose blind workforce averaged 13–19 per cent of its total workforce between 1968 and 1975, had become a "substantial profit-making enterprise" that paid minimum wages and was tainted by "allegations of negative bias towards blind workers, who had little choice but to accept poor wages with little prospect of earning raises or promotions."[24] BOOST observed, "The public is familiar with the image of a blind man behind the counter, dispensing candy or coffee in many public buildings, but the public does not know the problems faced by that man behind the counter."[25] Unionized blind workers at Caterplan even went on strike in 1979 over allegations of poor working conditions, subminimum-level wages, and in protest against the lack of consumer control in CNIB as evidence for the unjust working arrangements.[26] COPOH similarly maintained that it was necessary to promote consumer activism because the rehabilitation industry, including agencies such as the CNIB, was increasingly seen to represent barriers to self-determination.[27]

The establishment of Lyndhurst Lodge in Toronto in 1945 represented the national success of local veterans' groups that identified a need for comprehensive residential rehabilitation and community support for people with spinal cord injuries.[28] As DVA-sponsored patients and funding receded, Lyndhurst became part of an expanding network of rehabilitation services for people with physical disabilities. Under the leadership of Lieutenant John Counsell and others, rehabilitation facilities such as Lyndhurst partnered with local and national service agencies, notably the Canadian Paraplegic Association, to provide both veterans and non-veterans with disabilities with greater access to assistive devices, counselling, and other tools essential for successful community living.[29] In fact, Lyndhurst garnered a national reputation as a major centre for rehabilitation in the treatment of spinal cord injuries, leading Saskatchewan Premier Tommy Douglas, champion of universal healthcare in Canada, to pledge his support for residents of his province with spinal cord injuries to attend Lyndhurst in order to receive intensive rehabilitation therapy that was otherwise unavailable to them.[30]

Upon completion of physical rehabilitation many Lyndhurst patients, like other people with disabilities, faced the dilemma of inaccessible communities and workplaces. Many people with spinal cord injuries who attended Lyndhurst and were successfully discharged nevertheless encountered difficulty in their social and economic reintegration into society. Historian Geoffrey Reaume recounts the work of the medical director, Dr Albin Jousse, who wrote to the commissioner of Ontario's hospitals in 1964 complaining that many young patients had nowhere to go other than long-term care facilities following the completion of rehabilitation programs.[31] Jousse understood the difficulty encountered by Lyndhurst patients during the transition to community living and considered this a major barrier beyond the rehabilitation hospital, which he believed had a responsibility to assist clients find suitable work and living arrangements. In one instance he proposed that young females live in student nurse residences to avoid being placed with the elderly and in order to receive the ongoing care they required while providing the added benefit of employment opportunities as receptionists.[32]

As Lyndhurst clients discovered, rehabilitation was an incomplete response to communities that were not always willing or able to receive them. Indeed, most people with disabilities, regardless of the origin of their impairment, relied heavily on family support beyond the rehabilitation process.[33] One interview participant, "William," attended Lyndhurst in the early 1960s following a spinal cord injury. William, reflecting on his experience and those of his peers, found that the initial treatment and recovery he received only partly prepared him for community living. Following two years of rehabilitation at Lyndhurst, William returned to his hometown before attending university during a period in the early 1960s that he referred to as the "pre-accessibility days."[34] He encountered no curb cuts at street corners, "apartment buildings were very difficult," "bathroom doors were too narrow," and there was no accessible underground parking, "which is pretty much a necessity if you're living on your own," among other difficulties. William credited Canadian Paraplegic Association social worker Ross Beggs for providing essential support while he reintegrated into the community. Beggs, whose accomplishments and accolades from ex-patients were documented in Reaume's history of Lyndhurst, was a vocational rehabilitation counsellor responsible in the early 1960s for assisting people to find jobs and housing and to gain access to schooling.[35] William reported that Beggs even liaised with the university's engineering department on his and other students' behalf to design

3 & 4 Photographs of typical obstacles confronted by wheelchair users on the University of Toronto campus during the 1970s, as reported in *The Varsity* newspaper. Street curbs and long staircases presented barriers to access in the city and thus prevented many people with mobility impairments from fully participating in the life of the community.[36] © *The Varsity*, 1977. Reproduced with permission.

and install curb cuts at priority locations throughout the campus.[37] For William and other people with various disabilities, rehabilitation started his pursuit of social and economic reintegration rather than represented its terminus.

Disability became "big business" in the post-war period, as people with disabilities were situated at the centre of an extensive rehabilitation industry that "demands clients in order to justify [its] existence."[38] According to this perspective, disabled people were worth more to the economy as liminal figures, existing between exclusion and integration, than they would be if they were full participants in the labour market, given that each disabled person generates substantial employment within the various supports and services they use.[39] James Charlton observes that whole industries were established to rehabilitate, transport, house, educate, employ, and service people with disabilities. Charlton argues that disabled people "become commodities the moment their disabling condition acquires an exchange value that a few people profit from."[40] Originally a working-class occupation with little formal training, occupational therapy had achieved greater recognition as a middle-class profession by the post-war period, as rehabilitation workers organized themselves into professional associations. The success of the rehabilitation industry, however, was judged by its ability to reintegrate disabled people into society. In drawing attention to "special" needs arising from impairment, disabled people were singled out by rehabilitation through instituting various "corrective" regimes of therapeutic intervention.[41] However, many people with disabilities were often "rehabilitated from the time they are disabled to when they go to their graves," owing to the array of medical, psychological, rehabilitation, social, and therapeutic professionals that permeate their lives.[42]

The rehabilitation industry that emerged during the 1970s defined disability by an individual's difficulty in accessing employment. The US Rehabilitation Act of 1973, for example, defined disability in economic terms as denoting an individual who has a physical or mental disability that represents a "handicap" to employment and who can be expected to benefit from vocational rehabilitation services.[43] Rehabilitation was primarily directed at disabled persons, subjecting them to intensive training regimens that promised to help them better navigate an inaccessible world. The original conceptualization of vocational rehabilitation entailed training disabled people to be accommodating to employers, given that business enterprises were not expected to accommodate people with disabilities.[44] Clients in rehabilitation programs were expected to push the boundaries of their abilities to therapeutic effect, sometimes using devices and technology that supplemented or replaced "lost" abilities. Yet rehabilitation professionals during the 1970s and 1980s often found that local communities were ill-prepared to handle the needs and demands disabled people placed upon mainstream environments, thus jeopardizing the success of their therapeutic efforts.[45] Rehabilitation, then, was a twofold individualized process that reshaped deviant bodies to approximate normative standards while easing disabled people's access to mainstream environments.

By focusing on individuals' perceived deficits and struggles, rehabilitation redirected attention away from the reconstruction of exclusive environments and systemic practices that restricted disabled people's access to mainstream opportunities. Although many disabled people recognized the obvious benefits of rehabilitation, there was growing recognition that it could also preserve an exclusionary status quo.[46] Continuous intervention in disabled people's lives by medical and rehabilitation professionals ultimately perpetuated the belief that disability was a complex problem that precluded the ability to live and work independently in the community.[47]

This approach to disability began to change in Canada during the 1970s with the evolution of hiring initiatives towards broader awareness campaigns that highlighted socially constructed barriers to workforce participation. "Your attitude could be their biggest handicap" – so went the tagline of an unprecedented national awareness campaign undertaken by the leading disability advocacy organization in the early 1970s, the Canadian Rehabilitation Council for the Disabled (CRCD).[48] As the national voice of the rehabilitation industry, the CRCD was generally seen to speak on behalf of the disability community. Television and print advertisements rolled out across the country featuring, along with the provocative caption, people in wheelchairs, those wearing leg braces, and those manifesting other physical disabilities. Suddenly, the public were encouraged to discard accepted wisdom, which rooted disability in an individual's medical pathology, and to consider the concept that overcoming the limitations of impairment required a combination of professional intervention and adjustments in social attitudes. Just as the "Marching Mothers" campaigns of twenty years earlier had attempted to reconfigure general understanding about the impact of polio, the CRCD campaign ambitiously set out to create greater public awareness of the role of attitudes in the construction of barriers to integration. Indeed, many children with polio during the 1950s were now working-age adults facing attitudinal and physical barriers to employment that would have benefited from the greater awareness sought by the CRCD.[49]

This new perspective on disability was facilitated by shifting control over the representation of disability issues to the public. When federal responsibility for vocational rehabilitation programming moved away from the policy arena of labour towards the Department of Health and Welfare in 1973, rehabilitation services were more fully integrated with social assistance and disability support mechanisms. Funds were immediately made available to the CRCD to raise awareness of disability in a way that highlighted social barriers but ultimately underscored the role of the rehabilitation sector in the lives of disabled people. The type of awareness CRCD sought to create was that of disabled peoples'

One of these men is a burden to society. The other is disabled.

5 Cover of *Access* magazine, 1981, published by the Canadian Rehabilitation Council for the Disabled featuring two men in suits – one standing, the other sitting in a wheelchair – with the caption "One of these men is a burden to society. The other is disabled." Similar to the "Your attitude could be their biggest handicap" poster, this image plays on stereotypes of wheelchair users, forcing viewers to evaluate their assumptions about the association of disability with burden. Such images challenged assumptions about disability in the workplace with the aim of creating a more inclusive work culture.[50] © Easter Seals March of Dimes National Council, 1981. Reproduced with permission.

potential, unlocked by rehabilitation services and unblocked by prejudicial attitudes.

For the architects of the CRCD awareness campaign, disability was misunderstood and this ignorance perpetuated attitudinal barriers to inclusion in mainstream society. The campaign reflected a developing consensus in the rehabilitation industry that broader social barriers were partly responsible for the social and economic marginalization of disabled people. Rehabilitation professionals increasingly observed clients making their way through the rehabilitation system only to find their integration blocked by physical barriers and unspoken prejudices.[51] As a result, a lack of awareness about disability was seen to create and re-inforce "disabling" attitudes, which restricted the potential impact that rehabilitation professionals sought to achieve in terms of the meaning-ful social and economic integration of disabled clients.

The CRCD campaign built upon long-standing "Hire the Handi-capped" campaigns and associated events in the United States. Harold Russell, whose hands were amputated and replaced with prosthetic hooks following a war-related injury, wrote in his memoir about the de-velopment of the well-known awareness campaign.[52] Russell, who was born and raised in Sydney, Nova Scotia, achieved international celeb-rity status by starring in the acclaimed war-themed Hollywood film *The Best Years of Our Lives*; subsequently, he served as the long-time chair of the President's Committee on the Employment of the Handicapped. Russell recounted how the National Employ the Handicapped Week helped raise awareness of disability following the Second World War in order to encourage employers to change their attitudes and practices around the employment of disabled people.[53] The campaign typically constituted a number of local-level events that were endorsed at the national level, but by 1949 organizers had begun to promote the slo-gan "Hire the Handicapped – It's Good Business." The slogan achieved wide influence by means such as the skywriter, a famed zeppelin that travelled along the east coast carrying the message, a special invocation by the archbishop of New York City, and nationwide school essay con-tests that prompted students to write essays on hiring the handicapped, offering prizes including money and trips to Washington, DC.[54]

The ubiquitous slogan steadily made its way into the Canadian dis-course of disability issues and awareness activities surrounding the pro-motion of disabled people in the labour market. The Toronto Mayor's Task Force on the Disabled and Elderly noted in 1976, for example, "All of those Hire the Handicapped campaigns, however well-intentioned they may have been, have done little to alleviate the situation, pos-sibly because they were saying, in effect: 'Do the crippled a favour.'"[55] Goodwill Industries similarly noted that the slogan had become a "tired old line."[56] The Ontario Human Rights Commission asserted that despite long-standing campaigns to promote the hiring of dis-abled people, those with disabilities were "constantly being denied the opportunity even to try for jobs that are within their competence."[57] By 1980 the Ontario government was forced to distinguish wider pro-grams of affirmative action from "Hire the Handicapped"-style hir-ing campaigns in an effort to develop more intricate responses to the complex problem of unemployment in the disability community.[58] Still, the slogan continued to have wide purchase among promoters of disability employment initiatives. Local organizers with the Vocational Rehabilitation Advisory Committee in Belleville, for example, continued to hold their own Hire the Handicapped Week during the 1980s, confident that the popular slogan would resonate with local employers and the wider public.[59]

During the 1980s the slogan "Hire the Handicapped" continued to have broad influence in Canadian culture. A popular television program called *The Littlest Hobo*, for example, featured an episode, which aired in 1984 on the CTV Network. In Toronto construction foreman Victor Corrano (played by Canadian television legend Al Waxman) receives a phone call from an agent regarding promotional materials sent to him. Corrano shuffles through his mail to locate a pamphlet, which reads: "Hire the handicapped. It's good business." Distracted and agitated but pressed to display his sympathy, Corrano responds, "I got your brochure and the book. Well look Mr White I appreciate what you're trying to do, really I do, but this is ... well I got enough problems with normal guys. I don't need crutches and wheelchairs here. This is construction work here, Mr White. I don't make handbags here. That's alright. Goodbye."[60] The dramatized exchange revealed what would have been understood at the time as a commonplace response to disability by an insensitive employer.[61] Only when Corrano is later paralysed after falling from faulty scaffolding and confronts an altered self-identity does he realize that his preconceptions about disability were inaccurate.[62] In the end, the episode leaves viewers with moral lessons of acceptance and understanding about disability issues accompanied by a warning about the emotional and psychological consequences of prejudice and discrimination.

The reconceptualization of disability as the effect of attitudinal barriers constituted an entirely new paradigm that would take time to accrue in the public consciousness. Many people found it counter-intuitive to prioritize attitudinal change when the traditional approach to disability held that both social and economic exclusion were naturally correlated in excluding people whose individual impairments prevented access to work. In his landmark text *Handicapping America*, published in 1978, disability activist Frank Bowe wrote, "Resistance to hiring disabled people is as emotional as it is cognitive."[63] Bowe asserted that attitudes can be remarkably inflexible, even when people are presented with ample evidence regarding the effects of "disabling" attitudes.

Bowe discovered that attitudinal barriers were in many ways more resilient than architectural barriers because they could not be erased simply with legislation. Bowe concluded that more than thirty years of Hire the Handicapped Weeks and similar awareness campaigns across North America had resulted in little appreciable change in employer attitudes.

Deprived of a diverse set of experiences with people with disabilities, many in mainstream society relied upon stereotypes and culturally mediated notions about disability that reinforced the ideological and actual separation of disabled people from normative settings. In her address to the Seminar on the Employability of the Handicapped, Ontario Minister of Labour Bette Stephenson noted, "We may ramp the steps and widen the doors and redesign the washrooms, but until attitudes change, progress will be illusory."[64] Stephenson observed that attitudinal and psychological barriers could not be undone as readily as physical accessibility and rehabilitation, reflecting a developing consensus among rehabilitation professionals and disability rights activists regarding the attitudinal barriers to rehabilitation. Despite a collective desire to "help the handicapped," Stephenson observed that in Canada there was often a tendency to seek out simplistic solutions.

During the early 1980s a variation on the "Hire the Handicapped" campaigns emerged with a greater emphasis on the employability of disabled people. This new campaign promoted the abilities of the "able disabled," adopting a decidedly empowered approach to changing conventional attitudes, rather than focusing on eliciting sympathetic or charitable impulses implicit in the earlier CRCD campaigns. The phrase "able disabled" suggested that the "dis-" in the term "disability" wrongly characterized people with disabilities as incapable, when in fact a person's medical status did not necessarily reflect their capacity for self-determination and ability to be productive in the labour market. In 1973 E.I. Du Pont de Nemours & Company, based in Wilmington, Delaware, conducted a landmark study of its disabled employees. Du Pont included a sample of 1,452 workers and evaluated them against records of insurance rates, absenteeism, job performance, taxes, and motivation.[65] The highly influential report, titled "The Able Disabled" but widely known as the "Du Pont study," discovered that many fears around hiring disabled people and the impact on companies were unfounded, suggesting that disabled workers were just as "able" as nondisabled workers, despite widespread prejudice against them. The Du Pont study had wide international influence among the business community and rehabilitation industry, as the term "able disabled" quickly spread in disability advocacy circles in the United States and Canada as the successor to older "Hire the Handicapped" campaigns. A subsequent study conducted by Du Pont, released in 1981 and titled *Equal to the Task*, included a wider survey of 2,745 employees and confirmed earlier findings and reinforced the construction of disability in socially progressive terms.[66] Canadian authorities quickly picked up on the study's findings and message about disability. The Toronto Dominion Bank, for example, embarked on a nationwide hiring campaign following the Du Pont study, and human resource professionals in Toronto organized events featuring Du Pont as a model for Canadian employers.[67]

In preparation for the International Year of Disabled Persons (IYDP) in 1981 Canadian authorities picked up on the underlying message in the Du Pont studies in the development of promotional activities. Ontario Ministry of Labour's Handicapped Employment Program (HEP), for example, undertook a major campaign through its educational seminars, television commercials, posters, print advertising, and an exhibit that toured the province with the slogans "Label Us Able" and "We Are All Able."[68] The campaign recognized that disabled people were considered "unable" in many ways in the workplace and broader community, but it sought to reverse prejudicial "labelling" by emphasizing disabled peoples' capability for productive employment. The campaign involved a multidimensional exhibit funded by the province that toured the province featuring disabled people in everyday working environments.[69] The *Globe and Mail* used the publicity generated by the campaign to promote employers that demonstrated exemplary commitment to the campaign's slogans.[70] One television commercial aired in Canada showed a camera panning over a production studio where an advertisement was set to be shot. The scene bustled with the activities of various workers, including "carpenters, technicians and musicians preparing for the production." At the conclusion of the commercial, it was revealed that all the workers were disabled.[71] While television commercial producers apparently encountered difficulty in finding qualified disabled workers, the wider campaign built upon the foundation of public awareness about disability generated through long-standing hiring campaigns with concrete examples of productively employed people with disabilities.[72]

Despite active engagement and endorsement by rehabilitation professionals seeking to improve the state of social and economic participation

6 Actors in the "Label Us Able" television commercial campaign representing the diversity of the disability community and their capacity for productive employment.[73] © Archives of Ontario, 1981. Reproduced with permission.

among their clientele, some commentators warned that campaigns to raise awareness of the employability of disabled people might backfire, owing to a "distressing tendency of people to jump on a popular bandwagon, subsequently jumping off when it has run its course."[74] Rehabilitation thus became an increasingly politicized experience, and many people with disabilities began to question why disabled people continued to experience social and economic dislocation after many years (and dollars) spent on the expansion of the rehabilitation system and promotion of the rehabilitation approach to disability. An increasingly visible politics of disability during the 1980s reflected simmering tensions surrounding systematic practices to integrate disabled people and the control by the rehabilitation industry over the articulation and promotion of disability issues.[75] In an argument for a new collaborative politics of rehabilitation one commentator from the rehabilitation industry asked, "Who's Driving the System?" in a newsletter column in reference to the ongoing controversial debates around the merits and challenges of a "provider-driven" versus a "consumer-driven" vocational rehabilitation system.[76]

Disability rights activists in Canada increasingly argued that providers were focused more on the longevity of their programs and not enough on breaking down barriers to community participation.[77] The columnist quoted above noted that, despite appearances, consumer-controlled vs. provider-driven approaches were "not necessarily mutually exclusive nor do they need to be at odds with one another."[78] Disability rights activists argued that the commitment to medical and rehabilitation procedures that initially justified intervention in their lives often became a lifelong commitment to the rehabilitation industry that locked disabled people in a perpetually liminal state of separation from mainstream social and economic activities. Disability rights activists believed that medical and therapeutic responses to disability, while initially establishing control over disabled bodies through institutional mechanisms, also served to shape public knowledge about disability.[79] In particular, disabled people argued, they lacked control over a vast rehabilitation service system that broadcast its own definition of disability to a wider audience. Providers retorted that consumers were ignorant of the realities of the rehabilitation system and failed to appreciate the work of rehabilitation professionals.[80]

Similar to other activists in civil rights movements during the 1960s and 1970s, people with disabilities struggled with the search for a positive framework in which to foster an empowered identity to resist common experiences of oppression. Disability was linguistically and culturally conceived as the inverse of ability, freedom, and independence – all major cultural ideals in modern capitalist societies – since most forms of disability were regarded as states of compromised health that robbed individuals of their self-determination.[81] The prevalence of a largely negative ontology of disability stigmatized people with disabilities and undercut the development of a positive framework in which to build an empowered disability identity. Before the 1960s there were few alternatives to the ideology of rehabilitation and without a political voice of their own, disabled people were unable to effectively challenge this system.[82] Disabled bodies were objectified "through the gaze of deficits and deviance" that shaped the rehabilitation paradigm, since it was held that failure to adapt to normative functional standards also disqualified disabled people from full participation in social and economic opportunities.[83] Consequently, disability rights activism lagged behind other social movements, in part because many people with disabilities internalized negative associations between disability and dependency. Many people with disabilities lived, learned, and worked alongside one another during this period, in long-term care hospitals, residential institutions, rehabilitation facilities, and sheltered workshops. But the powerful influence of negative reflections of disabled bodies, due in large part to the interaction between a pervasive medical gaze and negative cultural attitudes, permeated the experience of disability and discouraged the collective empowerment of people with disabilities.[84]

Despite this negative framing of disability, rehabilitation associations played an important role in fostering the development of self-help consumer activism by supplying the opportunity for disability rights activists to come together in discussion of strategies to resist the status quo, which included the existing rehabilitation system. Disability activists' participation in CRCD, for example, stemmed from the solicitation of consumer feedback regarding rehabilitation services and areas for improvement. Marc Lalonde, then federal minister of health and welfare and highly influential member of Liberal Prime Minister Pierre Trudeau's government, provided an unprecedented endorsement of the disability rights movement in 1970 by suggesting that service agencies should consult with their disabled clients before coming to him with various requests.[85] Lalonde was unique in that he worked closely with disability rights activists and others in the disability community to focus on "the development of a citizenry attached to a single identity [being Canadian] through their differences."[86] Despite his endorsement, however, the CRCD decided to limit consumer input to issues around recreational services, since it was evidently less threatening than issues such as employment and education.[87] In 1973 the CRCD instructed consumer representatives to select six delegates to attend their inaugural conference in November in Toronto. The goal, however, was to establish an advisory committee, "not to share power."[88] Yet by this time disability activists had grown frustrated with the lack of people with disabilities as leaders in the CRCD and of any substantive recognition of the principles of consumer rights. Provincial consumer organizations of disabled people had already begun to take shape, establishing the basis for a national, cohesive force of disability activists through which the CRCD's hegemony in the sphere of rehabilitation services and promotional campaigns could be challenged. As a result, a group of activists in attendance at the CRCD conference demanded that the executive board reconvene with a majority of members with disabilities, or consumers would withdraw their support from the organization.[89] The board rejected the petition, causing consumers to leave the conference; yet the delegates left "more inspired by meeting each other than the thought of belonging to CRCD's advisory committee."[90]

The repudiation of professional control over rehabilitation services and disability advocacy fuelled an electric atmosphere of disability rights organizing in Canada. Activists affiliated with COPOH noted that disability advocacy during the 1970s was led largely by organizations representing the rehabilitation industry. Disability rights activists believed that rehabilitation professionals no longer represented the interests of people with disabilities, who, they argued, had failed to present a coherent and unified message on behalf of disabled people. Rehabilitation agencies and associations purportedly representing disabled people were seen to undermine the pursuit of social and economic participation. As evidence of the disunity, disability rights activists pointed to the domination of national organizations for disabled people, including the Canadian Paraplegic Association, the Canadian National Institute for the Blind, the Multiple Sclerosis Society, the Cerebral Palsy Association, the Canadian Coordinating Council of the Deaf, the Canadian Mental Health Association, the Canadian Association for the Mentally Retarded, the Canadian Association of Rehabilitation Professionals, and the Canadian Rehabilitation Council for the Disabled, none of which was consumer controlled.[91] Each of these organizations represented different groups of disabled people with their own priorities, mandates, and inter-organizational politics, which often had little to do with the concerns of their constituents. Although the CRCD was considered to be acting as the "national umbrella organization for many societies dedicated to rehabilitation," COPOH determined that in fact it represented the interests of rehabilitation professionals, who "failed to bring together the handicapped community" while denying consumer participation by "retaining real leadership in the new national vehicles created."[92]

Mounting tensions between disability rights activists and the CRCD led COPOH to refuse endorsement of the rehabilitation industry in any substantive way at the 1980 World Rehabilitation Congress in Winnipeg if consumers were denied the right to present their views as "autonomous consumer organizations."[93] The CRCD had managed to avoid

7 Interior of the Winnipeg Convention Centre, setting for the 1980 World
Congress of Rehabilitation International. It was here that COPOH made
history as the first disability rights activist organization to participate in
the congress as representatives of the disability community.[94] © Easter Seals
March of Dimes National Council, 1979. Reproduced with permission.

recognizing COPOH as an equal partner following disability rights activists' separation from the council in 1973 and, as the host member
for Rehabilitation International, the CRCD executive board took the
extra step of refusing COPOH's petition to speak as an autonomous
organization. Consistent pressure and endorsement by prominent political leaders in Canada finally convinced CRCD to reluctantly allow
COPOH to attend the conference as equal members of Rehabilitation
International and representatives of the disability community. At the
time membership in Rehabilitation International was limited to representatives of the rehabilitation industry and the workers' compensation
sector.[95] Thus, the move to include COPOH prompted American disability rights activists associated with the American Coalition of Citizens
with Disabilities (ACCD) to voice their concerns to COPOH, believing

World Congress of Rehabilitation
Held at the Winnipeg Convention Centre
1980

8 & 9 Participants at the 1980 World Congress of Rehabilitation International. For the first time disability rights activists from COPOH and individual consumers sat as equals alongside rehabilitation professionals, service agency representatives, workers' compensation board officials, and public policymakers. The inclusion of disability rights activists in Rehabilitation International was an unprecedented development in the field of rehabilitation advocacy.[96] © Easter Seals March of Dimes National Council, 1979. Reproduced with permission.

that their membership in Rehabilitation International constituted an endorsement of the rehabilitation industry.[97] The ACCD warned that, if COPOH proceeded, it should ensure that the principles of autonomy and consumer representation were fully respected.[98] Straddling this fine line between representational autonomy and endorsement of the rehabilitation industry, disability rights activists in Canada had won a significant symbolic hurdle in the promotion of consumer control.

In an effort to move away from the prevalence of a negative framework of disability partly reinforced by a medicalized rehabilitation system, disability rights activists argued that the emphasis in rehabilitation on self-care, mobility, and employment did not always serve the best interests of disabled people.[99] COPOH contrasted the rehabilitation model with an emerging independent living (IL) model during the 1980s, which stressed "wider outcomes such as living arrangements, relationships, consumer knowledge and assertiveness, outdoor and out-of-home activities."[100] The "IL approach" focused on empowering people with disabilities through core programs in a developing network of Independent Living Centres across Canada, which connected people with disabilities with a wide range of community resources.[101] Important resources such as peer support and self-advocacy skills effectively challenged the rehabilitation industry's reliance on professional intervention and control of services, ensuring that access to social and economic opportunities represented the best interests of people with disabilities.

Although rehabilitation challenged the segregation and exclusion of people with disabilities by demonstrating their potential for improvement, many disabled people increasingly resented the rehabilitation industry's fixation on "correcting" perceived individual deficits rather than attacking the social construction of employability. It also became increasingly clear that rehabilitation itself was often not enough to address the problem of chronic unemployment and poverty; a fact made evident to both rehabilitation professionals and people with disabilities, who began to question the legitimacy of their economic marginalization. As a result, a growing consensus developed around the need to supplement individual rehabilitation interventions with broader awareness campaigns designed to change the social and physical environments where disabled people lived and worked.

By the 1980s many disabled people harboured mixed feelings about rehabilitation as a process, industry, and philosophy. An emerging social movement of disability rights activists presented a new perspective of disability that placed individual people with disabilities at the centre of their own employment objectives rather than allowing rehabilitation professionals and their organizations to set the agenda for social and economic integration. Disability rights activists sought greater control over rehabilitation services and asserted a new perspective on disabled people that coincided with a more empowered and independent outlook. A new consensus began to develop in the disability community around independent living that situated the social and vocational objectives of individual people with disabilities ahead of the priorities that shaped the development of the rehabilitation industry. As a result, rehabilitation organizations were structured in a closer, albeit collaborative, position with consumers of rehabilitation services as they worked towards the objective of economic integration.

Chapter Four

"A Voice of Our Own": Disability Rights Activism and the Struggle to Work

I was nineteen when I was injured so I was pretty independent and pretty much on my way, knowing what I wanted to do and working out there in the world. I knew to get that same level of response there was a lot of self-advocacy that had to take place. You really do have to put yourself out there and prove yourself above and beyond other people, perhaps, because other people look at you with doubt.[1]

It is not a lack of skill, education or ability to work that is the problem, but the perception that people with disabilities are going to be a drain on the organization through extra services, medical care, leave, etc. Not only do I have to contend with my disability that I was born with or acquired through no fault of my own and all the difficulties and energies that entails, I feel like I am fighting a ghost that restricts me from taking my place in society.[2]

During the late twentieth century in Canada, the pursuit of paid employment among working- and middle-class people with disabilities dovetailed with a desire for greater levels of independence. A growing movement of disability rights activists emerged during the late 1970s promoting greater consumer control over community supports and services. Motivated by widespread poverty and unemployment in the disability community, many people with disabilities increasingly argued that their lack of control over employment supports and services undermined the objective of "full participation" in society. Inspired by American and British developments in social movement activism, disabled people in Canada began to assert their rights as citizens and consumers of rehabilitation services, arguing that most disability organizations claiming to speak on behalf of the disability community did not truly represent the interests of disabled people.[3] New activist groups of people with disabilities, often led by disabled women, emerged in Canada during the 1970s, articulating this vision of self-determination and civil rights and promoting new philosophies of self-help and consumer control over service and advocacy organizations. Disabled people discovered they could use their status as citizens and consumers of social, educational, and rehabilitation services to press for political and economic reforms while creating a public discourse around the capabilities and employability of disabled people that resisted the influence of charitable support and medical authority. Grass-roots disability rights groups at the local level engineered provincial and national coalitions of volunteer activists that shared a common goal of retooling the discourse of disability in the workplace and in broader society.

This chapter examines the rise and evolution of disability rights activism in Canada from the 1970s into the twenty-first century in terms of the impact on labour market participation. It begins with the articulation of this vision by an influential national coalition of disability rights activists who promoted new philosophies in contrast to the conventional image of disability advocated by family groups and professional agencies. The chapter then documents the evolution of disability rights activism in Canada with a particular emphasis on analysing the relationship between disability rights organizations and service agencies in Ontario. Initially evoking bitter animosity and resentment, working relationships between disability rights activists and service agencies eventually gave way to greater collaboration, understanding, and cooperation. The final section reflects on the evolution of disability rights activism in relation to the rise of independent living philosophies and their impact on the working experiences of disabled workers in Canada.

In the early 1970s representatives of the federal Department of Health and Welfare pondered in a government periodical, "Why is it so difficult for the disabled to organize?" The article answered that disabled people lacked a clear constituency in which to organize and asserted that individuals with disabilities were preoccupied with their own experiences and challenges dealing with the many obstacles to social and economic participation. It was stated that "the '60s was a time when the traditional minority groups organized to fight for peace, civil rights, and an end to poverty, but disabled people (physically handicapped in particular) were the last group to be activated by this kind of activism." While local groups of disability rights activists across the country worked towards similar goals around accessibility and inclusion, the federal government believed that these activists were largely disconnected from one another and did not represent a genuine social movement compared with other civil rights movements of the time. Nonetheless, the authors acknowledged a "new breed of handicapped person," characterized by acquired physical disabilities, middle- or working-class status, youth, and fully expecting to "return to their former jobs, schooling, and pursuits" after a period of therapy and training.[4]

Awareness of this "new breed" of disabled people reflected social and political developments during the 1970s that quickly transformed the discourse around disability issues. As in the United States, a new kind of disability rights activism emerged during this time, which differed from previous forms of disability advocacy. Disability rights groups were animated by identity politics and engaged in direct and indirect strategies to promote practical changes in the way disabled people lived and worked.[5] New political organizations in Canada led by disabled people were rooted in a youth-based culture of protest and identity politics that focused on dismantling physical and attitudinal barriers to greater economic participation.[6]

Canadian historians have examined the intersection of "rebellious" groups of youth and new political ideas that emerged in the post-war period.[7] A cohort of "rebel youth" from the mid-1960s to the early 1970s was energized by a culture of protest and forged a movement of New Left activists and young workers.[8] Labour was a defining feature of these social, political, and cultural developments, including a new wave of labour militancy and radicalism shaped by a defiance towards existing conditions and systems of belief.[9] An emerging youth-based movement of disabled people dovetailed with other social movements in Canada during the late twentieth century. The decades of the 1960s and 1970s reflected an upsurge in social movement activism, characterized by the introduction of varied new activist groups representing particular interests.[10] In contrast to the previous generation of parent advocates and professional-dominated lobby groups, disability rights activists forged new social movement organizations alongside their non-disabled peers. Canada's "rights revolution" was composed of women's liberationists, gay rights activists, and other civil rights activists who advanced a new discourse and culture of respect for social rights.[11] Disability rights organizations lagged behind other civil rights groups, but social activism by disabled people emerged directly out of an ongoing culture of protest that engulfed the 1970s political discourse of human rights in Canada.[12]

By the mid-1970s a new organization had stepped onto the national stage in Canada to lead this developing social movement of disabled people. The Coalition of Provincial Organizations of the Handicapped (COPOH) was established in Winnipeg in November 1976, with the aim of providing a "national vehicle through which provincially based consumer groups of handicapped people could speak to issues at the national level."[13] Led by Jim Derksen and Henry Enns, both of whom were characteristic of the "new breed" of disabled person, COPOH brought together disparate groups of disability rights activists operating locally across the country. Local groups were reconstituted as affiliate provincial organizations in order to share information and engage in coordinated initiatives to advance a shared agenda on disability rights. By the end of the 1970s COPOH membership included various disability-led organizations, including the British Columbia Coalition of the Disabled, Committee of Action Groups of the Disabled (Alberta), Voice of the Handicapped (Saskatchewan), League of the Physically Handicapped (Manitoba), United Handicapped Groups of Ontario, Carréfour Adaptation (Quebec), Council of the Disabled (Prince Edward Island), The HUB (Newfoundland), and League for Equal Opportunities (Nova Scotia).[14]

Despite geographic and political differences between these local organizations, COPOH helped forge a rights movement based on identity politics, laying the foundation for a national disability rights movement.[15] The growth of social movement activism, including the women's movement, the civil rights movement, the anti-war movement in the United States, and the LGBT movement, created an opportunity for disabled people to organize.[16] The Canadian disability rights movement was "founded on the transformative and liberation politics of the 1960s new left movements," following opportunities carved out by pioneering women's rights activism in particular, which created new dialogue on equity issues in the labour market.[17] However, Canadian disability activists argued that their movement was decidedly "less dramatic" than its American counterparts.[18] Under the national banner of COPOH, disability rights activists across the country adopted a reformist instead of a radical agenda, promoting incremental reforms to existing service and advocacy organizations in order to achieve greater consumer control over rehabilitation and other disability services.

Disability rights groups in Canada during this period eschewed a dogmatic approach in favour of pluralist positions that strengthened connections between coalition members, moving a progressive, integrated – but practical – agenda forward.[19]

In contrast to disability rights activists in the United States, those in Canada were relatively "state-focused," relying upon public funds for organizational development and lobbying for incremental policy reform. Led by groups of committed volunteer activists, an emerging disability rights movement in Canada lacked the necessary funds for organizational development but rejected charitable fundraising as a matter of principle, in order to move away from what was seen as a negative association between disability and charity.[20] Many disability rights organizations during this period, including COPOH, survived initially on a series of developmental grants from the federal government.[21] In fact, COPOH did not have an administrative office during its initial years and forwarded all its official correspondence to co-founder Jim Derksen's home in Winnipeg. An authority on the history of the Canadian disability rights movement, Derksen later identified public sector funding as "the single most important factor responsible for the tremendous growth in Handicapped Consumer/Monitoring Organizations across Canada."[22]

As the national representative of the Canadian disability rights movement, COPOH held its inaugural conference in 1978 based on the theme of employment, using the event to articulate its message regarding consumer-directed vocational services and disability rights to policymakers and employers across the country. COPOH still represented a loose coalition of volunteer activists, but developed its policies from the grass roots to avoid alienating groups within the fragile coalition. COPOH noted, "A prime concern which has been expressed by the membership to date is that of employment. For this reason employment has been chosen as the basic theme for this first national conference."[23] The decision to highlight the employment concerns of disabled people within a disability-controlled discourse was unprecedented in Canada, reflecting the growing influence and confidence of the Canadian disability rights movement. The title of the conference, "Employment – Action Now," articulated a consumer vision of labour market integration in which employment services, advocacy, and labour legislation were defined by the needs of consumers rather than the priorities of the rehabilitation industry. The conference also signified the first time disability rights activists, service agencies, bureaucrats, politicians, employers, labour groups, and others came together under the auspices of consumer activism to discuss labour market issues involving disabled people. A letter of invitation sent to the Canadian Labour Congress (CLC) by COPOH noted, "due to current uncertain economic times the right of every Canadian to meaningful employment is being undermined," the conference would help focus attention on disabled workers who "are often forgotten when jobs are scarce."[24]

The conference established COPOH's role as the national voice of the disability community, a position previously held by the Canadian Rehabilitation Council for the Disabled (CRCD), and asserted disabled people's right to participate in discussions about labour market participation and employment services. Determined to promote consumer rights, the conference revolved around the disability perspective of employment policy, affirmative action, human rights, and ways in which the government, private sector, labour movement, and disability rights movement could work together to improve the labour market participation of disabled people.[25] COPOH argued, "handicapped Canadians are no longer content to accept 'lip service' when it comes to participating in the decision making process."[26] COPOH representatives believed that policy resolutions from the conference would help craft a "greater role for handicapped representation within advisory and decision making federal bodies" in the construction of employment legislation, architectural barriers, and training resources for disabled people. Alongside many disability rights activists across Canada, conference participants included major stakeholders in the labour market such as senior representatives from the Treasury Board, Secretary of State, Department of Manpower and Immigration, Canadian Chamber of Commerce (CCC), as well as major companies and labour organizations. Conference organizers hosted Terrance O'Rourke, president of the radical activist group American Coalition of Citizens with Disabilities (ACCD), as the keynote speaker. O'Rourke underscored the legitimacy of consumer rights, speaking of the American precedent of successful working partnerships between industry and disability rights activists in the pursuit of meaningful employment integration. Reviews of the conference praised the unique cross-fertilization of ideas between participants within a consumer framework, which resulted in a highly productive exchange.[27]

The success of the COPOH conference led the United Handicapped Groups of Ontario (UHGO; later known as People United for Self-Help or PUSH) to hold their own employment conference the following year. UHGO wanted to build upon these national developments by cultivating similar cooperation with the public sector and employers at the provincial level. One such venture was a booklet developed in collaboration with the Ontario Ministry of Labour to help disabled jobseekers. The booklet, titled *It's Up to You... Disabled People Can Work! Job Hunting Hints for the Handicapped*, addressed reasons why employers often did not hire disabled people, including the "fear of the unknown." The booklet empowered readers to challenge these attitudes with a properly formatted resume and a confident, "positive attitude," explaining that "your handicap does not interfere with your everyday work." The feature photo showed a female office worker using a wheelchair at a modified workstation as she answers the phone and manipulates a typewriter. The image reflected the theme of the UHGO employment conference "We must stress our abilities ... not our disabilities" which is printed in a large font above the woman's workstation. It appeared on the cover of an Ontario Ministry of Labour booklet regarding job hunting advice for disabled workers and reflected the principles of self-help by educating consumers about ways to improve their search for employment.[28]

The COPOH employment conference resulted in the establishment of formal and informal partnerships between disability rights activists, major employers, and policymakers. Pointing to national radio, television, and newspaper media coverage of the conference, the inaugural chief commissioner of the Canadian Human Rights Commission, Gordon Fairweather, praised COPOH activists for sparking an extraordinary growth in public awareness of disability rights.[29] Fairweather was so impressed by meeting disability rights activists that he drafted a letter to Prime Minister Pierre Trudeau exhorting him to include substantive protections for people with disabilities in the new Canadian constitution. The current discourse on employment integration created momentum within the disability rights movement to push forward an emerging agenda focused on emancipating disabled people from the margins. In the wake of this increased attention, COPOH's funding was increased, which enabled volunteers to open a new office in Winnipeg and COPOH Chair Jim Derksen to embark on an outreach tour across Canada and the United States to build support for disability rights activists in Canada.[30] Derksen's journey took him to Washington, DC, to strengthen relations with American disability rights activists, including peers in ACCD, which he believed COPOH could model itself after by learning from their method of combining political lobbying with direct action.

On his tour Derksen attended meetings of the President's Committee on the Employment of the Handicapped (PCEH) whose "Hire the Handicapped" campaigns had set the standard for promoting the employment of disabled people. Seated far from the "high ranking officials" with his ACCD colleagues "at the back not eating steak like the others because they couldn't afford the banquet fee," Derksen found that the PCEH was the American equivalent of the CRCD: "A façade to hide the impotence of the various governmental employment programmes." Unlike the ACCD, COPOH and its affiliate organizations focused on lobbying for reform rather than direct action, adopting what Michael Prince describes as a typical Canadian approach to disability activism, which focused on "progressive administration and social democratic thought."[31] Nevertheless, the tour was a formative experience for Derksen in his leadership of COPOH, and he returned home with renewed enthusiasm to work with other activists to build a robust Canadian disability rights movement.

While rehabilitation and service professionals participated in consumer-driven conferences and engaged in dialogue with disability rights activists, they ultimately resisted the premise of consumer control over rehabilitation, employment, and other social services. This outlook reflected the fact that disability rights activism threatened the legitimacy of professionals' control over service agencies. Service agencies were often either indifferent or opposed to the notion of consumer-controlled services, often responding to disability rights activists with an attitude of "We already do that" or "Why would we want to do that?"[32] During the late 1970s people with visual impairments expressed their dissatisfaction with the ability of existing services to facilitate their economic integration. A landmark study in 1976 by Cyril Greenland, titled *Vision Canada*, determined that the state of services for blind Canadians reflected a situation of "unmet needs," causing growing numbers of people with visual impairments to question the Canadian National Institute for the Blind's (CNIB) monopoly on services for blind people.[33] Greenland discovered a younger generation of blind youth and young adults increasingly vocal in their opposition to the CNIB.[34] This cohort of blind youth, however, stood against an older generation of people with visual impairments who were emotionally and financially committed to the CNIB.[35] Greenland recommended that the CNIB take steps to proactively close this generational divide by decentralizing its services and improving consumer representation in the administration and provision of employment services.[36] While such steps were not immediately adopted, the Greenland report revealed significant gaps between consumer demands, rights, and the status quo.

In Ontario, for example, disability rights activists with visual impairments who were affiliated with the Blind Organization of Ontario with Selfhelp Tactics (BOOST) challenged the CNIB's virtual monopoly on services for people with visual impairments. In publications and media statements BOOST characterized the CNIB as an exploitative hegemony that inhibited the social and economic integration of blind Canadians. The group released its own report on the "unmet needs" of blind people, which amplified concerns articulated in the Greenland report. The BOOST report, called *Selfhelp and Government Commitment*, was part of a project to develop consumer-led alternatives to the delivery of services for blind people.[37] BOOST explained that several grassroots-based rights organizations of blind people emerged and quickly failed after 1970, owing to little political experience and an insufficient base of supporters. The incipient nature of disability rights activism in Canada during this period led many leaders of upstart groups to be co-opted by larger service agencies, such as the CNIB, who hired activists as staff members, effectively undercutting its opposition.[38] BOOST believed it had remained steadfast by building a mass base of supporters and avoiding a strictly dogmatic approach to the promotion of consumer control philosophies.[39] The extensive report included sixteen chapters of recommendations challenging the "single agency model" that supported an unbalanced reliance on CNIB services.[40] The BOOST report echoed previous recommendations by Greenland in his *Vision Canada* report, which concluded that the CNIB should be decentralized over time, devolving responsibility to local disability rights organizations and community partners, since local services were in a better position to assess and respond to the needs of consumers.[41]

BOOST's report projected "an atmosphere of disillusionment that was prevalent in the late 1970s among the mass of progressively motivated blind Ontarians."[42] Growing tensions among predominantly blind youth fuelled a wave of strikes that rocked the blind community during the late 1970s when unionized blind workers alleged that CNIB's Caterplan retail outlets provided unsafe working conditions and the $0.40 per hour wages exploited blind workers forced to endure an inadequate job placement program. Picketers' signs read "CNIB unfair to the blind"; "I only make .40 an hour. What do you make?"; "Strike"; and "Please, enough to live on."[43] One protest led by BOOST activist John Rae marched on CNIB Toronto headquarters on 14 March

10 & 11 Photographs of Anne Musgrave, a key member of BOOST and University of Toronto student, as she navigates St George campus in downtown Toronto. A member of the youthful "new breed of handicapped person," Musgrave was an outspoken self-help consumer activist whose involvement in consumer activist politics led *The Varsity* newspaper to feature her in an examination of the experiences of "U of T's handicapped students." ©*The Varsity*, 1977. Reproduced with permission.

1979 during a meeting of CNIB senior officials, demanding consumers receive open access to their confidential files, which were discussed with consumers only at meetings with job counsellors.[44] Rae argued that the "deplorable conditions which face most blind Canadians" were due to a lack of control over decisions that affected their lives. The CNIB refused to allow access to client files and barred BOOST from access to the meeting, which caused increased resentment and lack of collaboration between the organizations.[45]

Disabled people experimented with developing their own consumer-run alternatives to typical job training and employment service agencies. One such agency, called The World of One in Seven, established in 1973 in Kingston, Ontario, was named after the alleged "one in seven Canadians" who have some type of physical disability. The agency matched disabled jobseekers with "real work for real wages," providing specialized interventions on the basis of clients' variable needs and working closely with employers to ensure successful placements.[46] Led by disability activist Jean Moore and staffed by employment counsellors with disabilities, The World of One in Seven was unique among employment agencies in Canada in that it adopted a "client-centred" peer-support approach made possible by low counsellor/client ratios compared with mainstream services offered at Canada Manpower Centres.[47] Specialized employment counsellors acted as a liaison between disabled jobseekers and employers in an attempt to establish a positive working environment and to facilitate future job placements. Moore argued that by focusing on placing disabled people in paid jobs, they reduced the tax burden to fund welfare benefits, promoted awareness among a growing networks of employers, and boosted the self-confidence and skills profile of disabled people.[48]

The World of One in Seven's success was commemorated in a documentary film that profiled disabled workers who had been placed in paid employment through the agency, emphasizing how the organization worked towards reducing attitudinal barriers to labour market integration.[49] The *Kingston Whig-Standard* also profiled the agency in 1977, noting it had placed 324 clients in jobs, had an additional fifty on its waiting list, and interviewed former clients and employers who praised the agency for its many successful placements.[50] Despite this success, The World of One in Seven was disbanded in 1979 when the organization's funding contract with the federal government expired. Sixty active clients managed by two specialized employment counsellors (a 1:30 ratio) were transferred to the local Canada Employment Centre (CEC), where eight counsellors managed 5,000 clients (a 1:625 ratio). The transition plan included Moore working nine months beyond the closure of the program to advocate for the remaining clients, with no provision made for an ongoing role in future placements of disabled jobseekers.[51] Moore complained that the move did not make financial sense because the agency had in fact been doing the work of local CECs in addition to necessary advocacy work promoting "real work" opportunities for disabled clients, and it did so at salary levels considerably lower than CEC employment counsellors.[52] Nevertheless, the agency dissolved and a groundbreaking example of consumer-run employment services abruptly ended.

As the World of One in Seven shut its doors, a new relationship between consumers and service agency professionals developed at the provincial level. United Handicapped Groups of Ontario, founded in

1953 as an umbrella organization for social groups of people with disabilities across the province, transitioned in the early 1970s from "merely a means of encouraging recreational activities" to "an advocacy group promoting change in human rights, transportation, and employment."[53] On the heels of COPOH's successful employment conference at the national level, UHGO held a similar forum in 1979, which had a profoundly consolidating effect on disability rights activism in Ontario. UHGO's executive director, Lois Harte-Maxwell, a polio survivor who ran the organization from Room 28 at St Joseph's Hospital in Peterborough, noted in reference to the conference, "The 130 delegates, suffering from virtually every form of mobility disease, decided to press for better representation of the disabled in advertising and to see all buildings employing people in business and industry made accessible to the handicapped within seven years."[54] Determined to move away from the association of disability with charity, UHGO resolved that "fundraising by outside groups concentrates on pity and is paternalistic because the physically handicapped should have the capacity to raise their own funds."[55]

Despite its stance against advocacy and fundraising by those outside the disability community, a lack of resources required UHGO to lean on the Ontario March of Dimes (OMOD) as part of a nationwide project initiated by COPOH focused on building the capacities of local disability rights groups to respond to the changing employment needs of disabled people. The project, known as "Job Corps," operated under a federal grant administrated by COPOH to scale-up provincial disability rights groups and develop their capacity to provide disabled people with consumer-based employment counselling, training programs, and labour rights and to serve as a conduit for consumer input in the development of labour policy.[56] The Job Corps project was a critical developmental opportunity for disability rights organizations underequipped to build an effective social movement that could respond to the employment advocacy needs of disabled people. The Ontario branch of Job Corps involved fourteen fieldworkers, who assisted UHGO's twenty-one-member organizations to mobilize in pursuit of their own local political goals.[57] In addition to her role as executive director of UHGO, Harte-Maxwell served as project leader, earning just $5.40 per hour ($17.19 adjusted for inflation) to lead fourteen employees – ten of whom were disabled – to perform research and develop affiliate and potential UHGO member organizations.

Although the Job Corps project represented an important moment in the development of organized disability rights activism, it risked compromising the principles of self-help and consumer control because of its close association with professional-based service agencies. Although UHGO was provided with $100,000 (approximately $315,000 adjusted for inflation) for organizational development from the federal government, another $10,000 (approximately $31,000 adjusted for inflation) came from the OMOD, including access to OMOD office space across the province that enabled Job Corps Community Development Workers to carry out their work.[58]

Despite the positive intentions that brought these organizations together, the power imbalance between upstart disability rights groups and service agencies thrust activists and professionals into conflict. Tension quickly emerged that highlighted broader conflict between disability rights activists and service agencies in Canada at this time. Soon after UHGO agreed to work with OMOD officials, OMOD representative Lee Rullman dictated that Job Corps staff use official OMOD letterhead in all its written correspondence to justify OMOD's investment in the project.[59] However, Harte-Maxwell received complaints by UHGO member groups who complained that OMOD letterhead on Job Corps communications ran counter to consumer principles and reflected poorly on UHGO as an autonomous disability rights organization. Harte-Maxwell complained to Rullman that prospective disability rights organizations, such as BOOST, had chosen not to affiliate with UHGO and were likely discouraged from doing so when they received letters from fellow disability rights activists printed on OMOD letterhead. Beyond the poor optics of sending out UHGO Job Corps correspondence on OMOD letterhead, Harte-Maxwell grew increasingly concerned that the practice undermined the expansion of disability rights activism in the province. The federal government wrote to Harte-Maxwell, assuring her that despite her role as executive director of UHGO, Job Corps operated separately from both UHGO and OMOD.[60] Despite OMOD's objections and under the terms articulated to her by the federal government, Harte-Maxwell promptly changed its letterhead to "Self-Help Efforts – Handicapped Community, Ontario" and forwarded her correspondence with the secretary of state to Rullman in justification of her stance against OMOD letterhead.[61]

COPOH also observed that a degree of ambiguity existed in regards to how disability rights groups, service agencies and individual workers were supposed to work together. COPOH found that a lack of organizational cooperation and ideological divisions resulted in Job Corps taking too long to become operational, fuelling disagreements between disabled people and service agency professionals. These differences were highlighted during a meeting between Harte-Maxwell and OMOD executive director Lee Rullman on 13 August 1979:

> HARTE-MAXWELL: UHGO is attempting to spread their wings as a consumer group.
> RULLMAN: It doesn't make sense, business or otherwise, to duplicate.
> HARTE-MAXWELL: What are *you* doing?
> RULLMAN: Why don't you get in touch with me and find out? We are offering to support and consult with your people.
> HARTE-MAXWELL: We seemed to part company in Kingston over control– whether my staff would do anything contrary to March of Dimes principles, etc. The operative word there is "assist" versus "control." I am responsible to the government.
> RULLMAN: The province of Ontario is *our* bailiwick.
> HARTE-MAXWELL: It's *ours too!* As a consumer organization, we have a lot of strength.
> RULLMAN: You should take help where it is offered. It's our position that you haven't taken any help – we want to help.
> HARTE-MAXWELL: I don't see it as a positive help.[62]

Illustrative of a "we already do that" approach to disability rights activism, OMOD perceived its role as the dominant host that held both financial and professional authority. Despite this initial tension, however, disability activists and service agencies reached a tentative rapprochement, providing space for collaboration and understanding. UHGO and OMOD successfully completed their working agreement, regularly reporting on the development of the Job Corps project through a biweekly newsletter (aptly named *Wheels of Progress*). In December 1979 Rullman wrote to Harte-Maxwell offering OMOD additional financial assistance to ensure the successful completion of the project.[63]

Relations between UHGO and OMOD had thawed, partly owing to their shared participation in the spontaneous establishment of the Coalition on Human Rights for the Handicapped. The coalition had emerged to protest the introduction of new provincial legislation that sidestepped amendments to the Ontario Human Rights Code to include disabled people.[64] Rullman stated that the impromptu emergence of the coalition represented the first time service agencies and disability rights groups had come together under one banner to speak with a single voice.[65] As the relationship between service agencies and disability rights groups evolved towards greater mutual understanding, individual activists and people with disabilities redefined the parameters of their relationship with community-based service agencies in the shared pursuit of full participation in the labour market.

The struggle to fashion a consumer-led vision of economic participation at the national and provincial levels stimulated the expansion of self-help services for people with disabilities at the municipal level. This new concept of consumer-led services was informed by a new philosophy of independent living that emerged in Canada following its introduction at the 1980 COPOH conference on rehabilitation in Winnipeg. Independent living conceives disability primarily in social and political terms and seeks to empower disabled people to take control of the rehabilitation and employment services they need to participate in the mainstream. Proponents of independent living promoted peer support initiatives, believing that "people with disabilities can best identify their own needs and can have productive lives in the community through self-help, empowerment, advocacy, and the removal of barriers."[66] This perspective held that discriminatory attitudes and employment policies created social and economic barriers to full participation that could (and should) be resisted through the assertion of civil rights and equitable access to employment opportunities.[67]

The proliferation of independent living in Canada reflected the contours of an evolving social movement of disability rights activists who rejected the conventional rehabilitation paradigm.[68] Independent Living Centres developed during the 1980s and 1990s to ensure that a consumer-led approach to independent living to social and economic integration could assist people with disabilities in Canada find work and live independently in the community. Proponents of independent living empowered people with disabilities to assert greater control in their own lives by learning from other people with disabilities about how to live and work independently in the community.

These developments in disability rights activism were particularly visible in the Toronto area. Beryl Potter, a triple amputee, grandmother, and co-founder of the Scarborough Recreation Club for Disabled Adults in 1976, helped move local disabled people towards a more activist stance. Potter and her peers at the club, which included many working-age adults with physical disabilities, were optimistic about the potential of independent living to actively transform employment prospects of people with disabilities. To move this agenda forward, Potter established a new organization in 1980 called Scarborough Action

12 Beryl Potter, president of the Scarborough Recreation Club for Disabled
Adults, with the director and cameraman while shooting a documentary.
Potter was a key player in bringing to public awareness the self-help disabil-
ity rights movement in Toronto.[69] © Michael Slaughter/Getstock.com, 1981.
Reproduced with permission.

Awareness. Representing her organization and disability activists across
Toronto, Potter appeared before the Parliamentary Special Committee
on the Disabled and the Handicapped, contributing to its key report
that shaped the development of public policies regarding the social and
economic integration of disabled people in Canada.[70] Potter also took
advantage of growing awareness of disability issues in 1981 by organizing various activities in Toronto to promote disabled peoples' pursuit
of full participation in the community and the labour market. Similar
to disability rights activists at the national level, Potter conceived of
employment as the lynchpin around which other issues, such as transportation, housing, education, and recreation revolved. She argued
that people with disabilities must be incorporated into the workforce
in greater numbers, so that "we can become useful citizens and pay
taxes too," since a larger tax base provided by working disabled people
would help pay for demands for greater levels of accessibility.[71]

A leading disability activist on the local and national stage, Potter's highly public profile in Toronto heightened general interest around disability rights and independent living. She hosted her own local weekly cable television program called *Ability Forum*, which delivered news affecting the local disability community and featured local people with disabilities on a variety of topics.[72] Potter also received a major federal grant to establish the short-lived Scarborough Centre for Independent Living, which sought to put the principles of independent living into action.[73] By June 1981 Potter was also the public face of a provincial Employ-Ability campaign, which featured an exhibit that travelled around the city's malls and public plazas to promote awareness of disabled people's capacity to engage in paid work.[74] As a leading spokesperson for disability rights, Potter was also the subject of a documentary called *Life Another Way*, which aired on public television in October 1981, recording her work as "one of Canada's foremost crusaders for the rights of disabled people."[75]

Building on Beryl Potter's widespread appeal and influence, disability activist Sandra Carpenter also cited widespread "frustration with services offered in Metro Toronto" and a desire for an information centre to guide disabled people through the maze of services available to them in the city.[76] Co-founder of the national organization of feminist disability rights activists called DisAbled Women's Network (DAWN), Carpenter helped also worked to develop the Centre for Independent Living in Toronto (CILT). Reminiscent of the relationship between OMOD and UHGO at the provincial level, a steering committee at CILT was initially composed of disabled people and service agency representatives and opened an office in downtown Toronto at 182 Brunswick Avenue under the sponsorship of the Community Occupational Therapy Association (COTA).[77] The centre immediately began work on a service inventory and consumers' needs survey in the city to demonstrate the case for an independent living centre in the city based on consumer principles. By 1986 the organization had become totally independent of COTA, perhaps learning from the earlier conceptual pitfalls experienced by provincial organizations like UHGO. Similar to independent living centres in the United States, CILT was founded as a non-profit, cross-disability, consumer-controlled organization that worked to provide disabled people with opportunities to pursue integration and full participation in the workforce.[78]

Rather than building an insular movement of disability rights activists, feminist disability activists such as Carpenter, Harte-Maxwell, and Potter reached outside the disability community to provide a consumer perspective in mainstream organizations. In addition to her role as executive director of CILT, for example, Carpenter served on the board of the Canadian Labour Force Development Board (CLFDB) and the National Training Board, providing consumer input into the planning and implementation of employment training services across the country.[79] CILT also promised to offer disabled people in Toronto a place in which the principles of independent living could be realized through information sharing and networking among disabled people about various services that worked towards their full participation in the community. In 1987 CILT developed a local weekly radio program called *The Radio Connection*, which aired on CIUT-FM and was supported by the University of Toronto and the Government of Ontario.[80] The success of the radio program, which was operated mainly by disabled people working in the media, was part of a larger project during the late 1980s called Access Connections, which included CILT, Metropolitan Toronto, the Canadian Broadcasting Corporation, and the federal Canadian Employment and Immigration Council. The project led to the development of a permanent weekly national news program called *The Disability Network*, later rebranded *Moving On*, which first aired in 1989 on Saturdays from 12:30–1:00 p.m. and ran until 2006. The program focused on employment issues, acting as "an information vehicle to reach disabled job seekers about employment opportunities. It will increase the collective profile of people with disabilities as active labour-market participants."[81] Staffed and hosted by people with disabilities, the program reflected the principles of the disability rights movement while actively dispersing independent living philosophies to a wider Canadian audience.

Despite the expanded influence of disability rights and independent living, Carpenter and other activists confronted a largely unreceptive network of service agencies. As CILT worked towards building consumer-led services, rehabilitation professionals established their own groups such as the Toronto Independent Living Advisory Committee (TILAC), which served to reassert professional control of rehabilitation services. TILAC held its meetings at Lyndhurst Rehabilitation Hospital (formerly Lyndhurst Lodge) and was founded as a coordinating body of service providers and consumers to address the needs of physically disabled people who sought to live independently in the community.[82] However, despite appearances, TILAC was primarily composed of service agencies that promoted the rehabilitation industry's particular vision of independent living.[83] TILAC rebuffed disability activists' philosophies of consumer control, maintaining that people with physical disabilities who wished to direct their own care would experience a potentially negative impact on their lifestyle and quality of care, in addition to increasing costs to service providers and frustrating the administration of long-term care services.[84] Cognizant of the organization's stance on consumer control, Carpenter and other disability activists repeatedly refused to join TILAC, since it did not reflect the true nature of independent living principles.

Amid ongoing conflict between disabled people and rehabilitation professionals, Potter co-founded the Coalition on Employment Equity for Persons with Disabilities (CEEPD).[85] In April 1986 she led disability rights activists from across the country to Ottawa to protest the introduction of federal employment equity legislation, which she argued did "little to force federally regulated employers and Crown corporations to hire and promote disabled people."[86] Photographs featured Potter triumphantly in front amid placards that read "Dead like Bill C-62"; "No penalties, no justice"; "Jobs when?"; and "Black Monday, disabled person, no equality, no jobs, no justice."[87] During the protest, Minister of Labour Flora MacDonald addressed the Speaker of the House on behalf of Prime Minister Brian Mulroney, denying that the government had ignored disabled groups' attempts to discuss the bill with the prime minister and that he had personally written to Beryl Potter explaining the situation. In an extraordinary outburst, Potter, who was sitting in the back row of the public gallery, yelled out: "My name is Beryl Potter and I've received no such letter!"[88] The *Toronto Star* reported that the rest of her words were drowned out by calls from the Speaker for order while Potter was forcibly removed from the gallery. Indeed, individual direct action, such as Potter's parliamentary outburst, represented a larger spectrum of disability activism encompassing the actions of individual activists.

Potter was part of an increasingly vocal group of disabled women who struggled to find their own voice in a developing disability rights movement in Canada. Although many key disability activists in Canada were women, disabled women themselves came together in the mid-1980s to form their own organization in order to advance issues pertaining specifically to disabled women. Following a conference in Winnipeg in 1985, the DisAbled Women's Network was formed, dedicated to addressing poverty, violence, and discrimination experienced by disabled women.[89] In 1989 DAWN published "Different Therefore Unequal," presenting various troubling statistics that demonstrated the ways in

13 Protester in April 1986 on Parliament Hill in Ottawa with a placard affixed to the back of his wheelchair that reads "No equality. No penalties. No justice." As the message suggests, disability rights activists were upset that employment equity legislation did not come with any enforcement for hiring targets.[90] © Murray Mosher, 1986. Reproduced with permission.

which disabled women were much more likely to be unemployed and live in poverty relative to the situation of disabled men.[91] Throughout the 1980s and into the twenty-first century, DAWN sponsored several research and outreach projects concerning these issues, working with other disability activists and women's rights organizations to stimulate change. Many influential leaders in the national disability rights movement in Canada, including Pat Danforth, Diane Driedger, Donna Hicks, and Sandra Carpenter, assumed leadership positions in COPOH and CCD in addition to their membership in DAWN. This cross-fertilization of disability activism ensured that women's issues were represented in other disability rights circles and influenced a broader agenda of respect for diversity within the disability rights movement.

Activism by ethnic and racialized disabled people also emerged in the 1980s and early 1990s. As disabled women founded their own organizations, visible minorities and recent immigrants found their voices were silent in the broader disability rights movement and sought to build their own organizations. In 1981 disability activists in Montreal, Quebec, founded the Association multiethnique pour l'intégration des personnes handicapées (AMEIPH). AMEIPH was first funded in 1984 to expand its offerings of specialized French-language instruction, job-readiness workshops, and family support services to ethno-racial people with disabilities in Quebec.[92] In 1990 the National Aboriginal Network on Disability (NAND) was established as a cross-disability, consumer-led organization of Aboriginal people with disabilities dedicated to advancing issues affecting Canada's Aboriginal communities, including poverty, unemployment, education and training, addictions, mental health, and rural isolation from services. In the same year NAND participated in a Study Group on Employment and Disability alongside other leading disability rights organizations, shaping the disability rights movements' strategic objectives concerning the economic integration of disabled people. In 1993 NAND received a major federal grant to study employment issues concerning Aboriginal people with disabilities.[93]

Ethno-racial people with disabilities founded the Ethno-Racial Disabled Persons Coalition of Ontario (ERDCO) in 1993 as a cross-disability, consumer-driven, advocacy organization, whose mission was to advance the rights and opportunities of disabled people by confronting the racism and oppression experienced by ethnic and racial minorities. Growing out of a vibrant anti-racism movement in the 1980s and 1990s, ERDCO secured funding to support the establishment in 1995 of a specialized mental health centre in Toronto called Across Boundaries, serving ethno-racial minorities. One of the more enduring features of ERDCO's brand of activism involved the production and dissemination of research studies examining issues confronting ethno-racial people with disabilities. In 1996 ERDCO partnered with the Women's Health Project to launch a research effort to "educate and empower ethno-racial women who were vulnerable to abuse and violence" with the express purpose of using the research to prevent violence against women.

ERDCO's approximately 200 members also worked throughout the 1990s and into the twenty-first century to broaden the diversity of the disability rights movement in Canada, delivering workshops and informational materials on community consultation and methods of increasing inclusivity within the disability rights community.[94]

Increased support for independent living promoted by disability rights activists such as Potter and Carpenter transformed access to employment opportunities for many people with disabilities in Toronto. Interview participants in the present study maintained that the rise of disability rights activism and independent living during the 1980s created new employment opportunity structures in which self-determination through work became increasingly attainable. "Lily," who lives with quadriplegia and worked in the public sector, encountered steady improvements in physical accessibility, which led to increasing access to accommodations and greater attention to flexible working arrangements. Lily notes, "I require assistance in terms of attendant services to help me with clerical work, washroom, getting my coat on and off, things like that. When I first started working, that wasn't available so I had to rely on co-workers."[95] The introduction of accommodation funds that provided increased access to attendant services in the workplace as well as assistive technologies such as voice recognition computers, speaker telephones, ramps, elevators, and door openers, served to create a working environment that gave Lily greater control in her workplace.

Inspired by the growing disability rights movement in Canada, "David" entered the workforce in the mid-1970s in the area of non-profit community services, where he became involved in various aspects of disability activism. As a person with a visual impairment, David collaborated with others in the blind community and helped to establish coalitions with other disability activists motivated to forge an effective discourse on disability rights in Ontario. As a young activist, David poured his energy and talent into organizational development and cultivating networks of activists to improve the social and economic integration of disabled people. Ironically, but like many other activists in North America, David caught the attention of public sector employers. Encouraged by the deinstitutionalization movement, disability activism, and international developments in disability rights, various levels of government hired many disability activists to supply expertise in the area of disability issues. David explained that being a disability activist and public servant was "not the easiest ... because the movement's goal was to lobby external aid for changes in legislation programs and policies and I, as a civil servant, was expected [to] and actually succeeded in delivering programs to the best of my ability as a non-biased civil servant." Nonetheless, David spent the remainder of his career balancing disability and labour activism with public service.[96]

"Michael," who lives with mental health issues, similarly found that the growth of the disability rights movement coincided with the proliferation of job opportunities in the voluntary sector. Limited availability of flexible work for people with mental health issues caused Michael to search for employment within the disability rights movement, where employers and co-workers in consumer-run enterprises were more likely to provide accommodations rather than force him to self-accommodate in an inflexible workplace. He recalled, "I did make the point with somebody who was helping me with my personal experience speech and we were coming to the part where I was talking about the past. I had difficulty with work. Her suggestion was 'You weren't able to work.' I said, 'No, I had difficulty.' I'm comfortable with descriptive language. I had difficulty working. Generally, I've put myself in a consumer-friendly work environment."[97] Michael found that since he started working in the early 1980s, his path towards economic integration reflected a process of self-accommodation that incorporated income support with work that suited his abilities.

Michael found that despite the growing availability of consumer-friendly jobs, mental health issues were generally conceived separately from physical disabilities. He explained, "You get fruit baskets when you're in hospital for blood work or a heart test or some kind of serious health or physical health issue. But you get misunderstanding and fear with certain aspects of mental health recovery and support. That's a big thing. It's not a socially comfortable illness, condition or experience."[98] In contrast, Lily encountered a trend of increasing acceptance of her visible physical impairments in the workplace, "I'm pretty sure that most people when they first see me don't think I could be working at the type of job I've been at for thirty years. When I first started there was certainly scepticism about who I was and what I was capable of. [Since then] I think a lot of my co-workers don't really see me as a person with a disability."[99] Notwithstanding these differences, both Michael and Lily were empowered by the growth of disability rights activism in Toronto to achieve a level of self-determination through work. As Lily noted, "By working and having good income I'm able to make choices in where I live, if I want to go on a trip somewhere, it helps me purchase additional attendant care services that if I didn't work I couldn't afford. It allows me freedom and choice."[100]

"Charlotte" began working in the retail sector during the late 1980s to save money in order to attend university. Born with cerebral palsy, which limited her mobility, she earned a university degree and sought work in the social services sector. Despite having "all the good qualities of a good employee" and a personal strategy not to go to an employer with a "list of demands" outlining accommodation needs, Charlotte encountered difficulty securing a full-time position, finding only contract work. Regardless of her difficulties, Charlotte stated, "Thank goodness I was born when I was because if I was born earlier my life could have been very different ... I'm not saying there's not a struggle now, but that was very limited."[101]

In response to widespread poverty and unemployment in the disability community during the late twentieth century, people with disabilities, such as Michael and David, began to organize themselves into activist groups in order to pressure service agencies and policymakers for greater levels of self-determination in the pursuit of social and economic integration. Disability rights groups were often led by disabled feminists such as Beryl Potter, Jean Moore, Lois Harte-Maxwell, and Sandra Carpenter, connecting gendered experiences of disability and keen organizing skills to international women's activism critical to a growing disability rights movement. Although disability rights activists adopted a particularly statist approach, which enabled them to expand their activities through the provision of public funding initiatives, there were instances of direct action that directly challenged conventional approaches to helping people with disabilities find integration. Individual activists and disability rights organizations emerged as part of a growing social movement of working-class disabled people living in poverty on social assistance but seeking to live and work independently in the community. Significant consumer-led employment conferences in the late 1970s reconfigured the policy discourses that had long associated disability with dependence on social assistance.

The main objective of a disabled-led, rights-based approach to the "problem" of disability that first emerged in the 1970s in Canada pointed to the crushing effect that poverty and low expectations had on disabled people in their search for independence and self-determination in the labour market. Fledgling disability rights groups such as COPOH, UHGO, and Scarborough Action Awareness worked tirelessly to promote the employability of disabled people. Activists confronted prejudice and discrimination in the community as well as in their work with government officials, rehabilitation agencies, service organizations, and business and labour groups. Disabled people fought for the right to create their own agendas, arguing that they needed greater control over their lives in order to achieve better outcomes in the labour market. This approach caused conflicts between disability rights activists and rehabilitation professionals at the national, provincial, and local levels, which reflected growing resentment about the ways in which professionals and advocates spoke on behalf of the disability community.

Notwithstanding the internal politics that divided the disability community, disability rights organizations in Canada focused predominantly on pursuing reforms to public policy meant to stimulate change in state infrastructure and the lucrative industries of social, educational, and vocational supports. Disability activists broke from conventional patterns by articulating a vision of "independent living" in which services were not only client centred but consumer controlled, placing disabled people at the centre of supports and services they deemed necessary to achieve their goals. Service agencies and policymakers were initially reluctant to engage with these literally foreign concepts and refused to relinquish control over services, but consumer-based infrastructure developed anyway, creating alternative pathways towards labour market participation. As it turned out, Canadians with disabilities needed to engage in unique forms of disability rights activism in order to fully assert themselves in the workforce and bring about meaningful change to the physical, social, and political landscape. For many disability rights activists, "full participation" was impossible without securing "a voice of our own."

Chapter Five

Sheltered Workshops and the Evolution of Disability Advocacy

The present reality was "A little Hong Kong" because [workshops] provided a lot of contracts for companies that would send their products there to be packaged and they would be very happy to receive this work done by the handicapped people, but they wouldn't hire them. Supposedly, the goal of the workshop was to give people skills so they could be hired in a company and didn't worry about looking for placement. They could not earn more than $100 a month because otherwise their pensions would be cut down. So they were in a trap of poverty. They didn't have money ... and were very poor. Because of this repetitive work process and lack of attention to them as human beings, their physical handicap was also, in a way, driving them to become mentally handicapped.[1]

In 1978 Canadian disability rights activists wondered aloud, "Why, when we have the creativity and the resources to establish meaningful, long term jobs, do we continue to accept the status quo of the sheltered workshops as opposed to community integrated employment alternatives?"[2] A number of obstacles confronted people with disabilities in Canada during the 1970s and 1980s as they attempted to find "real work for real pay" in the labour market, including pervasive inaccessibility and a welfare poverty trap that perpetuated exclusion from opportunities to gain conventional work and life experiences. Deemed unfit to work by mainstream standards but requiring the social and vocational skills necessary for the transition to paid employment, many people with disabilities were channelled into the sheltered workshop system, where they performed gendered manual, routine, unskilled, or semi-skilled work for little or no pay. Emerging from middle-class moral essentialism and ideals of self-determination through labour, sheltered workshops reflected broader social, political, and economic dynamics that surrounded the "problem" of disability during this period. Ineligible for workers' compensation and other benefits of the standard employment relationship, sheltered workers were neither "patients" nor paid "workers" but laboured within a liminal token economy. This system was originally designed to ensure that "unemployable" disabled people could engage in unpaid or stipendiary work appropriate to their abilities and build skills that would eventually transfer to gainful employment. But sheltered workshops were neither able to alleviate the crushing load of chronic poverty and unemployment in the disability community nor reconcile critical problems that undermined the efficacy of the workshop model. The workshop system formed an integral part of an evolving welfare state, revealing the exclusive nature of the Canadian political economy, which routinely stigmatized people with disabilities unable to compete effectively in the mainstream labour market. Sheltered workshops highlighted the fact that many disabled people can and did perform essential work despite their exclusion from the paid labour market.

In this chapter we examine the role and evolution of sheltered workshops in Canada during a period in which the advent of disability rights activism created countervailing pressures on the workshop system. Changes in the discourse of disability and realities of community living situated sheltered workshops at the centre of debates around the rights and opportunities available to people with disabilities. An initial discussion of the purpose of sheltered workshops moves into analysis of the relationship between workshop advocacy and disability activism. The final two sections track the transformation of this relationship as workshops experimented with the industrialization of the workshop practices. The outcome of these struggles and changes helped move popular consensus away from sheltered workshops towards the concept of supported employment.

Sheltered workshops reflected the liminal position of people with disabilities in Canada. Workshops occupied a key position in the lives of many people who could work but whose disabilities rendered them unemployable and their labour uncompetitive in the mainstream labour market. The concept that work could be therapeutic was a popular theme in medical and social work practices stretching back to the establishment of Victorian institutions for people with disabilities.[3] Medical experts believed the provision of regular, if not demanding, labour served to stabilize "disturbed" or "distracted" minds by encouraging patients to focus on the immediate tasks of their occupation.[4] Physical work was seen to have rehabilitative effects for "emotionally disturbed" people with mental health issues.[5] Sheltered workshops in Canada evolved from mid- to late-nineteenth-century work programs for blind people, providing work deemed appropriate to their sex and abilities. Both sexes engaged in broom making and basket weaving, while women were expected to perform thread spinning and sewing tasks and men performed woodworking and other light assembly jobs.[6] The earliest workshops that survived into the 1970s in Canada dated to the aftermath of the First World War, when a surge in resources as part of the resettlement process for wounded soldiers created a demand for protected settings where injured and war-blinded veterans could acquire competitive work-related skills.[7] By the 1920s occupational therapists were staffing "curative workshops" (as sheltered workshops were originally called), which formed part of the steady growth of the rehabilitation industry in Canada.[8]

Sheltered workshops provided jobs and work skills for people whose impairments ostensibly disqualified them from competitive employment.[9] As part of a regime of therapeutic intervention in the lives of disabled people, work in workshops – though mostly unpaid, uncompetitive, and lacking employment benefits – was seen by medical and rehabilitation professionals to convey other desirable physical, psychological, and social benefits. For people with physical disabilities, workshops represented the later stages of the rehabilitation process, restoring physical ability and self-confidence while providing work skills to improve employability for largely working-class jobs and enable future entry to the mainstream labour market.

Physical labour was conceived by middle-class reformers, rehabilitation personnel, and physicians to protect people with disabilities unable to compete in the labour market from the supposedly morally, physically, and mentally deleterious effects of idleness on physical and social functionality.[10] Expansion of the workshop system in particular was partly motivated by middle-class widespread cultural fear of idleness and played an integral part in the development of the modern social welfare state. Workshops were an important component of long-standing middle-class interventions in the moral economy of the working poor, seen to protect disabled people from the moral hazards of idleness as a result of being deemed unemployable in the open labour market while providing structured opportunities for the development of social and vocational skills. Shut out of the competitive labour market and faced with few alternatives, many people with disabilities were simply forced to accept work in sheltered workshops.

Many workshops operated in conjunction with large residential institutions. The notion that people with disabilities were "better off" in long-term care facilities forced many families to relinquish their disabled children and relatives into total care of residential institutions and led policymakers to devote extraordinary resources to the development and maintenance of these costly facilities. Interview participant "Rachel" reflected upon her late father's experience at a local sheltered workshop in Toronto during the early 1970s, "It was place for him to go to spend his working hours rather than sitting at home."[11] When visiting her father at the workshop, Rachel encountered "people with cerebral palsy, people with seizures, another person who wore a helmet all the time, but no programs to integrate him back into the community or these other people in the sheltered workshop. There was no attempt to consider that they might have a mind to do something else." "David" also recalled, "A lot of [sheltered work] was light assembly work or putting labels on bottles or various things for which they were paid something, a piece rate, generally well-below the minimum wage."[12] Judith Heumann, a pioneering American disability rights activist, similarly reflects upon her visits to sheltered workshops. She recalls, "I remember one day we went to visit a sheltered workshop in Manhattan. We had a meeting with one of the executives. I remember this guy telling me that people had a choice. No one forced people to come to a sheltered workshop. If they really didn't like it there, they didn't have to come. I remember saying to him I didn't think people were really being given a choice if their choice was staying at home or coming out, at least being here. It didn't seem to me that was a choice."[13] Shut out of competitive employment in the mainstream labour market, many people with disabilities living in the community and in residential institutions were forced to accept work in sheltered workshops.

Disconnection from the competitive workforce frustrated the transference of skills and experience gained in workshops to mainstream work environments regardless of their apparent necessity or value as a response to disability. Sheltered workers gained little actual competitive work experience in workshops that provided few marketable skills in a rapidly evolving Canadian economy. Sheltered workers in Toronto at the CNIB and Corbrook Sheltered Workshops, for example, convinced the Toronto Mayor's Task Force on the Disabled and Elderly in the early 1970s that their work, which included the manufacturing, assembly, and packaging of various goods such as brooms, brushes, mops, and ceramics, was in fact not therapeutic at all.[14] The task force's 1973 report included the scathing conclusion that most "physically handicapped" people in the city "if they are working at all (often in sheltered workshops) are doing so at a level which insults their potential."[15] Regardless of the perceived value in "protecting" marginalized working-age people with disabilities in sheltered workshops, their separation from the competitive workforce ultimately frustrated their integration in mainstream workplaces.[16]

Workshop administrators, however, reasoned that sheltered work would serve as a springboard to "real work" in the paid workforce. Interview participant "Paul" began his work life as a teenager in a sheltered workshop operated by the CNIB, where he remained for "all of a week," packaging pipe filters for approximately $1.60 per day (approximately $8.70 when adjusted for inflation).[17] Disgruntled with the lack of employment options, he waited for two years until he was provided with the opportunity to work on a special employment project producing Braille textbooks for $90 per week (approximately $400 when adjusted for inflation). Which he described as "Fabulous money. The first time I actually earned money, so to speak." The experience had a transformative effect on young Paul, stimulating his enthusiasm to advance himself in the workforce. Working at the CNIB during summers while attending university, he acquired experience in the technological aspects of converting transcribed materials to tape that led him to further education and employment in the public sector, where he acquired various skills and confidence working with assistive technology for people with visual impairments. Disappointed with the lack of internal advancement in the public sector, he opted for self-employment in the technology sector, where he found that his skills, experience, and interests provided the foundation for a successful and rewarding career.

Fresh out of college in the early 1970s and looking for work, "Lucy" similarly attempted to find entry-level positions in the private sector. As a person with a visual impairment, she described how "at that time I used a cane but I could fake it and roam around with my cane folded up and I didn't appear to be visually impaired." Lucy described being cautioned "not to put in our resume or cover letter that we had a disability because your resume was pretty certain to go in the garbage." Despite her ability to hide her visual impairment, she consistently found that interviews ended abruptly when she disclosed that she lived with vision loss. Unable to find a job elsewhere, she found work at the CNIB and as a counsellor in a local sheltered workshop and for the next few years moved between the private sector and what she described as the "safety net" of the non-profit sector while attending university. In retrospect, Lucy believes that "had it been later I would have had a lot more options open." However, with her university degree, employment experience, and renewed confidence, Lucy finally secured a career as a professional in the private sector, where she held a series of progressively responsible positions, as proponents of sheltered workshops imagined.[18]

The sheltered workshop system experienced a number of transitions during the twentieth century in response to changes in the broader sociopolitical environment. The workshop model evolved over the course of two world wars and numerous medical advancements that drastically changed the lived experience of disability. Sheltered workshops were generally considered an unfortunate but essential strategy to promote the economic integration of people recovering from or adapting to some form of impairment. During the Second World War and the remainder of the 1940s the Department of Veterans Affairs injected massive federal funds to develop the rehabilitation industry in order to expedite the recovery of unemployable injured soldiers.[19] By the 1950s, with the expiration of this cash infusion, the rehabilitation system officially transitioned back to care for the civilian population as federal funding receded and injured veterans completed their programs.[20]

Sheltered employment was also a form of moral therapy delivered by therapeutic specialists who trained clients in appropriate social roles. Occupational therapy and vocational rehabilitation programs in the healthcare and social service sectors formed concurrent thrusts within the workshop model. Whereas occupational therapy typically involved social and physical therapeutic intervention to develop an individual's functional skills and tasks related to daily living, vocational rehabilitation reflected a more intensive focus on employment integration through job coaching, training, and placement.[21] Vocational rehabilitation extended from the work-as-therapy model in order to facilitate the integration of people with disabilities into the labour market. Although work-as-therapy was a universal concept that shaped the disciplines of both occupational therapy and vocational rehabilitation, sheltered workshops were originally designed to help develop work-related skills and good work ethics that would eventually enable labour market re-entry. Unlike "day centres" where many deinstitutionalized people

14 The Salvation Army sheltered workshop at 124 Lisgar Street in Toronto's Beaconsfield Village neighbourhood, c. 1960. Many sheltered workshops such as the one pictured above provided work to local residents with disabilities within local neighbourhoods in order to facilitate greater integration and community reintegration.[22] Public domain.

with intellectual disabilities attended to develop remedial life skills while living in the community, workshops were originally more closely focused on employment issues.[23] These dual currents meant that workshops employed people with a range of abilities, using the workshop model within their own trajectories of rehabilitation. As a result, the workshop system was capable of addressing the needs of a diverse population of people with acquired and congenital disabilities within a wide spectrum of different rehabilitation needs.[24]

The majority of sheltered workshops in the 1960s and early 1970s primarily served people with acquired physical disabilities living in the community, since many people with intellectual disabilities and mental health issues were still segregated in residential institutions or non-vocational community day centres. Workshops closely reflected a focus on vocational rehabilitation and workforce integration. The acceptance of vocational rehabilitation as a transitional process in one's physical and emotional recovery meant that sheltered work was primarily intended to facilitate social and economic reintegration. The emphasis on labour market participation contrasted with the nature of occupational work therapy regimes in residential institutions, which were focused more on long-term care and moral therapy than on skills-oriented, vocational rehabilitation programs.[25] Occupational work therapy had long been an integral aspect of patient life in psychiatric institutions under the direction of predominantly female "ward aides," as occupational therapists were known. Work therapy was considered by rehabilitation professionals to promote physical fitness and calm psychological turbulence by providing tangible activities, ensuring that patients were more compliant for staff while supplying cheap labour to subsidize the hefty operating costs of residential institutions.[26]

However, during the 1970s these separate systems began to converge. The introduction of the deinstitutionalization movement to Canada reconfigured the workshop model to meet new demands as thousands of people with developmental disabilities and mental health issues flooded into local communities, placing extra pressure on the workshop system. Goodwill Industries, which had been in operation since the mid-1930s, reported that deinstitutionalization transformed their organizational workforce to include unprecedented numbers of people with "mental handicaps."[27] Workshops became not just a transitional means to paid employment but a way for recently deinstitutionalized populations to participate in full-day programming and secure moral therapy that would enable them to live in the community.[28] Occupational therapists, who had been crucial to the running of residential labour regimes and community-based day programs, found new sources of employment in the expanding workshop system. Whether or not participation in sheltered workshops led to paid employment for deinstitutionalized people was no longer the primary focus, since workshop proponents were often more concerned with ensuring ex-patients had sufficient community-based resources to develop their capabilities.[29]

Initially focused on reform within psychiatric hospitals following mounting evidence of poor living conditions and quality of care, the popularization of community living philosophies turned many concerned parents, rehabilitation workers, and disability rights activists into vociferous advocates for the closure of psychiatric hospitals. The primary mandate in the movement to deinstitutionalize people with intellectual disabilities and mental health issues was the development of community-based social services, accommodations, and other supports. Parents' groups forged coalitions that evolved into service agencies, such as the Canadian Association for Community Living (CACL), which lobbied the state to replace residential institutions with community-based services.[30] Rehabilitation professionals, meanwhile, devoted much of their attention and resources to developing local and national organizations such as the Canadian Council for Rehabilitation Workshops (CCRW), Canadian Rehabilitation Council for the Disabled (CRCD; as discussed in chapter 2), other professional associations that fuelled political lobbying at provincial and federal levels, as well as extensive public campaigns to promote the rehabilitation industry on behalf of disabled people.[31] Rehabilitation professionals were also obliged to respond to the developing social movement of disability rights activism galvanizing groups of mainly youthful people with physical disabilities and visual impairments and psychiatric survivors within and surrounding the workshop system. Disability rights groups fostered social interaction among people with disabilities and helped to construct a sense of shared identity and common purpose against traditional beliefs and practices. As these groups grew and evolved over the course of the 1960s and 1970s, they drew upon a developing international discourse that envisioned greater opportunities for disabled people's full participation, citizenship, and equality protected by certain inalienable legislated rights.[32]

Psychiatric hospitals housing people with developmental disabilities and mental health issues, almost 70,000 individuals across Canada, began shutting down as early as the mid-1960s.[33] By 1981 nearly 50,000 people had been deinstitutionalized, a 71 per cent decrease. The highest number of institutionalized patients were located in Ontario, where an 85 per cent decrease occurred during the same period, or more than 16,000 people were discharged into the community within a span of ten to fifteen years.[34] Provincial governments steadily closed residential hospitals as a result of escalating operating costs, dwindling public funds, and the rise of deinstitutionalization and disability rights movements that rejected segregated models of care.[35]

Rehabilitation professionals observed the transition to community living with a combination of optimism and deep scepticism. The official newsletter of the Canadian Association of Rehabilitation Personnel (CARP) released a special issue of their newsletter in 1979 that took a detailed look at the closure of one major residential institution: the Lakeshore Psychiatric Hospital in Etobicoke, Ontario. The newsletter summarized arguments "for" and "against" hospital closures, noting in this case upwards of $30 million in projected *costs* of renovation compared with *savings* of approximately $2.5 million in immediate renovation costs and $6 million in annual operating expenses that would result from closing the hospital.[36] Such cost-benefit analyses reflected broader concerns highlighted by the deinstitutionalization movement, which argued that it "costs a great deal of taxpayers' dollars to keep people helpless."[37] Arguments against closure included the relative scarcity of alternative resources to supplement outpatient clinics and the likelihood that, without adequate expansion of community supports, ex-patients would end up in boarding houses and motels and on the street. The CARP editorial juxtaposed the demise of the hospital with the promise of sheltered workshops as "a place to work like any other" for deinstitutionalized ex-patients in a growing framework of community services.[38]

In the context of deinstitutionalization, people with disabilities were funnelled into workshops because they were an available source of community service workers, where few other options existed. Proponents of sheltered workshops included parents, rehabilitation professionals, and policymakers, who argued that an existing network of sheltered workshops could address the unprecedented demand for community services by providing a means for deinstitutionalized client populations to continue occupational work therapy or vocational rehabilitation programs. Joe Dale of the Ontario Disability Employment Network explained, "At the time, it was not understood that people who had a disability were capable of holding regular paid jobs and most of those who went to the Canada Manpower Centres or VRS [Vocational Rehabilitation Services] Employment Counsellors were typically referred to a sheltered workshop."[39] The residential institution system had created yawning gaps in community-based services, since many people's needs were presumably taken care of within segregated facilities. As a result, the deluge of people leaving closing institutions put a severe strain on existing community-based resources, which included the workshop system. At first glance, the legacy of workshops as a feature of vocational rehabilitation appeared fully compatible with the principles and goals of deinstitutionalization. New workshops were created to address the particular needs of people with developmental disabilities, many of whom had spent their entire lives in psychiatric hospitals.[40] Although workshops were never operated directly by the state, growing reliance on public sector funding meant the administration of workshop operations was increasingly shaped by political priorities. The workshop system experienced fluctuating levels of political support along with wavering support from the evolving welfare state. Prior to the 1970s, with the introduction of regular government funding through federal-provincial cost sharing agreements, most sheltered workshops relied on a combination of private subscriptions, public fundraising campaigns, and sales of goods and services.[41] Fundraising had long been an integral component of disability advocacy organizations, such as the OMOD, whose well-known campaigns helped support the development of a network of sheltered workshops across Canada.[42] Other organizations, such as Goodwill Industries and the CNIB, opened storefronts supplying goods and services provided by clients.[43] An emphasis on out-patient care precipitated by the growth of the community living movement during the 1970s led to a rise in government funding to enable the rapid expansion of the workshop system to meet new demands. Federal-provincial cost-sharing agreements established under the Vocational Rehabilitation Services Act (VRSA) led provincial governments to pass legislation, such as Ontario's 1974 Developmental Services Act (DSA), which fostered the development of community-based services such as sheltered workshops received the bulk of their funding.[44]

Private and public sector reviews of sheltered employment conducted in the late 1970s and early 1980s revealed an apparent revolution in the workshop system. In 1979 the Ontario Ministry of Community and Social Services (MCSS) released an authoritative survey of workshops confirming the extent to which an evolving workshop system reflected broader trends in the rest of the country. Between 1973 and 1978 provincial subsidies to sheltered workshops increased 674 per cent, which coincided with the introduction of new government funding through the DSA and VRS finance agreements;[45] where only twenty-five workshops existed prior to 1960, by 1978 there were nearly 150 workshops receiving provincial subsidies.[46] Such figures coincided with the rate of expansion of the American workshop system, where 85 workshops in 1948 swelled to 1,500, employing 160,000 workers in the early 1970s, ballooning to 3,000 workshops by 1976, and peaking at 650,000 workers by the mid-1980s.[47] Pre-1960s workshops in

Canada were predominantly dedicated to serving the needs of people with physical disabilities. By the end of the 1970s, however, approximately 75 per cent of workshops included or were exclusively devoted to serving people with intellectual disabilities.[48] At the peak of institutionalized care during the short, three-year period from 1974 to 1977, fourteen workshops for people with intellectual disabilities were established compared with only three workshops for other people with physical disabilities and mental health issues. By the early 1970s workshops for people with physical disabilities were eclipsed by workshops for people with intellectual disabilities, and it was often presumed that the newest workshops were designed for the latter. American observers also found by the early 1970s that the workshop system was predominantly oriented towards people with intellectual disabilities.[49]

While sheltered workshops originally focused on the vocational rehabilitation needs of physically disabled people seeking workforce re-entry, the workshop system was increasingly composed of clients learning life skills through occupational work therapy programs while living in the community. Frustrated with the apparent failure of sheltered employment to facilitate advancing clients into meaningful paid employment, people with physical disabilities increasingly turned away from workshops, pursuing other means of vocational rehabilitation and job coaching. By the early 1980s it was common knowledge among disabled jobseekers and disability rights activists that workshops were failing to live up to their original purposes. A spokesperson for People First, an activist organization for people with intellectual disabilities, noted, "They call it a training workshop. If you're there 10 years it's not training."[50] Critics argued that workshops engaged in practices that ultimately prevented workers from moving out into the labour market. Funding arrangements encouraged administrators to hold back productive workers to meet production targets set in contracts with government and private companies. When funding criteria changed to discourage these practices, critics again argued that workshop administrators focused their energies on finding work placements for the least disabled clients rather than helping those with greater needs, a practice known as "creaming."[51]

However, workshop advocates were less concerned with the original purpose of sheltered work than in using the workshop system to help recently deinstitutionalized populations and other workshop clients gain a foothold in the community. As Michael Bach of the CACL noted,

"Through the 1950s and 1960s our associations for community living built an impressive infrastructure of special education, sheltered workshops and activity centres, and residential care arrangements, inspired by a vision that people with intellectual disabilities were as deserving of support and a chance in life as anyone else. By the 1970s, there were some voices among families and leaders of our movement which began to challenge whether this was enough."[52] The 1978 MCSS workshop survey noted many major differences between workshops for people with intellectual disabilities and others for people with physical disabilities and mental health issues, particularly in respect to the influence of parents, program diversity, and complexity of tasks. Intellectually disabled sheltered workers were far more likely to have no work experience, spend longer duration in workshops on average, rely upon social assistance, and family members for participation in programming workshop managers for contract procurement.[53] As a result, older distinctions between sheltered workshops and occupational activity centres typically designated for people with "severe" intellectual disabilities were decreasingly relevant during this period as sheltered employment moved away from its roots in vocational rehabilitation.[54]

Workshops had experienced an unprecedented shift in density, clientele, and purpose as the workshop system was reconstructed to meet the needs of a changing disability community. Rehabilitation professionals and policymakers were forced to explore ways of improving the workshop system as sheltered workshops increasingly came under fire from disability rights activists, policymakers, and a wider public. By the 1970s the discourse surrounding workshops had become more frequently contested in Canada. American disability historian Paul Longmore observes, "The Disability Rights Movement is not a homogeneous or unitary effort. Rather, it is an assemblage of disability-based political movements that sometimes cooperate and sometimes compete."[55] The disability rights movement involved dynamic relations between separate groups with differing agendas, which occasionally worked in tandem but also conflicted with one another. Workshops in fact constituted a major struggle among competing disability movements in Canada as disability rights activists, family advocates, and the rehabilitation industry reflected separate and sometimes competing priorities. Workshop advocates endorsed sheltered employment as necessary for some people with "severe" intellectual, mental health, and physical disabilities in communities underequipped to respond to their needs. But disability rights activists and growing numbers of allies argued that sheltered workshops represented the vestiges of oppressive regimes of segregation that counteracted efforts to promote integration and full participation by "warehousing" sheltered workers and violating some of their basic civil rights.

Escalating public distrust concerning the legitimacy of sheltered workshops compelled administrators and advocates to respond by reinventing the workshop model. As early as 1981 the Canadian Mental Health Association (CMHA) recommended a return to vocational training in "real work" training in "normal work environments, using job creation programs and worker-run co-ops to assist psychiatric survivors find jobs in mainstream industry.[56] In 1980 the CCRW published a national inventory of sheltered workshops, which concluded that the workshop system was ripe for a total makeover. The $450,000 survey (over $1 million adjusted for inflation) was described as "one of the most extensive research and development surveys ever undertaken in Canada on the industrial and commercial potential of Rehabilitation Workshops for disabled persons."[57] The inventory was conducted as part of a proposal to stimulate the industrialization of the workshop system, converting workshops from expensive, unproductive mechanisms of social welfare into robust, self-sustaining, non-profit enterprises providing realistic work experiences for clients. The objective was to identify industrial and commercial work that could be performed "profitably" by workshops in order to establish programs to develop business skills and operational strategies to place workshops in a better position to compete for public and private sector contracts. The CCRW inventory determined there were over 600 workshops in operation across Canada serving 25,000 workers, approximately half of which (45 per cent) were located in Ontario in medium-sized communities. The majority (67 per cent) of workshops were dedicated to clients with "mental retardation," while only 7 per cent were focused on delivering services to people with "physical disabilities."[58] As the 1978 Ontario MCSS workshop survey indicated, workshops devoted to people with intellectual disabilities were less self-directed than other workshops in that they relied heavily on workshop managers to secure contract work.[59] As a result, the conversion of most workshops in Canada to an industrial model could take place in a rather straightforward fashion, given the hierarchical orientation of workshops serving intellectually disabled clients.

The CCRW's preliminary inventory culminated in "Project BIDS" (Business Industrial Development Strategies), in a collaborative venture

15 Sheltered workers at the Truro Butler Centre in Nova Scotia sorting waste paper as part of the Project BIDS program. The pilot project in Truro was one of four pilot sites across the country in the cities of Fort Erie (Ontario), Ottawa (Ontario), and Mission (British Columbia).[60] © Truro Daily News, 1980. Reproduced with permission.

between CCRW and the recently established federal Bureau on Rehabilitation to facilitate the transition of workshops from "mere activities" into actual "production lines."[61] The transformation of the sheltered workshop system was identified at an early stage in the development of the bureau as internal documents earmarked special funds to stimulate the industrialization of workshops.[62] Shortly after being created, the bureau began actively working with CCRW to develop Project BIDS, committing another $86,000 (or $260,000 when adjusted for inflation) to develop pilot projects in Ontario, Quebec, and Nova Scotia to assist selected workshops in the handling of recycled waste paper products in order to effectively compete for public and private sector contracts.[63]

As a preliminary measure in order to generate business for industrialized workshops, the bureau advocated that the federal Treasury Board and Department of Supply and Services enact policies favourable to the procurement of contracts from sheltered workshops on a government-wide basis.[64] The Ministry of Supply and Services initially raised concerns about the quality of goods and the inexperience of sheltered workers with fulfilling competitive contracts, but eventually consented on a trial basis.[65] A series of progress reports from 1979 to 1981 on the status of pilot initiatives in the recycling industry in the Ottawa region found that workshops increased their net productivity and profitability. Sheltered workers participating in the project, all of whom were recruited from the Ottawa District Association of the Mentally Retarded, demonstrated a more "industrious attitude" and developed new work skills. Feedback from the other pilot projects also appeared to confirm these findings.[66] Further studies conducted for the federal government indicated that disabled workers "performed equally well in sheltered and integrated settings" and that sheltered workshops were ideal for the recycling industry in that the work was "enjoyable and meaningful to workshop employees and is identifiable to them as 'real work.'"[67]

However, the reported success of a few workshops masked underlying problems and tensions that threatened Project BIDS. One branch of the project was located in Fort Erie because the "area was particularly depressed and needed the work." At one stage of the project, parents withdrew their support because of a funding crisis that endangered the financial solvency of the organization. When these financial difficulties were eventually resolved, parents reached a new consensus that the BIDS initiative represented a financial liability to the workshop and undermined its social objectives.[68] Owing to these and other concerns, the Bureau on Rehabilitation retained a private consultant to conduct an internal audit of Project BIDS. The scathing report, submitted in 1982, found that project terms such as "adequate remuneration for work performed" failed to address widespread concerns about the payment of subminimum wages to sheltered workers.[69] The non-partisan auditor noted other substantive problems, including extensive documentary inconsistencies, insufficient data, inadequate costing mechanisms, miscommunication between levels of government, and a number of procedural issues. The auditor concluded that the project had lost sight of the "individual client as the ultimate workshop product" by placing too much emphasis on the conversion of workshops into "competitive businesses" when reviews of the workshop system "suggest[ed] that few could [become competitive]."[70]

The report confirmed what some disability activists had been saying for years. As the national representative of disability rights activists in

Canada, COPOH was invited to provide regular input to the CCRW at each stage of the project.[71] Although initially optimistic about the prospect of providing consumer input, COPOH soon became disillusioned with the notion of using sheltered work to "produce commercial articles for contracted sales without paying production scale wages, insurance" and other benefits.[72] Suspicious that the industrialization of workshops legitimated "an outdated, detrimental concept," COPOH argued that, rather than retrofitting workshops into production lines, there should be "consultation with handicapped people as to what type of meaningful work they wish to be trained for and in what training atmosphere."[73] COPOH complained there was little indication that Project BIDS would address the issues of consumer control, minimum wages, fringe benefits, safety standards, and how it planned to work with private industry to find "real work for real pay." Since activists felt Project BIDS was not demonstrating sufficient commitment to "eliminating exploitative wages" despite negative feedback on minimum wage exemptions in sheltered employment, COPOH held its 1980 conference in Vancouver, where it resolved to extend greater "human rights to disabled workers."[74] For disability rights activists the industrialization of sheltered workshops represented an attempt to extend the life of a rapidly crumbling and essentially exploitative system.

Public opinion of workshops also was in serious decline by the early 1980s, as mainstream media and disability literature painted a bleak picture of sheltered work. An early retrospective by David Cooney, president of Goodwill America, noted that it was "disappointing but, not surprising" that those who favoured de-institutionalization were critical of sheltered workshops and that "attacking a program as successful and useful as the sheltered workshops system [was] both illogical and counterproductive."[75] Sheltered work became something of a "hot topic" in news outlets across the country, as complaints swirled about unfair labour practices, poor working conditions, mismanagement of funds, violation of minimum wage legislation, and funding disincentives that held back productive workers.[76] In a critical commentary on sheltered workshops in Ontario written in 1983 Lola Freeman observed that training in workshops was not related to current market demand for skills. Freeman concluded, "Parents often see the workshops as a place for the person to go during the day, rather like day care for adults. These parents neglect to take responsibility for enhancing or assisting their child's progress."[77] Workshops were even associated with "slave" or "sweatshop" labour in certain accounts, as the liminal labour market status of sheltered workers was further complicated by the revelation that industrialized workshops would continue to receive provincial minimum wage exemptions.[78] The National Union of Public and General Employees planned to organize sheltered workers, calling charitable organizations among the "worst employers in the country" and advocated repealing minimum-wage exemptions.[79] Payment of stipends instead of minimum wages while workshop-made goods were sold at a profit was a common practice in most workshops across North America, given their classification as training organizations. But disability activists in both Canada and the United States pointed to subminimum wages as evidence of the exploitative nature of sheltered work. For example, American disability activist Frank Bowe similarly noted that, ironically, the US Fair Labor Standards Act permitted sheltered workers to be paid half the minimum wage even when such employment proved "the only source of work he or she can secure."[80]

Minimum-wage exemptions proved to be the sticking point in the fight against workshops in Canada, exacerbated by the move to reorganize sheltered work into industrial-type production lines. CCRW discussed the wage issue at their national conference in order to help resolve concerns around Project BIDS, but concluded that, since insufficient funding caused workshops to experiment with industrialized production, it did not make financial sense to raise labour costs by paying sheltered workers minimum wages or anything above what they "earned."[81] A 1980 review of procedures used in granting provincial wage exemption permits by the Ontario Ministry of Labour, for example, concluded that the workshop system operated as intended but recommended that permits apply to individuals rather than entire workshop organizations. The report also found that, if workshops were required to pay minimum wages, it might actually create a disincentive for sheltered workers to search for employment in the mainstream workforce.[82]

Disability activists, on the other hand, were convinced sheltered workshops did more harm than good to disabled jobseekers. Activists demanded that provinces provide "real work for real pay" by instituting mandatory minimum wages, or provide welfare rate "top-ups," and that the workshop system should place greater emphasis on vocational rehabilitation and job placement services. The wage issue continued to remain a serious point of contention across the country until the late 1980s, when fair-wages legislation was first implemented in Ontario and then followed by other provinces.[83] The objective of this legislation included making it possible for disabled people unemployable at a minimum wage, including sheltered or supported workers, to be paid "according to his/her ability" with a provincial top-up.[84] By then, however, the reputation of sheltered workshops as segregated institutions that violated disabled people's rights was widely recognized.[85]

In 1981 Canada celebrated the International Year of Disabled Persons, culminating in an unprecedented degree of attention that centred on the capabilities and rights of people with disabilities. As disability rights activists across the country seized the moment to press their rights-based agenda on a number of fronts, work began on a unique, two-part documentary series entitled *The Disability Myth*. The documentary series contrasted common "myths" about disabled people with "facts" based on interviews with disabled people, activists, professionals, and politicians.[86] With a combination of public and private sector funding, the Toronto-based filmmakers landed Oscar-nominated actor John Hurt as host and narrator for the series, which aired in 1982 and 1983 on Canadian Television Networks (CTV). Public response to the program was "positively overwhelming" and CTV was "inundated with phone calls from viewers." One published review of the series noted, "Aylward [the director] paints a bleak economic picture. The handicapped in sheltered workshops earn between $1.50 and $5 an hour. Some are not paid at all; they're not considered worth the minimum wage. Yet the best workers are kept in the shelters because they keep the operations going, yet about 65 per cent of the disabled remain unemployed."[87] Part I of the series, subtitled *Segregation*, stated that it was a "fact" that "most people are better off in integrated settings."[88] Cinematographers cast workshops as having a particularly dark atmosphere accompanied by ominous music, and they portrayed workers as helpless victims of an unjust, if not downright Dickensian, institution. Part II, subtitled *Employment*, focused on employment issues and blamed workshops for inhibiting the integration of disabled people into the mainstream workforce, emphasizing the importance of finding alternatives to the workshop model. The sheltered workshop model was cast as outdated and challenged compared with modern training methods that provided more realistic work opportunities. Despite CCRW's investments in the industrialization of the workshop system only a few years earlier, representative Leroy Thompson appeared in the documentary, arguing that workshops negatively affected opportunities to have "normal life experiences." Such portrayals of workshops permeated the public consciousness, enabling disability rights activists and their allies to promote alternatives to the workshop model.[89]

With mounting pressure surrounding the model and the imminent failure of the CCRW's industrial experiment, workshop advocates and rehabilitation professionals entertained alternatives. The accepted wisdom was (and continued to be) that workshops were necessary for particularly "severe" cases of disability. However, it became increasingly clear that workshops had lost sight of the transitional nature of sheltered employment in moving away from the original emphasis on vocational rehabilitation. A study commissioned by the Ontario Ministry of Labour's (OML) Handicapped Employment Program (HEP) in 1980 explained,

> As a business operation ... the workshop relies heavily on its most productive workers. Workshop managers whom we interviewed confirmed that there is an immediate and noticeable drop in output when good workers leave. The workshop may then find itself in the peculiar position of not being able to meet the income target set in the agreed budget with MCSS, thus paying an economic penalty for achieving a prime rehabilitation goal. This contradiction is likely to intensify as the workshops expand their business operations.[90]

Working in a sheltered workshop was never intended to be a permanent alternative to competitive employment, yet it seemed this had become the reality for too many unemployable people who "trained" for paid jobs that never materialized. Among the key complaints were a lack of individual attention to workshop clients and inadequate resources for facilitating labour market integration.[91]

By the mid-1980s a new consensus among disability rights activists, family advocates, and rehabilitation organizations moved away from sheltered workshops, coming together around supported employment.[92] In 1984 the landmark report of the federal Royal Commission of Inquiry on Equality in Employment confirmed that, if workshops were going to continue to exist, they should pay minimum wages and provide better job placement services that assisted sheltered workers to find paid work.[93] Active dismemberment of the workshop system did not immediately materialize, as social policymakers were reluctant to abandon a "facility-based program" model.[94] Many parents of workshop clients also continued to support the workshop model and had "a strong voice in setting policy for workshops." These parents supported the workshop model, arguing that workshops provided important social and emotional benefits to clients, and they feared the loss of reliable

day programming services would negatively impact the social integration of their adult disabled children.[95] However, these cautionary voices
were eventually overtaken by opposition to workshops.

In response to growing criticism of the workshop model, the CCRW
undertook a major constitutional review by engaging in extensive consultations with key stakeholders, including government, employers, disability rights activists, advocacy organizations, and service agencies.[96]
A CCRW survey called *Updating for the 80s* solicited input "about what
the current vision was, and what role this national organization would
play in working towards making that vision a reality."[97] Results of the
review steered the CCRW away from sheltered workshops towards
a "new mandate of increased access to competitive employment."[98]
Signalling this developing consensus regarding the move away from a
workshop model, the organization changed its name around 1983 from
Canadian Council of Rehabilitation Workshops to Canadian Council on
Rehabilitation and Work.

Support for sheltered workshops was replaced by a new concept
called "supported employment." Practised in the 1970s by innovative
job placement organizations such as The World of One in Seven and further popularized in the early 1980s, supported employment presented
an alternative to sheltered workshops. By suggesting disabled people
needed "support" rather than "shelter" to achieve workforce participation and independent living, supported employment revolutionized
the role of professionals in the lives of disabled jobseekers. Supported
employment typically involved placing clients in work-training programs within mainstream industry for specific durations under the
co-supervision of employers and transitional placement coordinators.[99]
The disability news program *Moving On* profiled one such offering, the
Opportunities Program in Porcupine Plains, Saskatchewan. Funded
by the federal Opportunities Fund, the program provided minimum-
wage employment to forty people with developmental disabilities in
partnership with local businesses – a box assembly plant, laundromat,
storefront, and RCMP detachment – while reporting increased profits
against diminishing reliance on fundraising.[100] The general expectation was that clients would acquire skills and experience that would
enable a smoother transition to existing or similar paid employment
relationships. The supported employment model relied heavily on the
intervention of social workers, rehabilitation professionals, and job
placement workers to cultivate relationships with employers to create
work arrangements that met mutually agreeable goals.[101] The model

worked by gradually removing support mechanisms until clients became virtually independent workers in mainstream settings.

The popularization of supported employment built on years of demonstrated results by agencies practising the concept. In 1976 the Metro Association for the Mentally Retarded (MAMR) in Toronto successfully placed twenty-nine clients in supportive work arrangements.[102] MAMR representatives discovered that cultivating an open and honest relationship with employers led to successful placements in paid jobs.[103] Similarly, The World of One in Seven job placement agency, discussed in chapter 3, developed a national and international reputation for their highly successful client-centred approach, which included low client-counsellor ratios to ensure that job placements were successful experiences for both supported workers and participating employers. A documentary film of the agency featured clients working in a variety of factory, services, and media workplaces and included interviews with Kingston-area clients and employers praising the supported employment model.[104]

In another case, award-winning *Toronto Sun* columnist and disability activist Mona Winberg documented the rise of supported employment in the late 1980s in a series of articles on the decline of the sheltered workshop system. In 1988 Winberg reported on one program called STEP (Supported Training and Employment Program) in North York, Ontario, profiling their innovative and successful approach to finding "real work for real pay" for clients. STEP workers used a systematic approach to teaching and training job skills, finding jobs and cultivating networks of employers, advocating for clients on job sites, and managing the worker-employer relationship. Winberg noted, "Not only does real pay for real work help a person's self-esteem, but it can also transform him from a social assistance recipient to taxpayer and consumer."[105] The program was one of many such initiatives that cropped up during this period as the sheltered workshop approach increasingly fell out of favour.

In the late 1980s the CCRW declared, "Most of the sheltered workshops in this country are in a state of transition. They were founded by family members and concerned citizens because society was not willing to accept disabled people on other terms. It was, in part, through the achievements that disabled people demonstrated through the 'workshop' system that societal attitudes have evolved and that the early inroads to competitive employment were achieved." The CCRW highlighted their organization's role in designing new community-based services, but lamented the legacy of supporting an approach that addressed the economic "problem" of disability by "sheltering" disabled people in separate workplaces.[106] By the early 1990s the CCRW was actively promoting "real work for real pay," including one partnership between IBM and disability agencies, which ensured disabled workers were "competitively paid, giving them real work experience."[107]

Sheltered workshops were not "a place to work like any other." Originally designed by middle-class advocates and professionals worried about the moral hazards of idleness among physically disabled people, the Canadian workshop system was reconstituted in the 1960s and 1970s to provide a ready source of community-based programming as part of an under-resourced response to the deinstitutionalization movement. The same optimism for community participation that led people with physical disabilities and mental health issues away from segregation in residential institutions invigorated the workshop system. By the early 1980s however, it became increasingly clear that sheltered workshops were incapable of and perhaps no longer entirely devoted to helping resolve the economic displacement of disabled people. Many people came to workshops and never left. Others left quickly, crediting workshops for illustrating a directionless future they wished to avoid. Relatively few clients ever "graduated" from workshop training programs by moving onto competitive employment and it became increasingly difficult to differentiate workshops from older methods of "warehousing" disabled people. As criticism of workshops mounted during the 1980s, administrators and advocates attempted to salvage the workshop model by experimenting with the industrialization and commercialization of sheltered work. Seemingly unproductive and unprofitable workshops could be transformed into thriving capitalist nonprofit enterprises, they argued, capable of addressing both the vocational and rehabilitation needs of client workers. However, while policymakers spent thousands of dollars on the reconstruction of the workshop system, a growing movement of critics highlighted the apparent focus on making sheltered workshops more profitable as opposed to more effective vehicles of employment integration. Initial pilot projects were heavily criticized, and activist organizations argued that money would be better spent helping people with disabilities establish their own businesses or developing strategies to promote inclusive job creation.[108]

The unskilled, routine, and non-marketable nature of sheltered work meant that, in addition to gaining little competitive employment experience, workers were underpaid or, in some cases, entirely unpaid.

Sheltered workers were classified as trainees and most survived on state-sponsored social assistance, which justified the payment of stipends instead of wages. Consequently, the role of sheltered workshops in developing employability raised larger questions about reliance on sheltered work, indicating larger social and economic problems created by designating entire categories of the population "unemployable" due to physical and mental abilities. Since paid employment represented the typical path to independence in mainstream Canadian society, sheltered workers were effectively denied full citizenship in this system.

Sheltered workshops did not resolve the problem of chronic unemployment and poverty in the disability community, nor were they proven to be an effective mechanism for ensuring full participation in society. Despite the rapid expansion of the sheltered workshop system during the 1960s and 1970s in Canada to facilitate the community reintegration of recently deinstitutionalized populations, the social and economic marginalization of working-age people with disabilities continued unabated. Indeed, attempts to rescue the workshop model, such as the installation of industrial capitalist practices, failed to accomplish even the traditional social and economic objectives of sheltered work. As the labour market evolved, it became increasingly difficult for sheltered workshops to impart vocational skills that would be relevant and applicable to the broader economy. The social construction of employability also meant that the social and economic liminality of people with disabilities was rooted in the nature of labour market transactions in the capitalist economic system that fundamentally deemed able-bodied workers more attractive than many people with disabilities. As a result, the ideological basis of sheltered work simply reveals how unemployable disabled people became casualties of an economic system predicated on arbitrary standards of the working body. At the very least, it was reasoned that if people with disabilities sought greater participation and integration in the community, they needed to work in mainstream settings with the appropriate supports. The history of sheltered workshops in Canada reveals that protection can unintentionally lead to segregation, not "a place to work like any other."

Chapter Six

Employers and the Ideological (Re)Construction of the Workplace

"There are those who listen politely and do nothing, those who listen politely and want to do something, and those who will do something," stated the *Financial Post* in June 1981, predicting the business community's likely response to the upcoming International Year of Disabled Persons (IYDP).[1] The columnist concluded that few companies are actually engaged in full-scale organizational change, despite warnings that provincial governments might introduce mandatory affirmative action programs forcing businesses to adopt proactive measures to hire people with disabilities.[2] Earlier that year the *Financial Post* reported that disabled people were an "untapped resource" and encouraged employers to stop thinking of people with disabilities as "charity cases."[3] Editorials such as these reflected growing awareness in the Canadian business community that many people with disabilities were excluded from the labour market, not because of some inherent personal limitation, but because employers failed to hire them and also failed to ensure their workplaces were inclusive and accommodating to workers with a range of abilities.

Despite outward expressions of support for disability issues from the 1970s to 1990s, many Canadian employers held deep-seated reservations about employing people with disabilities. This resistance was evident in statistical records documenting the systemic exclusion of disabled people from the labour market. Widespread prejudice and resistance to actually hiring disabled people undermined the outcomes of awareness-raising activities and ultimately violated the rights of disabled people in the labour market. A comprehensive study conducted in 1975 by the Canadian Chamber of Commerce (CCC) provided foundational insights by identifying typical employer perceptions of disability and understanding how employer attitudes and practices excluded people with disabilities from participation in the labour market. Repeated studies from the 1970s to 1990s reprised these original findings, demonstrating few substantive changes in employer behaviours, despite intensified campaigns across the country to raise awareness of disability issues in the workplace and encourage employers to hire disabled people. Nonetheless, employers continued to engage in "disabling" recruitment and work practices during this period, leading disability activists and their allies to lobby for stricter, enforceable legislation concerning accessibility and employment equity.

This chapter examines the role played by employers in the pursuit of the economic integration of disabled people. Discussion of employer attitudes and responses to efforts to promote employability is followed by an examination of the ways in which awareness campaigns and appeals to corporate social responsibility were limited by the calculated pragmatism of an increasingly cut-throat capitalist market system. The third section considers how government employers promoted the moral economy of disability and ultimately modelled equitable work practices to the wider private sector. The final section examines the veracity of early predictions that new assistive technologies would "level the playing field" by diminishing the competitive disadvantage of disability in the labour market.

Successful implementation of disability rights initiatives relied on the cooperation of employers to change employment attitudes and practices, since employer perceptions of job candidates ultimately determined actual employment outcomes.[4] Perceptions of disability were conveyed through workplace policies concerning recruitment, compensation, accommodation, promotion, termination, and other fundamental features of the employment relationship. Recruitment preferences and the treatment of disabled employees reflected broader social attitudes regarding disability that influenced decisions by employers in the workplace. Although the Canadian job market is technically a meritocracy where workers are recruited on the basis of their skills and abilities, employers also consciously or unconsciously held negative attitudes that affected various employment-related decisions.[5] When confronted with disabled people in the workplace, employers' prejudices about disability influenced recruitment and employment practices.[6]

Many typical work environments during the 1970s and 1980s were physically and culturally inaccessible to disabled people. Canadian workplaces and employers responded more positively to able-bodied workers and jobseekers who were able to effectively navigate the work environment, whereas disabled people were put on trial.[7] Interview participant "Rachel" explained, "I feel like I'm in a catch-22. If I disclose, I may encounter the discrimination because it spooks them, but if I don't disclose, then they hear rumours in the industry; 'She's a real [problem] ... she doesn't know how to project manage ... you can't deal with her.' So it's a really tough thing for me to decide."[8] As these stories suggest, disabled people could face employers reluctant or unwilling to recognize the negative conditioning that interfered with the interview process. As a result, people with disabilities could find it necessary in interview settings to downplay the impact of their impairments on job functionality.[9]

In an effort to anticipate and challenge stereotypically negative perceptions of disability by employers, jobseekers with visible or disclosed disabilities had to be fully aware of the limitations of their impairments yet also display positivity and unflagging optimism. Interview participant "Olivia" reflected on her experience growing up in a residential institution and subsequent job searches during the late 1970s in Toronto. Olivia found, "Getting your foot in the door, you're dealing with everybody's preconceptions about what you can and cannot do. What kind of help you will need and how much trouble you're going to be as an employee. How difficult it's going to be to get rid of you if things don't work out. You're dealing with all that baggage just looking for a job."[10] American rehabilitation consultant Carolyn Vash similarly noted in the early 1970s that a disabled person is "stereotyped as one whose total body and soul are concerned with his disability and issues relating to that disability. And if this is the impression an employer has, there's no reason on earth he's going to hire a person who sits and broods all the time about *his own problem* [my emphasis]."[11] For example, a pamphlet on job hunting advice produced by the Ontario Ministry of Labour's Handicapped Employment Program (HEP) encouraged people with disabilities to understand how individual jobseekers were partly responsible for challenging employer attitudes. The HEP pamphlet asserted, "Your own attitudes are also important. Handle your disability in a positive way and employers will be more receptive to hiring you. You have to believe that you will be an asset to an employer and that productive work is fulfilling."[12] In 1981 Jean Moore, president of United Handicapped Groups of Ontario and former director of The World of One in Seven employment agency, commented on her experience with securing jobs for people with disabilities. Moore concluded,

"Employers can go just so far in hiring the handicapped – and they still have a way to go – but the handicapped, too, must have some responsibility."[13] Moore felt that social skills in the area of self-promotion were regarded as one of the keys to successful social and economic integration, emphasizing that "so many [disabled people] have been out of the labor market for so long that they have a low self-image" and fail to adequately promote themselves to employers.[14]

Once employed in mainstream settings, many disabled workers faced a variety of discriminatory attitudes and practices. Common experiences included overbearing supervisors, assignment to menial tasks, co-workercomplaints about perceived special treatment, and social isolation in the workplace. Interview participants for this study encountered clear, as well as more subtle, instances of discrimination by employers and colleagues in the workplace. Interview participant "Lisa" reflected on her experience working in the municipal public service since the mid-1970s, "It's the middle managers, the supervisors, whoever you have to deal with at the actual job site ... because they might not know about disabilities, they have already formed an opinion and idea of what they think you can do or should do."[15] Interview participant "Dan," similarly found discrimination, prejudice, and ignorance existed in his provincial public sector workplace. Dan lamented, "I've had to fight with superiors and go over their head to demand that accommodations be made in certain circumstances."[16] Interview participant "Richard" also warns, "I've always remembered that because when you have a disability or something else that's often discriminated against, you sort of expect to be discriminated against so you might see discrimination when it's not really there. So I'm always reluctant to say something is discrimination."[17] In spite of his cautious attitude, however, Richard recalled one "cut and dried" instance where he was denied an opportunity to compete for a new position because a supervisor had unilaterally decided the job was not appropriate for Richard because of his disability.[18]

Canadian employers often approached disability issues with a charitable outlook. This approach was reinforced by the decision made in 1973 to transfer federal responsibility for vocational rehabilitation from the Department of Manpower to the Department of National Health and Welfare (DNHW), effectively disconnecting disability workers from mainstream labour policy discourse. Since DNHW officials were focused primarily on public health issues and the provision of welfare benefits, they sought input from Canadian employers about the best way to move forward with the vocational rehabilitation portfolio and larger goals shaping disabled people's labour market participation.[19] As a result, DNHW commissioned the Canadian Chamber of Commerce (CCC) to conduct a study in 1975 to determine why employers did not hire disabled people. The request was made in the context of the federal Liberal government's income security review, since there was little current data on the subject of the employment of disabled people.[20] As the largest network of local boards of trade, business associations, and chambers of commerce across Canada, the CCC study filled a void of employment data on the employment of disabled people while representing the attitudes and practices of employers across Canada.

The CCC's groundbreaking report marked the first comprehensive examination in Canada of the relationship between employer attitudes and the employment of people with disabilities. The report, entitled *Employability of the Handicapped*, concluded that employers' attitudes were all-important in determining the marginalization of people with disabilities in the labour market. Thirty per cent of survey respondents acknowledged they had never hired or considered hiring a disabled person and were unaware that vocational rehabilitation programs might be a source for new employees. Nearly 75 per cent of employers stated there was no job that disabled workers could handle or that the nature of their business was inappropriate for disabled people, and 61 per cent stated that a disabled person had never submitted an application or contacted them about available jobs. Many employers believed that disabled workers were inherently at greater risk of accidents, that they might contravene fire regulations and increase company insurance premiums. Other employers believed the workplace was inaccessible to many disabled people and could not be appropriately adapted. In addition, many employers believed disabled workers would be chronically absent, cause greater staff turnover, have emotional problems, require too much supervision, or generally negatively affect production rates. Employers clearly believed that recruiting disabled people would represent "hiring the unknown" and expose their organization to unnecessary risk. Employers were perplexed by the needs of people with disabilities and how disabled workers negotiated an inaccessible workplace and broader environment, which fostered general uncertainty and the sense of risk that challenged their attractiveness as potential employees. The study concluded that, while there was a serious lack of awareness of disability issues among employers, there was also a general willingness to learn more about disability and possibly hire disabled people should the opportunity present itself.

The CCC report was highly influential within the business community in Canada, promoting awareness and a review of prejudices against disabled people. Subsequent to the report, a Seminar on Employability of the Handicapped brought together officials from all levels of government, service agencies, and disability rights activists in an attempt to brainstorm strategies for increasing the employment of disabled people.[21] In advance of the seminar, disability activists lobbied political officials to make firm commitments to reforming policies to promote the inclusion of disabled people in the labour market.[22] In her keynote speech at the seminar, Ontario Minister of Labour Bette Stephenson expressed the general feeling of optimism at the seminar, noting the attendance of many business leaders gathered to work with government officials and voluntary agencies in order to create realistic job opportunities for disabled people seeking work.[23]

Despite healthy attendance and widespread optimism about the potential to build consensus on disability issues within the business community, the seminar received uneven praise. The disability-led Ontario Advisory Council for the Physically Handicapped (OACPH) optimistically reported the creation of "ripples of public awareness" as major corporations announced new accessibility plans in response to the seminar.[24] The Ontario government responded by increasing resources to promote the employment of disabled people within the provincial public sector.[25] The Canadian Human Rights Commission also responded by delivering a series of employment seminars across the country that brought together private sector employers, various levels of government, unions, disabled people, and service agencies.[26] The CCC ultimately deferred to the professional-led Canadian Rehabilitation Council for the Disabled (CRCD) as the most appropriate agency to follow up with additional awareness campaigns, which it did in preparation for the 1980 World Congress of Rehabilitation.[27] Subsequent seminars and training events, such as those conducted in conjunction with the annual National Access Awareness Week beginning in 1988 and continuing through the 1990s, also represented continuing efforts to combat evidence of negative employer attitudes with awareness-building activities to confront emerging trends and issues.

Studies of employers subsequent to the definitive CCC survey documented a lack of change in attitudes and practices of employers while

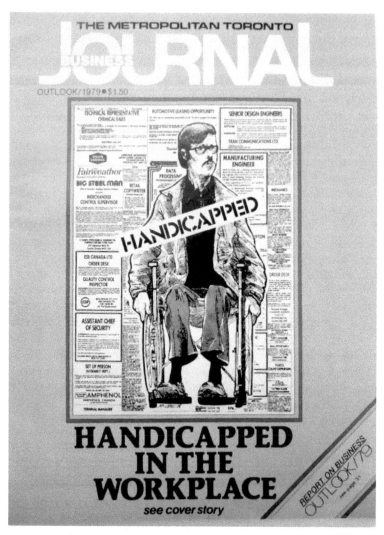

16 Cover of the *Metropolitan Toronto Business Journal* published by the Board of Trade of Metropolitan Toronto featuring a man in a wheelchair superimposed on a typical newspaper job opportunities section. The cover story revealed that employers in Toronto were responding to the growth in public attention to the various barriers faced by people with disabilities in their pursuit of employment.[28] © Toronto Region Board of Trade, 1979. Reproduced with permission.

promoting various initiatives to resolve the problem. Beginning in 1980, the Blind Organization of Ontario with Self-Help Tactics (BOOST) released a report entitled *Developing Alternative Service Models*, which encouraged employers to embrace a proactive approach to hiring disabled people.[29] The BOOST report reflected a prevailing attitude in the federal Liberal administration that supported innovative approaches to the problem of unemployment in the disability community.[30] In particular, BOOST envisioned the creation of a series of tax credits that would entice employers to hire disabled people and would provide new funds to develop public education programs aimed at increasing awareness of disability issues among employers, employment agencies, and employers' associations.[31]

The groundbreaking 1981 report of the Parliamentary Special Committee on the Disabled and the Handicapped (*Obstacles*) similarly reflected a climate of social change regarding people with disabilities in the government and broader public sphere. Following hundreds of submissions across the country, the *Obstacles* report included a number of recommendations aimed at alleviating barriers to disabled people's employment opportunities caused by employer policies and practices. The committee, chaired by Walter Dinsdale, father to a child with various disabilities and energetic ally of the disability rights movement, was created to develop realistic proposals for new initiatives to improve the social and economic integration of disabled people in Canada.[32] Similar to the BOOST report, the *Obstacles* report proposed special tax incentives to hire disabled workers and affirmative action contract compliance measures to ensure contractors respected the hiring preferences of disabled people and other identified minority groups. The report considered on-the-job training stipulations to expedite the movement of disabled people off welfare rolls and encouraged increased protection for injured workers who acquired disabilities at work as well as penalties for non-retention of disabled employees.[33] The *Obstacles* report thus highlighted the importance of employers in the promotion of the social and economic integration of disabled people.

In 1982 the Canadian Employment and Immigration Commission (CEIC) reported that there was little change among employer attitudes in Canada, despite hiring and awareness-raising campaigns. A CEIC report, titled *Employ-Ability*, detected "mounting pressure everywhere" and an "urgent need to increase employment opportunities for persons with physical disabilities." Through seminars involving disability rights activists, unions, service agencies, and employers, the CEIC

echoed earlier findings, arguing that employer attitudes towards disabled workers included: labelling, pity, inflated expectations of disabled applicants, beliefs that disabled people were "too much trouble,"
as well as general anxiety and myths around insurance costs, health
and safety, and productivity.[34] The 1983 report of the Ontario Task Force
on Employers and Disabled Persons entitled *Linking for Employment* envisioned the creation of community councils linking businesses with
local agencies and government departments in an innovative network
that promised to connect qualified disabled people with job vacan-
cies.[35] The task force, led by Jean Pigott, believed that the concept of
community councils situated employers as active participants with an
integral role in cultivating employment opportunities for people with
disabilities.[36] Pigott also envisioned a vocational rehabilitation system
that fully included employers in the process of finding job opportunities for people with disabilities.[37]

In the federal Commission on Equality in Employment, Justice
Rosalie Abella built on Pigott's findings by encouraging employers
in 1984 to redesign their recruitment and workplace practices to promote the employment of people with disabilities and other marginalized groups.[38] Abella issued a number of recommendations to promote
the improvement of employment opportunities for people with disabilities across Canada by challenging barriers to employment created in
part by employer attitudes.[39] In particular, Abella introduced the term
"employment equity" to refer to a system of special measures taken to
accommodate differences that would surmount barriers to participation in the labour market.[40] Employment equity, essentially based on
"affirmative action" programs but distanced from the stigma of hiring
quotas and enshrined in the 1986 federal Employment Equity Act, confirmed that employers' discriminatory recruitment, hiring, and promotion practices perpetuated an exclusive labour market.[41] Reminiscent
of conclusions in earlier studies, Abella found that disabled people
(as well as women, Aboriginals, and visible minorities) were denied
job opportunities, owing to systemic discriminatory attitudes of employers that presented obstacles to inclusion.

In order to combat troubling employment statistics and reports indicating high unemployment in the disability community, the federal
government sponsored the development of employer networks in
Canada to share best practices and facilitate job (re)entry. Two examples, the UK-based Employers' Forum on Disability and the US-based
Job Accommodation Network (JAN), indicated Canadian authorities'

17 The Canadian Council on Rehabilitation and Work (CCRW) produced the
handbook *Focus on Ability* in 1991 in response to recurrent reports indicating
that employer attitudes towards hiring people with disabilities had not
changed. The cover page, pictured above, featured disabled employees
of major employers such as the Royal Bank of Canada, Bell Canada, and
McDonald's. CCRW Executive Director Rob McInnes wrote in the introduction to the handbook "Why would your company want to employ someone
with a disability? Why wouldn't it?"[42] © Canadian Council on Rehabilitation
and Work, 1991. Reproduced with permission.

receptiveness to implement external initiatives. The Employers' Forum on Disability, a non-profit organization funded by 400 employer members and 100 global corporations that employed disabled people, was founded in 1986 in the United Kingdom and expanded into Canada in the 1990s.[43] The Forum worked by connecting employers in the interest of sharing industry-specific best practices around the development of progressive employment policies.[44] The Job Accommodation Network, established in the United States by the President's Committee on the Employment of the Handicapped, expanded into Canada by 1988 through a federal development grant.[45] JAN's services included the provision of consultative services to employers seeking to accommodate disabled workers by sharing best practices from other members with similar workplace profiles and experiences. It also provided private sector employers with tailored practical solutions to concerns about the employment of disabled people.[46] Through public sector support, JAN and the Forum reflected a pattern whereby the public sector provided outreach to private employers to promote the economic integration of disabled people.

Despite these initiatives, there was little evidence that neither the Employers' Forum nor JAN was particularly successful, as reports on the economic integration of disabled people during the 1990s continued to indicate little change in employer attitudes and employment practices. The federal Standing Committee on Human Rights and the Status of Disabled Persons released its report, *A Consensus for Action*, which indicated some noteworthy achievements but noted "modest" overall improvement in employment prospects for disabled people and suggested that the "economic integration of disabled persons ... is reaching an impasse."[47] The federal Disabled Persons Unit (DPU) reached similar conclusions following its study involving eighty interviews with employers, workers, service agencies, and other stakeholders. The study highlighted cases where employers had taken innovative approaches to employing disabled people. One example included the creation of a labour consortium in Ontario involving employers, service agencies, disabled people, labour networks, and the education sector, coordinated by a community steering committee. However, the DPU concluded that employer reluctance to adopt innovative measures to make the workplace accessible continued unabated, citing participant employers who believed most disabled people were "poorly prepared to confront the realities of today's labour market, and possess few of the skills and qualifications required."[48]

With the introduction of new human rights legislation protections and increased political visibility of recruitment and employment policies, public sector employers were often at the forefront of initiatives to hire disabled people and other underrepresented groups. By the late 1970s, disability activists called upon various levels of government to model employment practices to the private sector.[49] COPOH reminded public policymakers and the wider business community, "The federal government has since 1978 been saying that if voluntary affirmative action/equal opportunities programs are not achieved in the private sector as regards to employing disabled people then compulsory affirmative action will be imposed on the private sector."[50] The 1979 City of Toronto Executive Committee, for example, accepted the conclusion that "as a public sector employer, the City of Toronto has an obligation both to its own employees and to society at large to set an example in its treatment of injured and disabled workers into the workforce as full participants; those gains must begin with public employers."[51] Many public sector employers believed they were responsible for validating and promoting equitable employment practices by modelling them to the wider private sector. Given that the private sector represented approximately three-quarters of the Canadian workforce, government policies that actively promoted or demonstrated equitable employment practices had a large audience in Canadian industry.[52]

The Handicapped Employment Program (HEP) in Ontario was one state organization in Canada that promoted the capacity of public sector employers as models for progressive employment practices. The HEP's founding mandate in 1978 under Progressive Conservative Premier Bill Davis was to promote the employment of disabled people in the private sector while actively facilitating connections between employers and disabled jobseekers. In collaboration with the Ontario March of Dimes, the HEP developed an affirmative action pilot program in Hamilton, Ontario, that involved cultivating a group of participant employers whose awareness of disability issues would ripple outward into the business community.[53] The HEP paired participant employers with disabled jobseekers and service agencies that worked closely with human resources workers to reform their company's labour relations policies and practices.[54] The project resulted in the increased employment of disabled workers in Hamilton and cultivation of a network of area employers, and it provided Canadian-specific employment best practices essential to the production of promotional kits to liaise with private sector employers.[55]

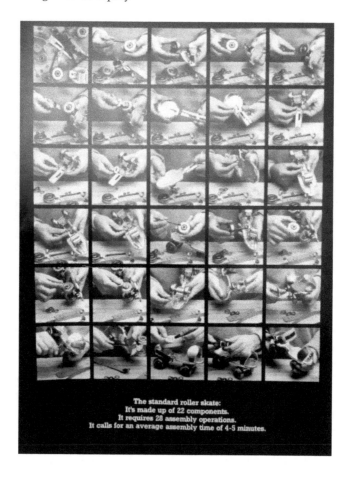

The standard roller skate:
It's made up of 22 components.
It requires 28 assembly operations.
It calls for an average assembly time of 4-5 minutes.

18   This first image demonstrates the skilled labour required in the assembly of roller skates, which involves performing twenty-eight operations within an average of four to five minutes.

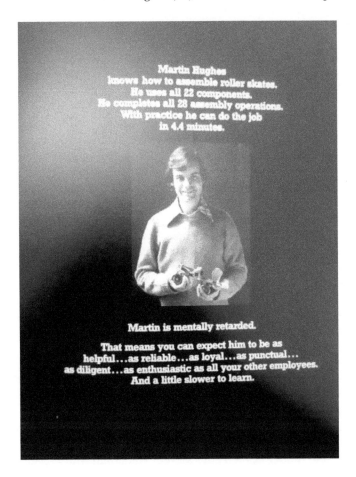

19 This second image reads, "Martin Hughes knows how to assemble roller skates. He uses all 22 components. He completes all 28 assembly operations. With practice he can do the job in 4.4 minutes. Martin is mentally retarded. That means you can expect him to be as helpful ... as reliable ... as loyal ... as punctual ... as diligent ... as enthusiastic as all your other employees. And a little slower to learn."[56] Both images © Marc Gold & Associates, c. 1979. Reproduced with permission.

At the urging of the HEP, the Personnel Association of Toronto (PAT) delivered a series of workshops to human resources workers and other representatives from Toronto-based headquarters of national companies and government departments, including AMX Canada, Shell Canada, Kellogg, IBM, Steinberg, Revenue Canada, Suncor, Sheraton Centre, Transport Canada, Canada Coast Guard, Du Pont Canada, Guardian Insurance, Labatt's, Kodak, Bell Canada, and British Petroleum.[57] In partnership with public sector employment bureaus and various disability organizations, workshops explored the impact of discriminatory attitudes in all aspects of the employment relationship and provided participants with practical tools for improving workforce participation rates and workplace culture regarding accessibility and inclusion.[58] Similar workshops were delivered throughout the 1980s and 1990s to thousands of employers across Canada in an effort to challenge employers in their resistance to hiring disabled people and others. Motivational speakers such as Richard Pimentel, whose awareness program called "Windmills" taught corporate and small business employers to understand the nature and impact of their attitudes towards disabled workers and jobseekers.[59] Pimentel argued, "I accept employers' comments about expenses and safety as valid concerns, but not as valid judgments. We hear the same tune every time we ask employers to hire someone. They didn't want to hire women because they don't know about business; they didn't want to hire blacks because they didn't know what would happen. It's the same song with different lyrics."[60]

The largest municipal corporation in the country and one of the largest public sector employers, Metropolitan Toronto public service was seen as a role model in the Federation of Canadian Municipalities and among private sector employers in the province. In 1980 a motion to introduce the Metro Bill of Rights proposed to "ban discrimination in hiring, assignment or promotion on the basis of race, creed, colour, nationality, ancestry, place of origin, age, sex, sexual orientation, marital or family relationship, physical disability or any other distinguishing characteristic." Aside from the obvious omission of intellectual disability and mental health issues in the Metro Bill of Rights, Metro Council opted for the weaker (though still unprecedented) declaration in support of equal opportunity employment to encourage the hiring of underrepresented groups in the municipal public service. The gay liberation paper *Body Politic* reported that the decision to reject the Metro Bill of Rights pitted the conservative boroughs against the liberal city centre;

a typical pattern that apparently reflected the bulk of decision-making in the Metro Council.[61] Although the Ontario Public Service had had a formal equal opportunity program and corporate policy on employment of disabled people in place since 1979, Metro Toronto was among the first municipal federations in Canada to formally incorporate the concept of equal opportunity into its general employment practices.[62]

Metro Toronto sought to confirm this position as a model employer in the region by adopting a progressive stance on employment practices. A pilot employment strategy in 1981 called the Disabled Program was quickly scaled up to a full Equal Employment Opportunity Division (EEO Division), which reported the recruitment of sixty-seven permanent and twenty-nine disabled employees between 1981 and 1984.[63] The division was primarily concerned with return-to-work initiatives for injured workers but also included proactive recruitment strategies and outreach recruitment of disabled university students for summer employment.[64] In response to reports by the mid-1980s regarding poor staffing levels of target groups and increased provincial oversight of employment practices, which resulted in the Municipal Employment Equity Program, Metro Council continually revised its goals and timetables to maintain its leadership position in progressive employment policy.[65] The second EEO Division report, subtitled *A Strategy for the 90s*, also reported that the current model of EEO resulted in "limited progress in achieving full equality in the workplace" and recommended the establishment of an employment equity task force to implement Municipal Employment Equity Program guidelines.[66] By 1990 the Employment Equity Implementation Task Force was in operation, involving city councillors, senior managers, union delegates, and provincial government officials in a joint effort to model employment practices for the wider private sector.

Metro Toronto also entered into a partnership with disability activists in the Centre for Independent Living Toronto (CILT) in a program called Access Connections, which was designed to "actively promote the greatly untapped human resources available within the disabled community." Employers were recruited to develop and demonstrate successful employment models with the goal of removing systemic barriers, developing support measures, enhancing existing training resources, and integrating employment equity measures at all levels of management. CILT reported, "By developing and sponsoring Access Connections, Metro Toronto is challenging employers across the municipality to equitably employ people with disabilities."[67]

By 1987 an employment equity program was introduced by the Ontario Progressive Conservative government in a policy statement that noted, "*With the exception of people with disabilities,* the representation of these groups in the OPS [Ontario Public Service] is already at or near their levels in the Ontario population [emphasis added]."[68] The provincial Office for Disabled Persons (ODP) argued that the best way to stimulate changes in employer attitudes and practices was by establishing public sector workplaces as models for other sectors and industries. However, given the voluntary nature of employment equity programs, it was held that sound evidence based on a tested equity program was the best way to influence a wider community of employers whose attitudes towards disability were consistently rated as hindering the employment of disabled people. Yet these attitudes did not reflect the predominant way of thinking among employers, who rated technological innovation as the means by which disabled people would achieve economic integration.

By the 1980s the progressive advancement of computer technology, assistive devices, prosthetics, and environmental controls began to radically transform the lives of many people with physical, sensory, and cognitive impairments, enabling them to live and work more independently in the community. There was widespread expectation in the late twentieth century in Canada that new technology would act as a great levelling force between able-bodied and disabled people. These predictions were applied particularly in regards to the workforce by providing unprecedented access to social and economic opportunities regardless of prejudicial employer attitudes. It was widely believed that "computers don't discriminate" and that the proliferation of computerized workstations would enable many disabled people to overcome inaccessible workplaces and challenge employer prejudices.[69] A substantial body of literature from the early 1980s predicted the development of a new technology-based economy, including many new tech-based job opportunities for people with disabilities.[70] Wilton explains that many people with disabilities, their allies, and others in the employment field believed "a post-industrial economy characterized by new technologies would facilitate the economic liberation of disabled people."[71] In 1980, for example, the Ontario Ministry of Labour told employers that computers were changing the entire labour market and that by the end of the 1980s, the "computer revolution will be here" and with a "substantial percentage of the population in the workforce will be using small desk-top computer terminals."[72]

During the late 1970s and early 1980s Canadian service agencies and government officials maintained that computers were "game changers," making it much easier for employers to hire disabled workers. Newsletters and journal articles spoke directly to Canadian employers, promoting the newest assistive devices and profiling people who used new computer technologies in the workplace. A 1979 column in the Canadian National Institute for the Blind newsletter *Employment Services News*, for example, reported that computers were enabling access to previously inaccessible jobs and even creating entire new job categories for blind Canadians. The article noted: "More and more companies in Canada are using computers for rapid information retrieval and storage. Now, thanks to modern technology, computer terminals can be used by blind as well as sighted employees." Synthesized speech boxes or "talking computers" installed at computer terminals enabled blind workers to type, edit, print, mail, and monitor incoming and outgoing data efficiently, challenging employers to reassess their beliefs about disabled people negatively impacting production rates.[73]

Despite this optimism, the application of new technologies in the workplace ultimately had an uneven and contradictory impact on the employability of disabled people in Canada. Incorporation of new technologies in the workplace did not necessarily overturn existing attitudes towards disabled workers, and there persisted a certain tension between accessible technology and employer prejudice.[74] Disability scholar Alan Roulstone warns, "The continuing presence of capitalist imperatives coupled with the global opportunities for corporate hedging presents major risks for disabled people and to traditional class-based social movements rooted in economic struggles."[75] While new computerized workstations may have benefited individual workers performing certain job tasks, technology did not address the "rationalisation of production at the societal level" such that employers in large enterprises, despite having greater resources, were in fact more resistant to individual needs because workplace technologies tend to emphasize standardization and efficiency.[76] Able-bodied workers continued to appear more attractive to employers because they did not elicit the same questions about the cost of accommodations and impact on productivity, despite the introduction of new workplace technologies or assistive devices.[77] For many employers, technology did not "level the playing field" because new assistive technologies signalled a lack of flexibility, which was in fact "a product of both recent changes to the structure and organization of paid work and enduring stereotypes about disability."[78]

20 & 21 A man and woman seated at an accessible workstation using state-of-the-art IBM equipment, including an audio typing unit consisting of an audio console, keypad, headset, and storage dial. The introduction of such assistive technologies, which interfaced with a rapidly evolving computerized workplace, offered the promise of new levels of access to job opportunities in the mainstream workforce for people with visual impairments.[79] © International Business Machines Corporation, 1981. Reproduced with permission.

Access to new assistive technologies was also often limited or prohibitively expensive. The Canadian Rehabilitation Council for the Disabled (CRCD) noted that many new aids introduced in the 1970s were not actually being used by the bulk of people with disabilities in Canada, owing to limited access and expense. As a result, the CRCD and the National Research Council of Canada established a non-profit provider of technical aids for disabled people in Canada called TASH (Technical Aids and Systems for the Handicapped).[80] TASH's mandate focused on marketing, distributing, and servicing assistive devices in the local Toronto market and nationally to facilitate the rehabilitation of disabled people and their goals in the workplace.[81] In Ontario, disability activists and their allies, complaining of an uncoordinated system for providing aids, lobbied the provincial government to develop an assistive devices program, which would improve access to assistive devices through targeted subsidies. The Ontario March of Dimes (OMOD) argued that the cost of assistive devices would continue to represent a "significant financial burden to the low-and-middle-income wage earners" and that "such a system would thus act as a disincentive to employment."[82]

The largest cohort of interview participants (eleven) entered the workforce during the 1980s, a decade in which disability rights, awareness of disability issues, and rapid technological change transformed expectations of disabled people seeking labour market integration. Most participants found work in the private sector, encouraged by the belief that an increasing number of companies were considered "equal opportunity employers" and many federally regulated businesses were subject to the (voluntary) provisions of employment equity legislation. Successive media campaigns that followed the IYDP were coordinated by service agencies and new provincial and federal departments focused on highlighting the needs of disabled people in employment matters. The prospect that technological innovation would erase most employment barriers for disabled people, particularly with the advent of computerized workstations, meant that many people who might have avoided the mainstream labour market sought greater independence in the community through paid work.

Interview participants found that the introduction of new technology did not necessarily "level the playing field" so much as it exposed the underlying reality of attitudinal barriers as the root obstacle to full participation. "Paul" noted, "Technology is supposed to be the game changer, but it hasn't worked out that way. I deal with it every day so I see the barriers and they're generally social. It's not that people can't do the jobs, it's convincing the employers that we can do the jobs."[83] "Alex" similarly found that the growth of new technologies did not necessarily result in greater access to employment. In his work as a youth focus group leader, Alex observed, "I see so many young people ... coming out of school who really do want to work badly and they can't get any jobs. That really distresses me because there's never been a time in our history where there was so much technology that's available."[84] "Mary" observed, "A lot of people with disabilities can't afford all the technology that you need to embrace and have access to. You have to learn it somehow or at least get access to it so you have a sense of it. Sometimes going to a job without knowing anything, sometimes that does work, sometimes it doesn't."[85]

A young woman in the early 1970s, "Emily" was determined to "get out in the workforce" as soon as possible, having been raised and educated in mainstream environments all her life. As a Braille reader and user of assistive technologies from a young age due to a congenital visual impairment, Emily became interested in the technical aspects of producing Braille and other accessible information prior to the proliferation of computer technology. She adopted a philosophy regarding employment accommodations to "ask for as little as I need and get the most out of it" as a personal challenge and to avoid presenting employers with too many demands.[86] Emily began working during her early twenties at various summer projects for employers in the education sector before moving into full-time employment with the CNIB where she held a series of positions that used her skills and training.

"Ashley" got her first job as a teenager during a period of technological innovation as computer technology revolutionized library science and other information technology. As a member of the Deaf community, Ashley found while attending post-secondary education that language and communication barriers caused her to choose and remain in an entry-level job below her level of competence and ambition.[87] Ashley learned that the lack of accommodation for sign language interpretation in her workplace and in other jobs limited her ability to advance within the labour market. When a physical injury forced her to leave her job, she encountered a labour market of underpaid contract work in the non-profit sector that encouraged her to return to work with the Deaf community, where her linguistic abilities and life experiences were valued.

Other interview participants reported inaccessible work terminal interfaces incompatible with mainstream technologies and being made redundant when employers decided to standardize workplace computer configurations. Paul concludes, "I can definitely cite many instances where people have actually been packaged out on jobs after several years of working for different companies because they can no longer do the job and bring value to the table so they were released because their software and technology couldn't access the internal systems in various corporations."[88] For example, "Lily" encountered greater access to employment through assistive technology that later evolved to be inaccessible, forcing her out of her job. She observes, "The IT systems are set up for the general working population and don't always take into account the special needs of people with access technology. They might make changes to a system and not give us advance warning, so my system is fine one day and not the next."[89] Lily concluded, "If there were the right attitudes then the computer technology problems would be resolved. If employers took the attitude that they should not and will not accept programs that will not work for everyone then they would push back to the manufacturers and vendors of said programs and say 'make it accessible.'"[90]

Employers figured prominently in disabled Canadians' pursuit of economic integration during the late twentieth century in Canada. Many Canadian employers adhered to the traditional moral economy of disability that associated disability with charity. In this respect disabled workers were relevant only in the realm of corporate social responsibility. Such attitudes shaped recruitment preferences and employment practices that rendered many people with disabilities unemployable in the mainstream labour market. The landmark report of the Canadian Chamber of Commerce demonstrated many of these employer prejudices, highlighting the undervaluation of disabled people's potential as productive members of the workforce. Subsequent initiatives brought public, private, and non-profit sector actors together to discuss ways to challenge negative employer attitudes. However, many studies of employer responses to disability from the 1970s to 1990s revealed that exclusionary attitudes and practices, particularly among a large pool of private sector employers, had not significantly changed unemployment rates in the disability community.

For their part, various levels of Canadian governments attempted to model equitable employment practices to the private sector by promoting a more inclusive perspective of disability. Various federal and provincial employment initiatives promoted a model of progressive employment practices that presumably rippled out into the wider labour market. Yet disability activists and others increasingly believed that voluntary measures including "employment equity" and the more laissez-faire solution – "equal opportunity employment" – were inadequate responses to the complex problem of chronic unemployment in the disability community. As with the failed hope that new technology would lead to a "level playing field" for disabled workers, employers often prioritized efficiency, productivity and standardization over the cultivation of an inclusive and accommodating workplace. Continued unemployment and poverty of disabled people in Canada, which persisted throughout the late twentieth century, led many critics to call into question the limitations of awareness campaigns and the value of sensitivity training for employers. The disability community's mounting frustration with "those who listen politely and do nothing" led them to pressure the state to adopt a more activist stance in protecting the economic rights of people with disabilities.

Chapter Seven

Rise and Decline of the Activist Canadian State

By saying that we live in an activist state, I mean to mark a special feature of our self-consciousness: an awareness that our society's existence depends upon a continuing flow of decisions made by politically accountable state officials.[1]

[The] commitment to an *activist state* which spent money to support organizations through which citizenship could be developed ... was part of its commitment to "participatory democracy" and achieving a "just society."[2]

State responses to rampant poverty and unemployment in the disability community changed because of a series of developments from the mid-1970s to mid-1990s in response to domestic and international developments in disability rights. Disability rights activists and their allies introduced the state to a new approach to disability issues based on their involvement as paid advocates, coalition-builders, public sector workers, and advisory committee members committed to the objective of greater participation in the labour market. A political discourse of disability rights was entrenched in the structure of the state, allowing various levels of government to assume – and strategically feign – its role in promoting a progressive vision of disability in the labour market. Formal vehicles of disability advocacy within government ensured a degree of continuous political visibility of disability issues in a constantly shifting political terrain. Special ministerial posts, bureaus, and advisory committees, however, disguised a lack of political action to improve the labour market integration of disabled people. Yet progressive deregulation of the economy effectively deactivated the activist state, undermining the capacity of the public sector to support the creation of an inclusive political economy.

This chapter charts the evolution and impact of disability rights on Canadian political institutions as pertains to the pursuit of disabled peoples' employment integration. The first section considers the influence of international developments in disability rights on the political ideology and response to the economic problem of disability in Canada. The second section discusses the function of special offices set up at all levels of government to act as a focal point in state-led advocacy and bureaucracy regarding labour market participation in the disability community. The third section considers the role of one such state organization, the Ontario Advisory Council for the Physically Handicapped, which served as the formal conduit between policymakers and the disability community in Ontario. The final section examines the decline of the activist state in Canada as the relationship between government and the disability community was transformed by the rise of a new political economy of disability.

During the 1970s international declarations by the United Nations stimulated the development of a political framework of disability rights in Canada. When the UN issued the Declaration on the Rights of Disabled Persons (DRDP) in December 1975, Canada lacked a comprehensive political outline in which to address the long-standing social and economic dislocation of disabled people. Despite growing consciousness of disability issues in Canada due to hiring campaigns and other awareness-building activities, there was no political framework that enabled Canadian policymakers to effectively address the exclusion of people with disabilities from the labour market. The DRDP addressed such gaps in policy, calling for "national and international action to ensure that [the declaration] will be used as a common basis and frame of reference for the protection of these rights."[3] The DRDP's thirteen-point resolutions regarding disability rights included the "right, according to their capabilities, to secure and retain employment or to engage in a useful, productive and remunerative occupation."[4] Canadian disability activists interpreted the section to mean "The right to work is not a privilege reserved for the non-handicapped," and they expected policymakers to use the UN framework to develop policies to promote the social and economic integration of disabled people.[5]

Canada played an important role in the development of the DRDP as the sponsor and member country that introduced the resolution to the UN General Assembly. Liberal Prime Minister Pierre Trudeau declared that the DRDP was an expression of federal policy in principle. The declaration presented Trudeau with a unique opportunity to publicly demonstrate his commitment to participatory democracy and the creation of a "just society," a famously vague but vigorously promoted platform during the 1968 and 1974 electoral campaigns.[6] In the book *Towards a Just Society*, Trudeau explained that his 1968 electoral campaign rested on a policy of universal equal opportunity.[7] In an attempt to clarify his intentions behind the creation of a "just society," Trudeau wrote, "How can we call a society just unless it is organized in such a way as to give each his due, regardless of his state of birth, his means or his health?"[8] He explained that a "just society" fundamentally represented a call for "anything that would make us more free and more equal."[9] Liberal support of a progressive program of disability rights thus flowed naturally from an existing political discourse at the national and international level. Fraser Valentine and Jill Vickers observe that changes in the conception of citizenship due to Trudeau's promotion of participatory democracy and "active citizenship" stimulated the development of disability organizations and encouraged disabled people and their allies to press the state to improve protection of their rights.[10]

To kick-start the policy formation process, the UN named 1981 the International Year of Disabled Persons (IYDP), devised to encourage all levels of government to formulate strategies and mechanisms to act upon the principles articulated in the DRDP. With the theme "full participation and equality" the IYDP promoted (among other actions) initiatives to "provide disabled persons with proper assistance, training, care and guidance, to make available to them opportunities for suitable work and to ensure their full integration in society."[11] Following the inclusion of people with physical disabilities in the 1977 Canadian Human Rights Act, which provided disabled people protection from discrimination in employment, Trudeau perceived the IYDP as Canada's opportunity to secure its reputation as an internationally recognized leader in the promotion of human rights.[12]

In Ontario the New Democratic Party (NDP) promoted affirmative action legislation as a means to secure progressive advances in labour market participation. Under the leadership of Michael Cassidy and Bob Rae, the NDP repeatedly proposed legislation in the 1970s and 1980s titled "An Act to Provide for the Employment of Disabled Persons." However, a lack of enthusiasm for affirmative action, particularly in the political climate dominated by decades of Progressive Conservative governments, repeatedly killed the bills before second or third readings. Despite this opposition, private members' bills were frequently introduced, beginning in 1978 by Toronto MPP Odoardo Di Santo and later by Hamilton-East MPP Robert Mackenzie (both labour leaders and members of the NDP's core membership in the labour movement).[13] The legislation required that at least 3 per cent of an employer's workforce include people with serious or prolonged disabilities with allowances for variable percentages, and individual employers or entire classes of employers could be exempted by the minister of labour if they were deemed eligible. A register of "employable disabled persons" constituted the labour pool from which employers could select qualified workers and employers who violated the act were liable to fines ranging from $1,000 to $10,000.[14] Although each bill died after being tabled, they represented a concerted attempt by the NDP to provide a legislated floor to support disabled people chronically trapped in unemployment or unwillingly dependent on welfare assistance. Mackenzie admitted that affirmative action was understandably "controversial but stems from my frustration with efforts to provide employment for the handicapped."[15] Ontario NDP leader Michael Cassidy similarly defended the creation of a legislated program of affirmative action in the province, noting "the principle, it seems to me, is an important one, and that is that major employers should be required to have an affirmative action program to ensure that people who are disabled do, in fact, have as a matter of reality, not just [in] principle, access to employment from which they are now barred."[16] Modelled after public and private sector affirmative action legislation in Britain and the United States featuring the imposition of hiring quotas, the introduction of NDP-sponsored affirmative action bills continued until 1987, when dwindling political interest in mandatory hiring quotas shifted support in favour of voluntary employment equity legislation.[17] As the NDP labour critic in the late 1980s, Mackenzie recalled, "Back in 1976, I think, which was the first year I asked questions about the percentage of disabled and handicapped people who were working, it was something like 15 per cent; 85 per cent were not working. The figures just last year were almost identical. Year after year ... we would find that the figures were not changing."[18]

Although affirmative action was not introduced in Ontario, the political terrain in Canada did shift over time, in large part owing to the work of the Parliamentary Special Committee on the Disabled and the Handicapped. The federal committee was struck in 1980 to guide the implementation of specific measures to improve the social and economic participation of disabled people. The committee's landmark report, titled *Obstacles*, made twenty recommendations related to employment (130 recommendations in total) and called on all levels of government to undertake specific actions to improve employment opportunities for disabled people.[19] The committee received hundreds of submissions from disabled people, their families, service providers, and others across the country who urged greater cooperation between federal and provincial governments, noting "jurisdictional boundaries were no excuse for avoiding necessary actions."[20] As part of a strategic framework for policymakers at all levels of government, for example, Recommendation 74 of the *Obstacles* report directed the Federation of Canadian Municipalities to lead municipalities towards improved functional accessibility of social and economic opportunities. The *Obstacles* report personalized its message by interspersing the recommendations with pictures and narratives of individuals with disabilities that made submissions to the committee, explicitly attaching a "human face" to a complex set of issues. Committee members concluded, "There are no insurmountable obstacles to prevent Canada from taking a world leadership role in providing disabled persons with the practical means for greater independence."[21]

The *Obstacles* report was accompanied by an atmosphere of enthusiasm, in large part owing to the "last minute" inclusion of disability in Section 15 of the Charter of Rights and Freedoms. Trudeau's announcement that new human rights protections would accompany the patriation of the Canadian constitution led disability activists to believe that the disability community would benefit from new human rights protections. When news indicating that disability was not included as a protected category in the draft charter was leaked, an intensive lobbying campaign erupted to force Trudeau's hand. Trudeau and Minister of Justice Jean Chrétien resisted the inclusion of disability in the charter, fearing it would create an enormous financial burden on federal, provincial, and municipal governments, which would bear the costs of retrofitting existing infrastructure in order to accommodate the needs of disabled people. In response to political resistance, members of the *Obstacles* committee, disability rights activists, and their allies initiated a nationwide letter-writing campaign and staged protests across the country to demand the inclusion of disability in the charter, and at the last minute Trudeau and Chrétien relented.[22] David Lepofsky asserted it was disability activists' reference to "Canada's international obligations" and its support of the IYDP that finally swayed Trudeau to live up to his original promise of participatory democracy.[23]

22 Protesters outside federal Employment and Immigration Minister Lloyd
Axworthy's office in Winnipeg in October 1981 carrying placards that read
"Disabled Demand Dignity." Such demonstrations occurred across the
country as disability rights activists demanded the inclusion of disability as
a protected category in the forthcoming Charter of Rights and Freedoms.[24]
© Ken Gigliotti/Winnipeg Free Press, 1981. Reproduced with permission.

Following the IYDP, the UN adopted a World Programme of Action in 1982 and a Decade of Disabled Persons (1983–92) in which activities related to the prevention, rehabilitation, and equalization of opportunities for disabled people could be implemented and measured.[25] In response to the *Obstacles* report and these new UN resolutions Trudeau created a cabinet position to coordinate the federal government's response. When Canada finally signed onto the Decade of Disabled Persons in 1985, federal and provincial governments created ministerial posts (called minister responsible for disabled persons) that coordinated initiatives to "accelerate progress toward the full participation and integration of disabled persons."[26] The selection of well-known reformers, including former Toronto mayor David Crombie at the federal level, reflected the cooperative reform tenor of the ministerial post, which required balancing collaborative relationships with several government departments to succeed in achieving progressive reform on disability issues.[27] Importantly, these special cabinet posts represented positions of advocacy within government that facilitated reform of public policies by ensuring the government was both "complete" and "effective" in its response to disability rights.[28]

A central feature of the Canadian state's response to disability activism during the 1970s and 1980s included the establishment of special offices at each level of government mandated to develop measures to improve job opportunities for people with disabilities. Special offices educated employers and the wider public about the needs and abilities of disabled people in the labour market and served as official liaisons between government, employers, and the broader public sphere. The offices, including the federal Disabled Persons Unit (DPU), the Ontario Handicapped Employment Program (HEP), and the Metropolitan and Toronto Office of Services for the Disabled and Elderly ("Toronto Office") included disability advocacy as part of their mandate and thus represented a vanguard in the promotion of disability rights in the government. New initiatives to promote awareness of disability issues were often devised within these offices and exerted pressure on other parts of government to modify or eliminate barriers to social and economic participation. Simultaneously acting as civil servants and paid disability advocates, workers in these offices combined the responsibilities of running a government office with an activist agenda marked by progressive widespread reform that targeted multiple sectors of the state.

In response to the energetic political discourse of disability following a "lengthy" period of development during the 1970s, the federal government created the Bureau on Rehabilitation ("the Bureau") to coordinate disability policies and programs across Canada.[29] The Bureau's mandate focused on harmonizing federal policies and practices around the prevention of disability and support of rehabilitation services given that responsibility for rehabilitation services was fragmented across several ministerial jurisdictions including employment, income, housing, transportation, and accessibility. The Bureau advised the federal government on policy and initiated special projects to facilitate the development of employment opportunities for disabled people. Federal resources were funnelled through the Bureau into collaborative partnerships with rehabilitation agencies such as long-standing media campaigns by the CRCD and CCRW's initiatives, which promoted improvements to the sheltered workshop system.[30] However, the Bureau did not initially foster a close relationship with the disability rights community, given its primary focus on developing relations in the rehabilitation industry. Toronto producer Alan Aylward, for example, received a rather chilly reception when he approached the Bureau in 1981 seeking funds for the documentary series *The Disability Myth*. As noted in chapters 2 and 5, the series adopted a particularly critical stance on the rehabilitation system in Canada and showcased the agenda of disability rights activism with its focus on seeking greater consumer control over rehabilitation services. Despite wide acclaim after being aired on the CTV Network, including an endorsement by the provincial HEP office, the Bureau felt that the premier episode, subtitled *Segregation*, was "somewhat lengthy and repetitive," arguing that Ontario had been "filmed to death" in light of the recent proliferation of films about disability issues.[31] The Bureau ultimately rejected Aylward's proposal on the grounds that its funds were already committed to the non-consumer-led CRCD for its advertising campaign.[32]

In response to significant restructuring in the early 1980s the Bureau, renamed the Disabled Persons Unit (DPU), was downscaled and increased its engagement with disability activists. During the mid-1980s the DPU provided crucial funding that stimulated the development of a national network of consumer-run Independent Living Resource Centres (ILRCs). The Centre for Independent Living Toronto (CILT), for example, received core funding from the DPU, which enabled the organization to provide crucial peer support to disabled people in Toronto. CILT's executive director, Sandra Carpenter, wrote to the DPU, noting

"You have no idea what a new sense of stability and purpose this money has given us. It will be so valuable in the years to come as a foundation from which to help our fellow consumers."[33]

At the municipal level, grass-roots organizing by an eclectic mix of citizens during the early 1970s led to the formation of a special office in Toronto. A dynamic group of professionals, volunteers, and family advocates led by Alderman Anne Johnston coalesced during the 1972 mayoral election that lobbied candidates to commit to improved accessibility and job opportunities for disabled Torontonians.[34] The successful election of reform Mayor David Crombie was seen by disability advocates as the commencement of a new era of positive change in the promotion of disability rights in the city. Crombie's inaugural address acknowledged the influence of the group in the formation of his political platform, arguing that what we "can no longer afford to ignore is the physically handicapped." He proclaimed, "This City is for all its citizens no matter how palsied their step or frail their grasp."[35] In his analysis of the 1972 Toronto election, dubbed a "populist victory," Jon Caulfield argued that Crombie was in fact forced to "court" reformists such as Alderman Johnston, since he lacked support among those in their camp and, despite his entreaties, Crombie was "never seriously regarded … as one of them."[36] As part of his pursuit of a political alliance with other reformists, in 1973 Crombie created the Task Force on the Disabled and Elderly, following strong recommendations by Johnston. The task force was mandated to investigate ways of improving disabled people's access in the city, and its report included a comprehensive series of recommendations encouraging city council to facilitate social and economic integration through improved accessibility, housing, education, transportation, employment and income, leisure and recreation, and city services. By the time the task force's first newsletter was released in 1977 to provide the public with an update regarding the ongoing work of task force members, the initial impact of the report on physical accessibility had already been made apparent in the installation of over 1,000 curb cuts at sidewalks across the city with plans for a further 124 ramps by end of year.[37]

After the report was adopted in principle as a policy statement of Toronto city council, the Toronto Office continued in its advisory role. Metropolitan Toronto (encompassing the City of Toronto and neighbouring boroughs) appointed Belinda Morin as coordinator for the Metro Toronto Working Committee on the Disabled and Elderly, which was responsible for collaborating with members of the Mayor's Task

Force to broaden the mandate of the city task force to serve the entire Toronto region.[38] A North Toronto resident and ally of the disability community, Morin abandoned a budding political career to work as a social justice advocate for the United Community Fund (forerunner of United Way Toronto), where she became known for her progressive views.[39] Morin represented the municipal equivalent of federal and provincial ministers responsible for disabled persons, acting as a paid advocate for disability issues in the region by monitoring employee recruitment and selection, providing input to municipal departments on the needs and concerns of disabled employees, coordinating the education of supervisors and personnel regarding the employment of disabled people as well as acting as an adviser to the Mayor's Task Force. Morin argued that the primary challenge of her position was "The bureaucratic expectation is to keep the lid on while you have a mandate to keep the lid off."[40]

By the late 1970s the work of the city task force and Metro coordinator had earned a national reputation for Toronto as a leader in promoting accessibility and inclusion. In 1981 the Toronto Office boasted that its work "has had an impact on not only the citizens of Toronto, but other municipalities as well. It helped spur other levels of government to review their policies and legislation affecting disabled people."[41] Indeed, the influence of the Toronto Office on other levels of government reflected the importance of intergovernmental relationships in the development of new policies at both municipal and provincial levels. As Jon Caulfield explained, "Toronto's Metropolitan federation is a provincial invention. Ontario municipalities are 'creatures of the province,' subject to its absolute control."[42] As a result, most major programs including new initiatives to deal with disability issues were fundamentally dependent on provincial funds, revealing the extent to which political priorities defined at the provincial level shaped the implementation of new initiatives devised at the municipal level. Progressive Conservative Premier Bill Davis's 1978 Speech from the Throne outlined the Ontario government's new plans to place greater emphasis on promoting job opportunities for disabled people throughout the province. Davis discussed various issues regarding the "full participation" of disabled people in Ontario (borrowed from the UN Declaration on the Rights of Disabled Persons), including the need for greater accessibility, access to assistive devices, welfare assistance, and vocational rehabilitation programs, all of which required cooperation with municipal authorities.[43]

Davis's Throne Speech provided the impetus for the establishment of an innovative new provincial office that would act as a catalyst for change in the Ontario government to address the economic displacement of people with disabilities across the province. The Handicapped Employment Program (HEP) was located within the Ministry of Labour, strengthening its mandate, which focused on facilitating employment integration for disabled people. The HEP was devised as a crucial link between multiple key stakeholders in the provincial labour market, including employers, unions, disabled persons, special interest groups, voluntary programs, social agencies, related government programs, educators, and health professionals. It promoted cross-sectoral awareness of disability issues among these stakeholders, providing education materials and consultation on specific matters while facilitating the development of new initiatives in government. Eager to establish itself as a catalyst for change, the HEP undertook a whirlwind of activity in its first year of operation, including fielding more than 2,000 inquiries from disabled people; development of an information centre for employers; publication and distribution of several reports, fact sheets, and pamphlets; initiation of contact with major employers, service agencies, and labour organizations; television appearances; and strategizing models for job matching.[44]

Despite their responsibility to pursue an impressive yet intimidating objective, these federal, provincial and municipal special offices were restricted by relatively small budgets. However, even with limited resources and staff, special offices steadily fleshed out the political framework around disability rights with the promotion of initiatives to improve job opportunities for people with disabilities. The HEP maximized the effectiveness of its small staff complement of approximately three people by reaching out to the disability community, cultivating connections with consumer-run organizations and disability rights leaders. For example, the Ontario Ministry of Labour hired blind activist John Rae to work as a consultant to implement many of the program's objectives and to act as the program's public face at various conferences, training seminars, and client consultations.[45] In his role as the HEP consultant, Rae combined his experience as a disability rights lobbyist with his new role as a civil servant, channelling his skills and connections with the disability community into the HEP's mandate advocating for change within government and the provincial labour market.[46]

Special bureaus naturally came into contact with one another, given their similar overlapping objectives. Yet these exchanges also exposed

23 From left, John Southern, Susan Forster, and Don Peuramaki at the CIUT-FM studio on the University of Toronto campus, where their weekly show, *The Radio Connection*, was first broadcast in January 1988 as part of the Access Connections project. The show shared employment-related news and other current affairs affecting people with disabilities in Ontario and the Toronto region and included a phone-in segment during which disabled people could voice their opinions on various topics.[47] © John Wood/Globe and Mail, 1988. Reproduced with permission.

underlying tensions that resulted from differing bureau priorities and clashes between individual advocates. Within the scope of federal-municipal relations, a collaborative venture during the late 1980s brought the Toronto Office for the Disabled and Elderly into a closer working relationship with the DPU as part of a joint employment initiative. As the federal Progressive Conservative government geared up for Prime Minister Brian Mulroney's second-term electoral campaign, funding was made available for the development of an initiative to promote the employment of disabled people. The result was an innovative project called Access Connections, conducted in partnership with CILT and the Toronto Office.[48] The project used a double-barrelled approach to increasing employment opportunities and awareness of disability issues by developing a radio program called *The Radio Connection* and a television show called *The Disability Network*, both of which employed disabled people while raising awareness of various issues affecting the disability community.

Designed to "actively promote the greatly untapped human resources available within the disabled community," the project was staffed by people with disabilities behind the scenes as well as showcasing the talent of disabled people on air. Initially broadcast out of local stations in Toronto, Windsor, Ottawa, and London during its thirty-month pilot, *The Disability Network* received such wide acclaim that the CBC expanded carriage to a national audience, made possible by renewed funding through special government offices.[49] The success of *The Disability Network*, which ran for another fifteen years, and *The Radio Connection* demonstrated the extent to which productive partnerships between government-based advocacy offices played an important role in developing employment opportunities for disabled people and awareness of disability issues in the public sphere.

Intergovernmental relationships between disability bureaus were tested during the IYDP when a new provincial awareness campaign, initiated by the HEP, revealed conflicting personalities and politics. The HEP devised a media campaign with the slogan "Employ-Ability" as part of its mandate to raise awareness of disabled people in the labour market and in celebration of the IYDP. The HEP commissioned a set of four posters by renowned paper sculpture artist Jonathan Milne, designed to be incorporated into various events and activities across the province that promoted awareness of disabled people's needs in the workplace, encouraging the retention of disabled workers, and modelling equitable hiring practices.[50] As an ally of the disability rights movement, Milne offered to cut his usual rate in half in support of disability rights and the "promotion of the needs and abilities of disabled people."[51] The final set of posters featured the depiction of a male worker on crutches, a blind female secretary, and a dark-skinned female "executive" wheelchair user.[52] The posters were subsequently distributed to the HEP's client list, which included more than 4,000 employers across the province, whose reception was reportedly extremely positive.[53]

Shortly after the set of posters was released, controversy erupted in Toronto regarding one poster that allegedly dealt insensitively with representations of disability and race. The questionable poster featured a dark-skinned female wheelchair user dressed in a suit sitting in front of Toronto City Hall, which Milne stated was intended to depict a female "executive." Although Milne explicitly sought to situate all his subjects squarely within the context of disability awareness rather than race relations, the poster sparked strong negative reaction from activist groups representing visible minorities who alleged the imagery reflected an insensitive portrait of race, given the "degree of blackness of the subject."[54] The simmering debate erupted into a full-blown controversy, ignited primarily by Belinda Morin, then-Metro Toronto coordinator for the disabled and elderly, who publicly voiced her displeasure with the poster to the media. Morin, who was interviewed by the *Toronto Star* in an editorial titled "She's Black, She's in a Wheelchair and She's Causing a Ruckus at City Hall," advised that she had written to the HEP office complaining that the posters were "in extremely poor taste."[55] A copy of Morin's letter stated, "The message conveyed, particularly by the Employ-Ability poster [depicting the female wheelchair user], cannot be taken seriously. It looks more like something from the National Lampoon and does not elicit thoughts of competency in a job."[56] Milne later recalled that in the ensuing furore he received angry phone calls from black-rights activists in Toronto who told him that he "didn't understand how black people looked."[57] Progressive initiatives that promoted the employment of disabled people were thus reconfigured once they entered the public sphere and were repositioned within a broader discourse involving other disadvantaged groups.

As the controversy unfolded, the Ontario Human Rights Commission, led by pioneering senior bureaucrat and politician Dorothea Crittenden, also refused to endorse the HEP's awareness campaign.[58] Crittenden faced a precipitous rise in complaints dealing with discrimination against visible minorities during her tenure, and the commission was already under intense public scrutiny at the time regarding its perceived lack of efficacy in handling cases and promoting new human rights legislation.[59] Minister of Labour Robert Elgie instructed the HEP to remove the offending poster from its campaign in order to refocus public attention on the substantive issues of the awareness campaign.[60] The posters, however, were already touring Toronto area plazas as part of Disability Awareness Month in the city when Scarborough Action leader Beryl Potter learned of the debate. Instructed to remove the poster, Potter instead wrote "CENSORED" across the disputed poster and "Not so proud are you, Dr Elgie?" across an accompanying message from the minister of labour in reference to what she perceived as political damage control that undermined the strength of the awareness campaign.[61] The "Potter incident" and the wider controversy that now surrounded the campaign prompted the HEP officials to prepare apologetic media statements. The incident, fuelled by their colleagues in the Toronto Office, demonstrated that questions of race and disability had not been thoroughly examined and that disability bureaus did not necessarily share a uniform outlook on the representation of disability issues; nor were the actions of each office immune to reproach.

As reactions to the economic "problem" of disability changed in response to an evolving political economy, it became increasingly important to maintain formal relations with the disability community through state apparatuses. One such apparatus included the consumer-led Ontario Advisory Council for the Physically Handicapped (OACPH), established in 1975 by second-term Progressive Conservative Premier Bill Davis to fulfil his electoral promise to improve government relations with the disability community.[62] An influential yet controversial body, the OACPH's role in the reform of disability policy reflected the degree to which government bodies existed problematically in the contested sphere of disability politics. The OACPH was a formal advisory body that streamlined relations with disability activists and their allies, holding regular public hearings across the province on various issues that served the consultative goals of policymakers and gave disabled Ontarians an official voice in the policy development process. As the *Toronto Star* reported, the OACPH "serves as an umbrella organization for all handicapped groups and is *the* channel through which the disabled of Ontario and the government communicate with each other" (emphasis added).[63] A consumer-led council composed of disability rights leaders across the province and their allies, the arms-length structure of the council made it responsible to the disabled population of Ontario, which it purportedly represented.

The OACPH established a special subcommittee on employment, which formulated recommendations to improve the economic integration of disabled people across the province.[64] With a mandate to improve government policies and practices around labour market integration, the subcommittee learned of many "organizations involved in looking at the employment needs of the physically handicapped" but found little definitive data on actual employment rates.[65] In response,

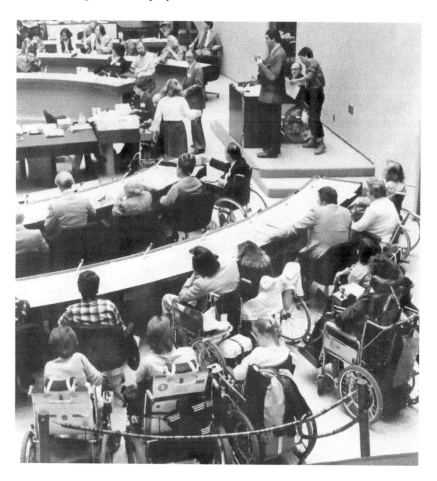

24 Participants in wheelchairs at the public forum organized by the OACPH at Toronto City Hall during Disability Awareness Week. The packed auditorium demonstrated the extent to which Torontonians with disabilities actively participated in the promotion of disability issues and advancement of their rights in the city.[66] © Sidney Katz/Getstock.com, 1979. Reproduced with permission.

OACPH Chair Jack Longman organized a public forum at Toronto City Hall as part of Disability Awareness Week to fill this information gap and allow "people get to know us [OACPH] and what our problems are."[67] The well-attended forum, which attracted national media attention enabled disability activists, local and provincial officials, individual constituents, and others across the region to collaborate in the formulation of new recommendations to improve the employment of disabled people in the province.[68]

However, this spirit of optimism was quickly tempered when OACPH members came to "reluctantly appreciate the necessity for the slow pace of change" in the public policy process.[69] The council resolved that public policies should focus on encouraging employers to hire disabled people, ensuring job opportunities existed, and enabling disabled people to acquire more competitive skills.[70] Following five years of consultations with disabled Ontarians by 1980, the council determined that the existing work disability policy system favoured the protection of workers who had become disabled in the workplace, while marginalizing disabled people outside the labour market. The OACPH concluded that once employed, disabled people "seem to be able to continue satisfactorily provided that the necessary adaptations to their work facilities are made."[71] As a result, the council sought to develop a closer working relationship with special disability offices, such as the HEP, by assisting in the development of employer resource kits and recommending policies that revolved around the improvement of training and job placement services for disabled people.

A major test of the OACPH spontaneously emerged when a bill was introduced to create separate human rights legislation for people with disabilities. Progressive Conservative Minister of Labour Dr Robert Elgie introduced Bill 188 in 1979 to create the Handicapped Persons' Rights Act.[72] The bill responded to recommendations of the 1977 Ontario Human Rights Commission report *Life Together*, which cited the province's "proud record" as a national leader in human rights but lamented the extent to which Ontario had recently lagged behind other provinces in new human rights legislation.[73] David Lepofsky explains that the bill was actually devised as a "parliamentary sleight of hand" to avoid opening discussion about amending the Ontario Human Rights Code to include the protection of sexual orientation.[74] Simultaneous to the rise of the disability rights movement, lobbyists had met stiff resistance from policymakers since the early 1970s in their struggle for new rights for gays and lesbians. To avoid these concessions to the gay and lesbian community, the Davis government proposed Bill 188 as a means to provide the disability community with new rights protections without opening the more contentious debate around gay rights, effectively sidestepping the issue of amendments to the Ontario Human Rights Code.[75] Critics argued that the bill legitimated a "separate-but-equal" approach to disability rights issues that lacked primacy over other legislation that would follow from inclusion in the Code.[76] An unprecedented coalition of disabled people and disability organizations called the Coalition for Human Rights for the Handicapped emerged to defeat Bill 188, marking an important milestone in the evolution of disability rights activism in Canada and demonstrating the disability community's opposition to separate human rights legislation.[77]

In stark contrast to the overwhelming consensus in the disability community against separate disability rights legislation, the OACPH decided to back Bill 188, endorsing the legislation as a welcome advancement of disability rights in the province. Disability activists responded angrily to the OACPH endorsement, arguing that council members were either unaware of sentiment in the disability community or had been politically co-opted by the Progressive Conservative government. Premier Bill Davis distanced himself from the controversy by declaring that his government had secured OACPH approval prior to introducing the bill, a revelation that further undermined the council's legitimacy as a representative voice of the disability community.[78] Faced with overwhelming opposition by the coalition and unable to rely on the OACPH for guidance, the government withdrew Bill 188 and Premier Davis entered into direct consultations with the coalition to amend the Ontario Human Rights Code. The move, which circumvented the OACPH, nevertheless represented a major victory for direct action in defence of disability rights legislation and demonstrated the continued relevance of an "activist state" in Canada.[79]

As the Canadian political economy shifted towards austerity in the 1980s and 1990s, this "activist state" began to erode. Disability-related ministerial posts were restructured, while specialized bureaus and advisory councils were dramatically scaled back or eliminated. Severe budgetary cutbacks drastically altered many parts of state dealing with disability issues, effectively dissolving structured relations between the state and disability community through specialized bureaus and advisory councils. A pattern of steadily retreating resources for disability programs was also partly concealed by pervasive state restructuring that transformed the government's approach to disability issues. In a massive round of restructuring in 1993 at the federal level the DPU was effectively abolished when its responsibilities were subsumed within a new "super-department" called Human Resources Development Canada (HRDC). Progressive Conservative Prime Minister Kim Campbell wrote to the Council of Canadians with Disabilities (CCD; formerly COPOH) about the drastic cutbacks and mergers, explaining that "the major restructuring of government that I announced on June 25 [1993] reduced the number of departments from 32 to 23 and ... are designed to ensure disability issues are considered within the wider context of human resource development, and in particular are linked strategically to programs such as income security and employment services."[80]

With the elimination of the DPU and the portfolio of minister responsible for disabled persons due to the streamlining of federal responsibility over a complex array of labour issues, the disability community's relationship with the state was diluted, undermining the capacity of the HRDC minister to undertake targeted measures to address poverty and unemployment in the disability community. The inclusion of disability alongside a broader spectrum of human resources issues meant specialized initiatives and close consultation with the disability community, which had taken place since the late 1970s and cultivated productive working relationships, was increasingly unlikely. While the CCD was initially supportive of the inclusion of the disability portfolio within the new HRDC, given promises to "include both welfare and employment focuses," it was quickly apparent that disability issues had "become lost" in the massive department.[81] The CCD expressed its dissatisfaction to Liberal Prime Minister Jean Chrétien in 1996 and 1997, complaining of "dramatic off-loading of responsibility to other levels of government and the reduction of federal standards and principles" and protesting that "the CCD should be celebrating its 20 years of achievement, but instead we are witnessing the systematic dismantling of the successes of the past twenty years."[82]

The Ontario NDP government introduced employment equity legislation in 1993, encouraging employers to voluntarily eliminate practices, policies, and job requirements that constituted barriers to disadvantaged groups.[83] The legislation was introduced as part of a "social contract," which included program cuts, tax increases, and administrative restructuring to deal with an escalating budgetary deficit – a move that served to alienate the NDP from their traditional base of support.[84] Employment equity also supported the efforts of existing specialized agencies, including the Training Coordinating Group for People with

Disabilities (TCG). Established in 1991 by consumers, service providers, business, labour, and training agencies in the Dundas West neighbourhood of Toronto with funding from Employment and Immigration Canada, TCG's goal was to promote access to skills training and employment opportunities for disabled Ontarians, an objective made easier with employment equity legislation.[85] The legislation required employers to institute comprehensive plans to revise recruitment, job qualifications, hiring, training, transfer and promotion, hours of work, compensation, workplace design and access, organization of work, technology, seniority, childcare, and leave of absence. NDP Premier Bob Rae created the Employment Equity Commission (EEC), which was responsible for administering the provincial Employment Equity Act (EEA) and enforcing fines against non-compliant employers who failed to adhere to mandatory reporting stipulations.

However, withdrawal from state activism as it pertained to the championing of disability employment issues was particularly visible in Ontario when the newly elected Progressive Conservative government under Premier Mike Harris replaced the NDP and initiated an infamous campaign of budgetary cutbacks and departmental closures that rocked the province. Dubbed a "Common Sense Revolution" by the Tories, the extensive cutbacks rolled back existing disability programming and employment initiatives introduced by previous governments.[86] Some disability activists and commentators hoped that Harris, whose son lived with cerebral palsy, would demonstrate a particular sensitivity to disability issues.[87] But Harris, being a vocal opponent of employment equity legislation, believed the existing approach to the chronic unemployment of disabled people replaced "merit and fairness in the workplace" with "arbitrary government intervention."[88] In his previous role as leader of the Opposition, Harris articulated a neoconservative perspective, claiming that employment equity legislation represented "reverse discrimination" by protecting minority groups against "good business practices" that prevailed in an open free market economy.[89] The Progressive Conservatives ran on an electoral platform that framed employment equity as an unfair and punitive obstruction to employers that threatened to create an onerous financial burden on small businesses and scare off potential investment revenue in the province.

As a result, in his first act as premier of a majority government in 1995 Harris repealed the EEA and abolished the EEC, claiming to have liberated the province with free-market economic ideologies in opposition to the imposition of supposed hiring quotas in Ontario. Harris believed that employment equity stalled economic development and that it was his party's responsibility to actively shrink the size of government and choreograph the reduction of the state's "interference" with the economy. Harris's plans in fact cut much deeper into existing programming that affected people with disabilities. The government introduced an "Equal Opportunity Plan" (EOP) in order to "restore the merit principle to Ontario's workplaces" and as part of an attempt to move away from the NDP's controlled reduction in spending, which did not involve a dramatic restructuring of government.[90] Despite earlier warnings within the PC party in the early 1980s from Minister of Labour Robert Elgie that "equal treatment won't necessarily guarantee equal opportunity," Tory policy under Harris shifted markedly towards unfettered deregulation of the economy, offering "equal treatment" to disabled people and other disadvantaged minorities.[91]

Part of Harris's electoral success came from the province's substantial disability community who, he promised, would enjoy new measures to improve their social and economic integration. In particular, Harris pledged to introduce an Ontarians with Disabilities Act (ODA) that would establish specific timelines for the imposition of accessibility standards in public spaces and workplaces.[92] Harris's EOP also involved "redirecting resources to training programs" to support greater self-reliance in disabled people's engagement with the labour market.[93] However, a proviso that accompanied all his electoral promises limited the introduction of new disability programming within the confines of "the economic goalposts of the Common Sense Revolution."[94] As disability activist David Lepofsky observes, the EOP represented the rebranding of existing disability-related initiatives and employment programs while dramatically scaling back other programming affecting disabled people.[95] The acclaimed Innovations Fund, for example, which supported "pilot initiatives to demonstrate new and non-traditional approaches to employment" and funded many organizations providing employment to disabled people was deemed outside the "economic goalposts" of the Common Sense Revolution. It was eliminated during an initial round of cuts to social programming.[96]

The new approach to disability issues represented a major setback to the existing mode of engagement with the disability community. Both the Ontario Advisory Council for Disability Issues (OACDI; formerly OACPH) and the Centre for Disability and Work (CDW; formerly HEP) were abolished, leaving an unrecognizable residual framework for the advancement of disability issues in the province.[97] Similar to the

25 Spectators at the Ontario Legislature in May 1996 watching MPPs debate
the future of the Ontarians with Disabilities Act – a key electoral promise
made by PC leader Mike Harris in 1995 shortly before being elected premier.
Wheelchair users were forced to watch the debate on a television screen outside the visitor's gallery, which had room for only four wheelchairs. Although
the non-binding resolution to move forward with the legislation passed 56–0,
disability rights activists and their allies waited until the year 2001, when
Harris finally relented and enacted the ODA after many amendments.[98]
© Andrew Stawick/Getstock.com, 1996. Reproduced with permission.

absence left at the federal level by the elimination of the DPU, the disbanding of the OACDI erased twenty years of consultation-based disability policymaking in the province. The CDW was an unlikely target
for austerity measures, since its mandate historically revolved around
increasing employment rates for disabled people – and hence moving
clients off welfare rolls. Yet the office's disappearance severely undermined the method in which the promotion of labour market integration

had previously occurred within the provincial government. Prior to its elimination the CDW regularly delivered training seminars to private sector employers and maintained a strong relationship with business community, streamlining its activities to focus on core programming in employer training, student education initiatives, and employment accommodations.[99] In the end, the centre was another victim of the Common Sense Revolution. When the announcement arrived that the centre was to close, CDW staff worried that "whether intentionally or not, the move to dismember the unit represented yet another step over the past years in this government's dismemberment of its infrastructure to deal with disability policy issues." The loss of CDW following on heels of the loss of the OACDI meant a dwindling policy infrastructure "diminished beyond recognition" to deal with disability issues.[100]

Federal and provincial restructuring ultimately manifested as social costs at the local level. In a paper titled "The Disabled and the Common Sense Revolution," the Daily Bread Food Bank in Toronto, which previously had reported that disabled people constituted at least one-quarter of its client base, pointed to the abrupt cutbacks as responsible for a sudden demand in their services by disabled people.[101] The organization profiled a sample of approximately twenty clients with disabilities whose reliance on the food bank became necessary only following the introduction of stricter eligibility rules and a 22 per cent cutback in social assistance rates. In an interview with *The Disability Network* following several media interviews about the reorganization of the provincial government, David Crombie, former Toronto mayor and ex-minister responsible for disabled persons, noted how the cuts had saddled cash-strapped municipalities with provincial responsibilities.[102] As chair of the Ministry of Citizenship, Culture, and Recreation committee designed to provide guidance to transitioning provincial-municipal relations due to the provincial cuts, Crombie argued that responsibilities for disability issues were more properly kept at the provincial level in a context of austerity, where the impact on disabled people could be made more consistent.[103]

International developments, such as the United Nations Declaration on the Rights of Disabled Persons, International Year of Disabled Persons in 1981, and Decade of Disabled Persons (1983–92), sparked a flurry of activity in Canada. Various levels of government installed a politically active framework to facilitate the social and economic integration of people with disabilities. Consultative relationships with the disability community were forged by special government offices and advisory committees set up during this period at the municipal, provincial, and federal levels to coordinate activities and initiatives encouraging "full participation" in the labour market. As interest and awareness of disability waxed and waned from the 1970s on, the offices and committees remained to facilitate an active state agenda on disability issues. But as the Canadian political economy was restructured by neoliberal laissez-faire philosophies and a period of austerity during the 1990s, the state's capacity for addressing labour market integration in any meaningful way declined as the economic inclusion of disabled people became increasingly precarious. By the mid-1990s a "common sense" revolution rolled out across Canada, effectively terminating the existing relationship between the state and disability activism by closing special offices and disbanding committees. The attendant loss of the disability community's voice in government jeopardized the future of disability activism and marked a shift towards a new politics of disability.

Labour Organizations, Disability Rights, and the Limitations of Social Unionism in Canada

A national trade union has its own self-interest in trying to overcome the employment discrimination encountered by disabled persons. Many of our members now have a disability of one type or another; all of them face the possibility of becoming disabled. It is our responsibility to fight for the social and economic well-being of all our members.[1]

Disability rights are a mainstream issue for our union in much the same way as contracting out or workplace safety and health issues ... Our working group is active with other labour groups ... and with groups outside of our union because our group is advancing the rights of disabled workers and indeed all members of society.[2]

The above statements by Canadian unionists, separated by more than twenty-five years of ad hoc coalitions with the disability rights movement, reflect an evolving politics of disability in the labour movement during the late twentieth century. Key players in the labour market, Canadian labour leaders tentatively reached out to disability rights activists during the mid-1970s as disability rights organizations, service organizations, employers, and the state initiated a new collaborative relationship. Unions were cautious about how disability rights would disrupt traditional "union business" such as collective bargaining and job accommodations. Core union practices such as collective bargaining and advocacy on behalf of injured workers reinforced the traditional medical pathology of disability and drained attention from other disability rights issues. The medical complex within which employers and insurance providers operated to provide accommodations and benefits to injured workers meant labour leaders were compelled to take a cautious approach to disability issues in order to avoid upsetting these arrangements. Canadian unions increasingly prioritized the interests of their members over broader class-based and social justice objectives, including disability rights. This approach was repeatedly revealed by unions' vigorous defence of seniority provisions in collective bargaining despite claims demonstrating these provisions marginalized other disabled workers. Despite conflicting ideological approaches, including the role of medical authority over disabled bodies, union leaders in Canada extended conditional support to the Canadian disability rights movement. A gradual shift towards social unionism facilitated by the growth in feminist organizing during this period created new opportunities for the labour movement to engage the disability rights movement without abandoning its convictions. In an attempt to synthesize traditional union priorities with the rejuvenating potential of social unionism, Canadian labour leaders harnessed disparate bases of activism that challenged long-standing approaches to disability issues.

This chapter examines the Canadian labour movement's responses to disability activism and the ideological dilemmas the engagement presented. Despite hesitant and non-committal partnerships, unions and labour leaders took a progressive public stance by celebrating disability rights, but they repeatedly fell short of concerted action. A thematic non-chronological analysis surveys the labour movement's involvement with disability rights activism during this period. The chapter examines the influence of public sector unions in the development of a progressive discourse on disability rights as well as emergent conflicts between disability rights, collective bargaining, the role of injured-worker activism, and strategic partnerships between disability and labour activists.

The Canadian labour movement underwent a remarkable transformation in the late twentieth century. Public sector unions secured progressive wage increases for members who staffed expanding government bureaucracies during the 1960s, which soon outnumbered the traditional "blue-collar" base of union membership.[3] Clerical workers, professionals and para-professionals, hospital workers, social workers, teachers, and others in the growing public sector flocked to unions as relations with management became increasingly fractured and hostile. Federal and provincial legislation passed in the mid-1960s and the1970s stimulated the unionization of the public sector by granting the right to certification, to collective bargaining, and to strike.[4] Union growth in the public sector coincided with the declining strength of

private sector unions as employment rates fell in core unionized in-
dustries such as manufacturing and in response to vigorous anti-union
offensive in the private sector.[5] By 1975 the Canadian Union of Public
Employees (CUPE) was the largest union in Canada, followed by the
Public Service Alliance of Canada (PSAC) and the National Union of
Public and General Employees (NUPGE).[6]

Public sector unions breathed new life into the Canadian labour movement by breaking down the long-standing domination by American
unions and imparting a reinvigorated sense of militancy gained by a
new position of strength and national leadership. By the 1970s and
1980s women represented roughly half the membership of public sector unions and steadily filled key leadership positions. Shifting gender
and racial dynamics in unions dramatically altered labour organizations. CUPE, for example, elected the first female national union president in 1975, established a National Women's Task Force in 1981, held
a National Women's Conference in 1984, and created the 'Rainbow
Committee' in 1988 to coordinate efforts to promote employment equity.[7] Canadian labour historian Craig Heron observes, "Women played
a crucial role in sensitizing their union leaders to the fact that not all
members were white, English-speaking, heterosexual men."[8] The democratic structure of unions meant that women used their numerical
strength to initiate an energetic and decisive dialogue on equality. This
new generation of labour activists nurtured the idea that the labour
movement should prioritize a reconnection with its working-class roots
in social justice issues at a time when unions were grappling with the
emerging threat of globalization and neoliberal politics.

The growth of unionized public sector work presented new economic opportunities for the disability community in terms of available
work, type of workplace, and nature of employer. Many persons with
disabilities had been rendered members of a surplus population whose
difficulty selling their labour for wages at once made them liminal figures in the competitive labour market and dependent on the productive
able-bodied population.[9] The expansion of government bureaucracies,
schools, hospitals, social services and affiliated work created an extraordinary demand for workers in a variety of workplaces. On one hand,
most of this work was presumably out of reach for disabled persons because public sector workplaces were just as likely as other sectors to be
physically inaccessible and unaccommodating to people with cognitive
or developmental disabilities. However, public sector employers were
often leaders in developing employment equity and accommodation

policies because they were held to a higher standard than the private sector in terms of the political nature of public sector employment. Metropolitan Toronto, for example, was one of the first "equal employment opportunity employers" in Canada to declare its support in 1980 for the principles of employment equity in advance of the International Year of Disabled Persons.[10] "White-collar," female-dominated public sector unions and federations also responded more favourably to the development of progressive disability policy than "blue-collar," male-dominated unions.[11] The public sector, then, provided a climate that was particularly amenable to the growth of progressive responses to disability activism.

By the early 1980s the discourse of equality initiated by women evolved towards the broader notion of "equity," with its more comprehensive focus on securing opportunities for women, visible minorities, Aboriginals, and persons with disabilities. Although employment equity promised to reduce workforce barriers for all target groups, labour leaders pursued what they saw as a pragmatic approach to social justice issues that legitimated an emphasis on improving the lot of unionized women. The discourse of equity that developed in the Canadian labour movement strategically prioritized women's equality over other target groups because Canadian unionists felt compelled to focus on the most attainable and least divisive goals in a period of concerted attacks on unionized jobs. A CUPE education manual from 1976 explained to readers, "To attack all problems at once may result in none being solved. Furthermore the large number of women in CUPE suffering from discrimination assures us that concentrating our energies on them – at least for the time being – will bear the most fruit."[12]

Although women's issues took the lead in the employment equity debate, people with disabilities did contribute to a progressive discourse on equity in the labour movement. As its national voice, the Canadian Labour Congress (CLC) introduced new policies in the early 1980s that provided the labour movement with a framework for addressing social justice in the disability community.[13] The CLC prioritized income security for disabled union members, creation of fair and appropriate jobs, new guidelines to enable members and affiliates to work with the disability community and their organizations, and the pursuit of other activities that stimulated job opportunities for people with disabilities in the labour market. Disability labour activist Patty Holmes observed in 1981 that the CLC attempted to codify the labour movement's long-standing support of disabled people within and beyond union rank and file.[14] Holmes warned, however, that while unions exert their influence through collective bargaining, the implementation of progressive disability policy required the full participation and cooperation of the entire labour movement.

The political discourse of disability rights thus directly influenced the heavily unionized public sector, where it combined with existing pressure from women and visible minorities in both public and private sector unions to prioritize employment equity. Social activists and equity-seeking groups pushed against the traditional organizational culture of unions in order to create space for disadvantaged groups. Unions, however, perceived social movement activism as peripheral to the primary work of collective bargaining, a perspective that stunted the adoption of stable connections with disability rights organizations. The politics of business unionism thus limited the extent to which unions were willing to engage in proactive measures concerning disability rights issues.

Constitutional changes prohibiting discrimination on the basis of disability introduced during the early 1980s coincided with a rapidly developing disability rights movement, which attracted the attention of unionists across Canada. The Charter of Rights and Freedoms ("the Charter"), one of the key vehicles that supported the legal protection of disabled people from discrimination in employment, also presented a major obstacle to disability activism in the Canadian labour movement.[15] Section 15 of the Charter included the provision of equality rights that stipulated, "Every individual is equal before and under the law and has the right to the equal protection and equal benefit of the law without discrimination and, in particular, without discrimination based on race, national or ethnic origin, colour, religion, sex, age or mental or physical disability."[16]

Many unionists believed the equality provisions of the Charter represented an attack on the collective rights of labour unions and a move to undermine the foundation of the Canadian labour relations system. Justice Rosalie Abella, architect of federal employment equity legislation, noted that the Charter contributed to legal tension between individual and collective rights. Abella observed, "We imposed unelected, unaccountable jurists to decide whether rights and freedoms no one understood, but everyone passionately believed in, were being violated."[17] Unionists worried that individuals and other equity-seeking social groups might use the Charter's protection of individuals as a tool to advance social change at the expense of collective enterprises, such as unions, and mire them in catastrophically expensive legal proceedings.[18]

Canadian unions argued that the Charter advanced a particularly individualistic notion of rights that was incompatible with the collective basis unions relied upon to represent workers. The 1991 case of *Lavigne v. OPSEU*, for example, confirmed many unionists' worst fears when Francis Lavigne, a schoolteacher and member of the Ontario Public Service Employees' Union (OPSEU), argued that his individual right to freedom of association under the Charter was violated when the union used part of his dues to finance various political campaigns.[19] The case essentially pitted the lynchpin of the post-war labour relations system – union security through mandatory collection of dues – against the Charter. Although the case eventually failed at the Supreme Court of Canada, it aroused serious anxiety among labour leaders about how legislation in the name of equity and human rights might be used against unions. Reflecting on these concerns, the Ontario Federation of Labour (OFL) noted, "The *Charter*, then, could turn out to be a two-edged sword. The leading edge may well carve out decisions that end discrimination against disadvantaged groups of people, or complete the economic and political freedoms of public sector workers now denied both the right to strike and political activity as citizens. The trailing edge of the sword, however, when wielded by reactionary minorities would cut down the whole framework of modern industrial society within which trade unions have helped to build a more humane environment."[20] Most Canadian unionists believed that the Charter, as well as other human rights legislation, should provide a "proper balance between collective and individual rights" rather than weighing heavily on individual rights and undermining the basis of collective action in a democratic society.[21] Disability rights commitments in union policy statements, therefore, raised deep-seated concerns about how those rights might be exercised to the detriment of the labour movement.[22] As a result, many unions avoided implementing concrete measures to increase workforce participation rates of disabled people.

In particular, many unionists felt that the duty to accommodate conflicted with seniority rights.[23] Cases such as the closure of the Lakeshore Psychiatric Hospital (LPH) in Etobicoke, Ontario, in 1979 demonstrated how unions chose to protect seniority ahead of larger social issues affecting people with disabilities. The closure of LPH pitted disability activists in Toronto against unionists concerned about the loss of unionized jobs in the healthcare sector as a result of the closure of residential hospitals. In 1978 the Canadian Council on Hospital Accreditation (CCHA) described LPH as an "excellent hospital" and provided a rare three-year extension on its accreditation.[24] The catchment area for LPH was one of the largest in the country at the end of the 1970s, handling approximately 230 admissions per month initiated by individuals, families, hospitals, and police in the Greater Toronto Area.[25] In the case against closure LPH was described as a "truly community hospital" that had developed extensive connections with local service networks and community-based programming. Satellite programs such as DARE (Daycare, Assessment, Rehabilitative Education) provided vocational training and counselling to 200 residential and non-residential clients in conjunction with the Workers' Compensation Board, CNIB, Canadian Paraplegic Association, Goodwill Industries, and other community-based disability organizations.[26]

As per his 1977 electoral commitment to expand the community healthcare network, Ontario Progressive Conservative Premier Bill Davis commissioned a study of LPH to assess the potential political fallout and impact on mental health services that might result from the closure of the hospital.[27] The investigation, undertaken by McKinsey & Company consultants, determined that psychiatric hospitals served a crucial role in provincial mental health services, which could not be readily replaced by community services. Yet, as was noted in a 1982 Legislative Assembly debate on the subject, the McKinsey consultants "acknowledged a defect of their study in not being able, because of limited terms of reference, to look at the role of the psychiatric units in general hospitals as part of the total picture."[28] Despite this admission, the report concluded that existing hospital services across the province could accommodate the extra demand, while the government stood to collect significant savings in operational costs.[29] In the months following the report, the minister of health stated that the decision to close LPH was made during the McKinsey investigation when it was determined that "there were more excess beds at the Queen Street Mental Health Centre and Hamilton Psychiatric Hospital than there were patients at Lakeshore."[30] The Queen Street Mental Health Centre had been undergoing extensive renovation since 1970 and was proposed as the new "super site" in which community-based care initiatives could be implemented.[31]

Alarmed at the prospect of extensive layoffs, OPSEU, which represented rehabilitation workers and support staff, commissioned its own study of the closure. Recognizing the developing consensus on disability rights in the Canadian labour movement, the OPSEU study trod a fine line between supporting the deinstitutionalization movement while condemning the manner in which policymakers had responded. OPSEU argued that the hasty closure of large institutions such as LPH accompanied by the failure to replace them with adequate community-based services staffed by qualified, experienced (and unionized) workers flew in the face of community living philosophies.[32] The OPSEU study found that the hospital closure would negatively impact a large provincial labour pool of healthcare workers, given that several bargaining units would be downscaled or eliminated completely. Minister of Health Dennis Timbrell assured OPSEU the government would try to avoid job losses through a province-wide hiring freeze, prioritized transfers to other jobs in the Ontario Public Service, and additional assistance in accessing employment. To support the government's position, yet in contradiction to the CCHA accreditation decision, Timbrell asserted in a speech to Metro Toronto Mental Health Services on 22 January 1979 that LPH had long been considered a "substandard" hospital.[33]

OPSEU's investigation ultimately concluded that the closure of the LPH meant 189 staff and several unit directors would be laid off and the redistribution of patients to other area institutions had more to do with cost savings for the province than seriously addressing the principles of deinstitutionalization. Indeed, OPSEU argued that hospital closures often occurred prematurely and without adequate consideration of the impact on existing services. OPSEU concluded that the government would eventually circle back to reopen the hospital, but by then many staff would have been laid off and the cost of rebuilding LPH or a new hospital would pale in comparison with renovation costs.[34]

Similarly concerned by the impact of disability rights initiatives on Canadian unions, the OFL undertook a comprehensive investigation of its membership in 1978, which provides insight into the ways in which Canadian unions incorporated disability issues in collective bargaining. Although the study did not identify specific unions, OFL membership included a wide range of public and private sector unions and selected representative examples for each type of clause. The study found that most collective agreements included provisions for disability, but clauses regarding disabled workers generally fell into two broad categories: those dealing with recruitment or employment conditions and others concerning the retention of employees who became disabled. Contracts regarding recruitment included hiring ratios, such as "For every 50 workers the employer employs he must hire at least 1 who is handicapped." While many collective agreements included anti-discrimination provisions, some unions negotiated wage adjustment clauses that provided special wage concessions as incentives to hire disabled people below the typical wage in a given department. Cognizant of the possibility that such clauses threatened to undermine other provisions of the collective agreement, these contracts were careful to restrict the use of such clauses with the proviso "subject to the approval in each instance of the employee and the union." Finally, many collective agreements established special jobs for disabled workers. For example, one clause read, "The company agrees with the union that all future employees who are hired into the Cleaning and Lubricating Department shall be 40 years of age or over and/or handicapped persons."[35]

The OFL study found that the most common disability-related clauses were those addressing the retention of disabled or injured workers. Typical clauses included the transfer of disabled workers to "lighter" or "more suitable" work. A typical clause read, "The Company shall make every reasonable effort to find work for handicapped or superannuated employees which they are able to perform." Where disabled workers were transferred to different work, many contracts attempted to limit the negative effects on wage rates through the establishment of structured wage rate adjustments "at appropriate rates of pay by mutual agreement between the company, the union, and the employee." In cases where alternative work was unavailable to disabled workers, some collective agreements protected employees from being fired through clauses that read, "Employees producing less than 90 per cent efficiency are subject to dismissal. However, in the cases of aged or handicapped employees now on the payroll, a reduction in wages comparable to the rate of efficiency can be adopted by mutual agreement of the company and union." While the study found most contracts respected the importance of seniority as a principle in collective bargaining, some collective agreements expressly exempted disabled workers from seniority rights. One typical clause read, "In the event of any layoff, handicapped or superannuated employees will be retained regardless of seniority and will be exempt from the seniority provisions of this agreement in that respect."

Disability activists and labour market analysts increasingly argued that seniority provisions in collective agreements often blocked disabled people's access to unionized workplaces. Entry-level work was typically more physically intensive than work jobs for more senior employees, discouraging or disqualifying many disabled job applicants.[36] In 1979 disability activists, service agencies, employers, unionists, and government officials gathered at Queen's University under the auspices of the United Handicapped Groups of Ontario (UHGO) to discuss employment issues affecting the disability community. A general consensus was reached among delegates, including provincial union representatives, that seniority rules contributed to workforce barriers by inhibiting disabled people's ability to acquire employment in unionized workplaces.[37] Jean Sparling, a rehabilitation consultant and disability rights activist who attended the conference, told the *Globe and Mail*, "Companies and unions do not discriminate against a handicapped person after the person has a job"; rather, it is in the attempt to acquire a job that problems are encountered.[38] Representatives from the Ontario Handicapped Employment Program (HEP), for example, noted that it was common for people with disabilities to be "screened out when union contracts require that a worker's first job with a company involve heavy physical work. Those workers usually are promoted into less physically demanding jobs as they gain seniority."[39] As a result, the HEP resolved to work with unions to reform their collective agreements to promote the interests of disabled people within and outside unionized workplaces.[40]

Despite the existence of "seniority-bumping" clauses documented in the OFL study, such provisions were generally uncommon, since unions took seniority clauses seriously, regardless of their impact on disadvantaged groups. As legal scholar Michael Lynk noted, "Seniority is considered a prized employee right and only very clear collective agreement language would permit an override ... The prevailing view is that seniority is a cornerstone of any collective agreement, and cannot be interfered with lightly."[41] By the mid-1980s, the OFL was assuring its members, "We believe that we do not have to give up seniority in order to achieve affirmative action ... Union support of affirmative action therefore can be seen as a means to round out the union's collective bargaining objectives: to retain those, who, because of physical or other barriers would have to terminate their employment and to offer opportunity for employment and advancement to those who so far have been excluded from the workforce."[42] Lynk determined that Canadian arbitrators largely denied grievances from disabled employees by bumping more senior employees in order to access accommodations and thus circumventing seniority provisions.[43] As confirmed in the 1992 landmark Supreme Court case of *Central Okanagan School District No. 23 v. Renaud*, unions could deny a human rights-based accommodation when it conflicted with the collective agreement. Consideration of the "disruption of a collective agreement" was usually included in tests of undue hardship in cases where disabled employees sought accommodations from the employer. As in the *Renaud* case, unions could thus claim undue hardship on the basis of the contravention of contract provisions even if an employer theoretically had agreed to the accommodation.[44]

Such persistent concern about seniority in spite of the stated transition to social unionism revealed that rhetorical commitments to engage disability activists did not distract unions from their chief objective protecting members, especially against elusive threats to collective security as embodied in employment equity legislation and the Charter protections. Beyond the bargaining table, however, unions were compelled to address a developing disability rights movement that sought greater engagement with the labour movement.

"Being a disability activist in the trade union movement was lonely," declared one interview participant in Toronto.[45] "David," who began working in the provincial public sector during the early 1980s noted, "As an activist and advocate for disability, I saw some definite similarities in the work I did in the community and the work of labour unions … When unions did work back then, they did not really see their work as working with folks with disabilities."[46] Another disability activist in the labour movement, interview participant "Lisa," found in her experience working in the municipal public sector since the mid-1970s that there was limited participation of people with disabilities in the labour movement.[47] Partly owing to the low visibility of disabled people in union circles, Lisa encountered little conversation about disability rights at the local level beyond issues that affected injured workers and current employees such as worker's compensation and occupational health and safety. Both David and Lisa encountered a culture within unions that encouraged distinctions between injured workers and other people with disabilities.[48] Such distinctions created a gulf between emerging social movements among injured workers and those of disability rights activists, whose shared goals were clouded by separate sites of allegiance.

The Canadian labour movement straddled an increasingly divisive and politicized medical and social model of disability. On one hand, unions supported injured workers that endorsed the medical categorization of their bodies to qualify for access to workers' compensation, job accommodations, seniority entitlements, and to facilitate dialogue on occupational health and safety issues. Union members who experienced an injury in the course of employment found a labour movement

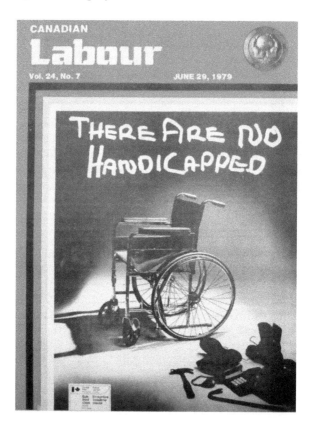

26 & 27 Cover and inset image of the *Canadian Labour* magazine published by the Canadian Labour Congress, juxtaposing conventional symbols of disability and work. Beneath the apparently handwritten caption "There are no handicapped" sits an empty wheelchair and various work tools, including

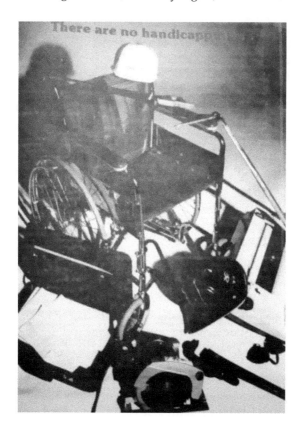

a hammer, a crowbar, work boots, and other "tools of the trade." The message communicates a sense of solidarity with disabled workers whose impairments prevent them from working.[49] © Canadian Labour Congress, 1979. Reproduced with permission.

anxious to protect workers through strong collective agreements.[50] Union literature promoted slogans such as "An injury to one is an injury to all" in reference to the bonds of union solidarity and the expectation that labour organizations would protect injured workers.[51] Unlike injured workers who used the medical model to highlight their demands, people with pre-existing or congenital disabilities within and outside unions sought to redirect attention to the impact of systemic barriers in the workplace and broader society. The conventional understanding of disability as a medical impairment that afflicted individuals was challenged by disability rights activism with its promotion of the reconceptualization of disability as a manifestation of socially constructed barriers to full participation based on arbitrary notions of normative fitness.[52] Many disability rights activists held that the understanding of disability as a matter of individual impairments reinforced the medicalization of disability while ignoring or minimizing the role of social processes whereby impairments become obstacles to social and economic participation.[53] In response to these opposing agendas, unions chose largely to deal with measures that affected injured workers, owing to the widespread belief that unions should focus on "practical" union business in an era of downsizing, outsourcing, and the scaling back of historic wins at the bargaining table.

Activism by injured workers in Canada stretched back to the origins of workers' compensation at the turn of the twentieth century, but its contemporary resurgence coincided with an upsurge in disability rights activism. Compared with a less influential minority of workers with self-identified pre-existing or congenital disabilities, injured workers were far better organized and insinuated within union culture.[54] Injured workers formed their own unions, for example, while invigorating labour activism on a number of relevant issues, including job accommodation, modified work schemes, and workplace accessibility. Union leaders were obliged to negotiate on behalf of their members for higher disability pensions and modified work schemes. Workers' compensation boards drew up payment schedules, derogatorily referred to as "meat charts," which ascribed monetary figures to the loss of digits, limbs, range of motion, and other physical impairments.[55] The *Toronto Star* reported that over 100,000 injured workers in Ontario and an additional 10,000 per year got one lump sum payment (or "lifetime pension") calculated on the basis of universal "meat chart" payment schedules.[56]

During the late 1970s and early 1980s injured workers in Canada led a social movement, composed primarily of Italian immigrant trades-people, against perceived attempts to dismantle the existing system of pensions for disabled workers.[57] A precipitous rise in workplace accidents during the 1970s put pressure on the workers' compensation system, leading to a stiffening of payment and benefit structures. These developments provoked protest from a vocal cohort of injured workers.[58] Injured workers argued that they did not receive proper rehabilitation and training supports, as many were rendered unemployable following workplace accidents. Another common complaint included the argument that Workers' Compensation Board wage subsidies provided on a sliding time scale encouraged employers to fire workers when they stopped receiving a subsidy for employing injured workers. As a result, many injured employees correctly believed they were being exploited by subsidy arrangements and effectively trained in jobs with no future for them.[59] As memorialized in the documentary film *A Right to Live*, injured workers led a protest to the Ontario Legislature at Queen's Park on 28 October 1975, where protestors threw themselves on the floor of the legislature in a desperate attempt to attract attention to their movement's struggle for greater entitlement to adequate levels of compensation, accommodation, and measures to reintegrate them into the paid workforce.[60]

The idea that physical disability was somehow a loss in need of financial reimbursement or could be so plainly quantified through medical testing and "meat charts" was clearly at odds with the ideologies underpinning much disability rights activism in Canada. The conventional understanding that disability was a medical impairment that afflicted individuals was supported by injured workers but fundamentally challenged by disability rights activists, who saw disability as part of the sociocultural construction of barriers. Many disability activists also held that the conceptualization of disability in purely medical terms legitimated long-standing institutional mechanisms of social control and oppression.[61]

The manifestation of injured workers' groups and disability rights organizations followed similar paths, despite their different ideological approaches. Both injured workers and disability activists formed legal advocacy fronts to push their respective agendas through the court system by sponsoring key cases that would create favourable legal precedence. A legal clinic called the Injured Workman's Consultants (IWC) was established in Toronto in 1973; it assisted injured workers in dealing with the Worker's Compensation Board, courts, and employers in their pursuit of compensation, accommodation, re-employment, and other matters.[62] After the IWC merged with other local groups of Italian injured workers, the organization became the Union of Injured Workers (UIW), uniting social movement activism with legal advocacy.[63] With 900 founding members, the UIW was established to "fight to bring about needed changes" to the workers' compensation system with four major demands: job security, cost of living increases, no workers' compensation board doctors, and better safety conditions.[64] Similarly, the Advocacy Resource Centre for the Handicapped (ARCH) was established in the late 1970s by a coalition of disability rights activists, disability rights groups, and service agencies, which perceived the need for an organization dedicated to law reform and test litigation that would help entrench disability rights in the legislative framework of the country.[65] As a cooperative venture involving disability activists and service agencies, ARCH was born in the spirit of collaboration, whereas the UIW and other injured workers' groups reflected a more antagonistic relationship with employers and the Ontario Workers' Compensation Board.

Disability rights activists lamented by 1990 that an effective relationship had not been established with injured workers. COPOH had not established a liaison with the UIW or other injured workers groups and ARCH blamed the situation on disability activists, stating "The disabled community has not included injured workers in its work. It is essential to have them involved."[66] The Canadian Association for Community Living (CACL) pointed to a "dual track system" for employed and unemployed disabled people that distanced injured workers from the rest of the disability community. Nonetheless, ARCH began to make inroads with injured workers' groups in the early 2000s, when it intervened on behalf of the Ontario Network of Injured Workers' Groups in two cases against the Nova Scotia Worker's Compensation Board, signalling a move towards a common understanding of how equality provisions affected all people with disabilities regardless of the origins of their impairments.[67]

Jurisdictional jockeying between provincial and federal workers' compensation systems had long been a source of contention among injured workers' groups, and the need for a national voice was seen as increasingly necessary.[68] To coordinate their lobbying efforts the Canadian Injured Workers' Alliance (CIWA) was founded in 1989 in Thunder Bay,

Ontario, by a coalition of injured workers groups, community legal aid clinics, unions, health and safety professionals, and government officials.[69] CIWA believed that "being injured at work is much more than a medical event" in that it involves the loss of income and self-esteem as well.[70] Solidarity in the face of serious injury was highlighted in CIWA's inaugural conference, through scenarios proclaiming, "I am a logger, a nurse, a welder, a miner. I was on the job when: 'a tree swung around and caught me in the back'; 'I lifted one too many patients'; 'I slipped off a roof'; 'I got hit in the back of the head with a steel rod.' Now I am an injured worker. In an instant my life has been dramatically changed. What do I need now?"[71] Reflecting the growing influence of disability rights activism and the social model of disability, CIWA adopted several resolutions that revolved around disability rights and consumer control in rehabilitation, compensation, re-employment, and pursuit of universal disability insurance.[72] This orientation was carried forward with calls for a universal disability insurance regime that recognized the struggles of disabled people outside the labour movement seeking greater participation in the labour market.[73]

By the 1990s and early 2000s unions and labour federations had established disability caucuses with the express purpose of building a strong and progressive dialogue on equity issues affecting disabled people. Delegates at labour conventions were required to self-identify as disabled in order to attend caucus meetings and vote on pertinent matters. However, many injured workers did not see themselves as disabled, nor did they necessarily share the goals of disability identity politics, instead viewing themselves as "fallen workers."[74] Indeed, the UIW film *A Right To Live* "chose the name 'union' because they believe injured workers are workers and should be treated as workers, not like charity cases."[75] Sociologist Robert Storey observes that in developing a "master frame of injustice" the injured worker developed a new self-identity as the "proud but beaten man who, because of a disabling workplace injury, could no longer provide for his family as he wanted and was supposed to do."[76] One injured worker interviewed in *A Right To Live* lost his job at a mattress manufacturing company after sustaining a back injury; he spoke to the "physical and emotional side-effects" of his injury, tearfully expressing that he was no longer "useful" and did not "feel like a man" in relation to his family.[77] Preoccupied with their experience of disease or injury and drawing strength from their peers in the labour movement and injured workers' associations, injured workers aligned themselves with a collective outlook that was distinctly different from

28 Unionized CNIB workers on the picket line outside an Edmonton sheltered workshop. Media coverage of the strike challenged the public perception of sheltered workshops, while solidarity with others in the labour movement strengthened their bargaining position. © Alberta Handicapped Communications Society, 1979. Reproduced with permission.

disability rights, identity politics, and equity activism. While the labour movement was attuned first and foremost to the needs of its able-bodied and disabled members, the transition to social unionism led to the formation of impromptu partnerships with disability activists.

Despite ideological differences with the disability rights movement, the Canadian labour movement did engage in a series of strategic alliances with disability activists as part of a trend towards the acceptance of social unionism. As labour organizations increased their involvement in the promotion of disability rights and labour market integration, they came into direct conflict with disability service agencies that employed disabled workers. One such conflict arose in 1979 when unionized blind workers who were members of the Canadian Union of Blind and Sighted Merchants (CUBSM) went on strike in Edmonton,

Alberta. Strikers alleged that paltry wages, dangerous working conditions, and substandard vocational training and placement services at CNIB and Caterplan retail outlets kept them in perpetual poverty and undermined their pursuit of independence. Some CNIB workshops were alleged to have an array of health and safety problems, including gaping holes in the floor, narrow aisles between stacks of sharply pointed surveyor stakes, and dangerous levels of airborne sawdust. CUBSM argued that, while impoverished workers earned approximately $0.40 an hour as a result of being classified as trainees in a rehabilitation program, the CNIB stood to gain considerable profits from the sale of goods and services. The strike began in August and quickly escalated as other blind workers and disability rights activists across the country railed against local CNIB offices, alleging the CNIB was a secretive and dictatorial monopoly that dominated services for blind Canadians while failing to improve their level of social and economic integration.[78]

In response to the strike, CUPE National sent delegates to march alongside strikers and pledged to provide financial support to strikers in solidarity with CUBSM's struggle against Caterplan. CUPE's move to support blind workers dovetailed with the labour movement's growing opposition to sheltered workshops, which was perceived as inherently exploitative and potentially threatening to overall Canadian labour standards. Opposition by Canadian unions to sheltered employment created an excellent opportunity for the labour movement to demonstrate its support of disability activists who also rejected sheltered workshops. The National Union of Public and General Employees (NUPGE) announced a national campaign in 1981 to lobby all levels of government to review and abolish legislation that permitted exemptions from minimum wage standards, calling such permits hypocritical and exploitative.[79] NUPGE criticized the argument by service agencies that sheltered work was therapy and thus not a "real" employment relationship, pointing to the fact that many sheltered workers put in full days in regular work settings, were supervised, punched time clocks, took regular lunch hours, and produced products that were sold for profit. NUPGE President John Fryer stated, "If the work is indeed therapeutic, and prepares them for other employment, then why are so many of them in these workshops for so many years? They are in fact dead-end jobs, with no hope for advancement." NUPGE and the CLC thus instituted a plan to organize sheltered workers across the country in order to press for better wages and working conditions. In one instance, ARC Industries, a sheltered workshop in Fort Erie that specialized in recycling paper waste, nearly shut down when civil service staffers represented by CUPE demanded a 50 per cent wage increase for their members, who, they argued, were extremely underpaid by provincial standards.[80]

Workshop administrators and advocates reacted to the union campaign with a combination of anger and disbelief. The Canadian Council of Rehabilitation Workshops (CCRW) resented unions' incursion into social service programming and challenged unions' attempts to organize sheltered workshops, citing the classification of sheltered workers as trainees in vocational rehabilitation programs.[81] CCRW President Kenneth Cope told the *Globe and Mail* that his organization was "very disappointed that the labor movement appears to be limiting itself simply to organizing disabled workers who ask for help, while there are other actions labor could also take which would be of far greater benefit to all disabled people whether they are employed in workshops or not."[82] Cope argued that unions were ignorant about the realities of sheltered work and the rehabilitation industry, pointing out that the CCRW supported the principle of upholding minimum wage legislation, but it was impossible to justify the payment of minimum wages in workshops, since the average worker contributes approximately 50 per cent below the productivity of a minimum wage.[83] The CCRW concluded that it would develop ways to cooperate with the labour movement in order to facilitate a meaningful exchange regarding the labour market integration of disabled people. But by 1990 this collaborative relationship had failed to materialize, and the CCRW repeatedly argued that unions "generally frown on arrangements where workshops and supported employment agencies receive non-union subcontracting work from unionized employers."[84]

The escalation of the minimum wage exemption issue had the effect of driving labour organizations and disability rights organizations into closer association. In their shared outrage against sheltered workshops, COPOH and the CLC boycotted the 1982 CCRW conference, simultaneously holding their own press forum to voice their opposition. The CLC also sent a strong message of support for disability rights activism by adopting a resolution in the early 1980s that recognized COPOH "as the representative voice of disabled Canadians" and called for "a strong working relationship" with COPOH to bring about "social justice for all disabled Canadians."[85] The resolution motivated COPOH to reach out to labour unions, encouraging the CLC to appeal to affiliates about the need to prioritize the negotiation of clauses in collective agreements that protected all people with disabilities to ensure they have access to training.[86] The CLC also resolved to focus on recruiting disabled unionists as activists and to ensure that its labour conventions were fully accessible. The CLC collaborated with COPOH on a number of consultations with federal ministers regarding changes to the federal labour code, including assistance in developing a one-week training course for labour activists on disability issues.[87] A notable example of the new relationship between disability activists and the labour movement included the CLC's solicitation of input for the Canadian delegation to the International Labour Organization in its deliberations on vocational rehabilitation policy.[88]

The early 1980s also saw Canadian labour organizations develop a new consensus on disability rights and employment equity issues. In 1980 the CLC called on the broader labour movement to encourage and support the employment of disabled people. The CLC noted, "One only has to look at the many thousands of disabled Canadians who are employable but not working to realize that they have not been given the chance to use their abilities." The CLC believed it was necessary to act as a "catalyst among groups or services representing the disabled, for the purpose of developing a national body to deal with all matters of concern to the disabled." The CLC also made a submission to the Parliamentary Special Committee on the Disabled and the Handicapped in 1980 that called for full protection of people with disabilities under federal and provincial human rights acts, full employment and job opportunities for disabled people, income security, affirmative action programs, employment incentive programs, review of sheltered workshops for evidence of exploitation, improved accessibility to public and private buildings, consultation with disabled people, and generally more consideration of people with disabilities.[89] In 1983 NUPGE and COPOH issued a joint report entitled *Together for Social Change*, which represented the culmination of an unprecedented collaboration between disability rights activists and the labour movement. The report promoted awareness of workforce barriers faced by disabled people and included a set of recommendations that served as a framework for policymakers, unionists, and disability activists undertaking a more informed plan of action to increase the employment of persons with disabilities. In particular, the report recommended the enactment of employment equity legislation, development of accessibility policies, more education on disability rights, and a commitment to ongoing cooperation.[90]

As important as the *Together for Social Change* collaboration was, the absence of follow-up reports or similar collaboration revealed the ad hoc nature of the partnership, which undermined the potential significance of the venture. By the early 1990s the Council of Canadians with Disabilities (CCD; formerly COPOH) observed, "there were many more instances when unions appeared to be more interested in getting involved with charity boosting, even to the extent of supporting telethons, than they were in making their employers sit down at the bargaining table and hammer out employment equity provisions."[91] Disability activists grew increasingly frustrated with the lack of change in the high unemployment rate of disabled people and unions' noncommittal relationship with disability activism. A conference held in 1994 involving the Manitoba Federation of Labour and the Manitoba League of the Physically Handicapped observed, "an underlying tension that, in spite of all the good will [*sic*] in the world, is bound to exist between 'haves' – those with jobs, trade unionists in this case – and 'have nots,' the vast majority of the population of people with disabilities."[92] The first National Workplace Equity for Persons with Disabilities Symposium organized by Human Resources Development Canada in 1998, for example, reported that despite years of lobbying by social activists to set the labour movement on a fundamentally social unionist path, it was instead the introduction of employment equity legislation that in fact motivated unions to include equity provisions in collective bargaining. One employer in attendance at the conference cited the example of a labour relations committee consisting of management, union representatives, and disabled employees in his workplace that "worked closely together to establish and review employee plans on a regular basis. Employees were invited to volunteer to participate on a task force to identify and reduce barriers, and the collective agreement includes language about accommodation."[93]

By the end of the Decade of Disabled Persons in 1992 CUPE concluded, "As the decade started out ... there was a rise in expectations – that there would be an increasing awareness about disabilities, leading to meaningful change, especially in the area of employment. This has not been the case, and the persistent realities in the lives of disabled persons have given way to new levels of bitterness and frustration."[94] In a study of how Canadian unions responded to social movement activism, Carroll and Ratner argued that the labour movement carried a certain amount of responsibility to take the initiative by virtue of its dominant position in terms of size and funding.[95] They discovered a labour movement in the process of dynamic change in 1995, presumably balancing its primary objective to defend its members as well as grass-roots activism presented by social movements.[96] A 1998 background paper for the CLC also concluded, "The question of income security for persons with disabilities, regardless of their origin, has been waning and waxing in Canada for at least two decades ... While CLC interest in this issue has been consistent over time, it has also been a relatively low priority."[97] Disability activist Yvonne Peters submitted a report commissioned by CUPE, which concluded that there were indeed union members with disabilities, that some locals were devising strategies to address the needs of these members, but that most locals needed more resources and information on strategies and methods for protecting the rights of members with disabilities.[98]

By the turn of the century labour organizations realized that passive and impromptu relationships with disability rights activists and organizations did not cultivate productive and valuable partnerships. In 2000 the CLC held its first Disability Rights Conference, bringing together labour leaders and disability activists to establish a more formal dialogue on disability rights in the labour movement. The result was an ongoing campaign entitled MORE (Mobilize Organize Represent and Educate), which culminated in the publication of the aptly named *The MORE We Get Together: Disability Rights and Collective Bargaining Manual.*[99] The manual, researched and written in large part by leading disability activist Pat Danforth, outlined what unions were doing to assist members with disabilities access accommodations, worker's compensation, contract benefits, return-to-work arrangements, and prevention of disability through health and safety provisions.[100] The manual was intended to facilitate further understanding of persons with disabilities and the discourse of disability rights while guiding union locals as to the best means of identifying and lowering workplace barriers. The manual also demonstrated the shift towards inclusive dialogue with disability activists since the late 1990s and early 2000s with the establishment of disability rights working groups in many major public sector unions and labour federations, and it shared several case studies where labour organizations had initiated programs to protect disabled workers and established partnerships with community organizations.[101]

A central player in a changing labour market, the Canadian labour movement reflected the extent to which disability rights shaped the discourse of work and working-class interests from the mid-1970s onward. The emergence of disability rights in Canada coincided with the transformation of union membership, the rise of social unionism, and unprecedented changes in the organization of work. Among union leaders these changes facilitated purposeful dialogue about the role of disability rights in the workplace and within union structures. However, as social institutions embedded in local communities of working peoples, unions reflected the predominant understanding that disability affected the individual. Despite their defence of workers injured by capitalist enterprises, the Canadian labour movement ultimately failed to adequately defend the interests of a broader disability community injured by an exclusive capitalist system. Inherent divisions in the broader disability community also manifested themselves in unions. Core union practices such as advocacy on behalf of injured workers reinforced the medicalization of disability, which undercut declarations in support of disability rights. The business of union work increasingly ran up against a new generation of labour activists championing social justice and the extension of civil rights to traditionally disadvantaged groups. In an attempt to combine union business with social movement activism, the Canadian labour movement was caught between its support of medical authority and the social model of disability and presented no clear way forward.

The labour movement was larger, more stable, and better funded than the loose coalition of volunteers leading the Canadian disability rights movement. These differences in structure and size meant that labour organizations tended to solicit the input of disability activists and rights organizations when the opportunity arose and forced the terms of these momentary partnerships to fit within an existing set of priorities. Disability activists in the labour movement also pointed to this unidirectional power relationship as the source of inherent tension and chronic inaction on disability rights.[102] Despite these disappointments, social activists and equity-seeking groups continually pushed against the traditional organizational culture of unions in order to create space for disabled workers regardless of the origin of their disability. As a result, the labour movement afforded greater attention to the advancement of disability rights issues in response to a new generation of labour activists who sought to extend the boundaries of social unionism to include all people with disabilities.

Conclusion

In late twentieth-century Canada the experience of disability was profoundly shaped by work, including the pursuit of employment and exclusion from the labour market. Waves of awareness about disability issues advanced and retreated from the 1960s to the 2000s, while the social roots of the economic "problem" of disability remained intact, prompting a search for creative responses to the under- and unemployment of disabled people. Multiple disability movements challenged attitudes and mechanisms that perpetuated the long-standing marginalization of disabled people in the labour market by actively engaging employers, governments, and labour leaders in the redefinition of the social and economic problem of disability. Canadian disability rights organizations were decidedly grass roots, but their energy fed a national social movement focused on attaining new rights and protections in pursuit of meaningful social and employment opportunities. Disability rights activists were recruited by special government bureaus and labour organizations and tasked with helping to recondition public attitudes and practices of policymakers and employers. Physical and social obstacles were reconceptualized as socially constructed barriers that hindered disabled people from undertaking mainstream education, skill development, and other opportunities essential to advancement in the labour market. If barriers were socially created, however, they could be systematically dismantled. Within and outside structures of power, disability rights activists and their allies promoted a progressive dialogue on the importance of disabled peoples' increased participation in the labour market, as it was believed that economic integration was a crucial element in disabled people's pursuit of full citizenship.

Despite forty years of contemporary disability rights activism in Canada, the continuing problem of chronic poverty and unemployment in the disability community prompts us to question the degree to which disability rights activists and their allies actually influenced the labour market and broader cultural responses to disability. This book demonstrates that there were a variety of responses to disability rights activism that produced many new changes. The disability community spoke with many voices, often in cooperation but sometimes in conflict. Yet the message remained the same: people with disabilities are capable of more than prejudicial stereotypes allow, and they should be provided with free access to opportunities in which to develop these capabilities. Despite the varied experience of disability and the nebulous character of disability movements, disability activists found common ground in the struggle for access to employment opportunities. This struggle produced widespread changes in the built environment, policy landscape, and social discourse of disability that made it possible for people with disabilities to find jobs. An important battleground in the struggle for integration was fought at the workplace by individuals and disability groups seeking to create new identities based on the provision of gainful employment. The work of disability organizations and government bureaus that highlighted the employability of disabled people formed a larger collective project that included hiring and awareness-building campaigns. These initiatives evolved in response to changing labour conditions and legislative protections. Whether on the picket line, protesting working conditions in sheltered workshops, or in meetings with employers and policymakers, disabled people and their allies continually focused on devising solutions to labour market accessibility.

A capability-based discourse of disability initiated by parents and the deinstitutionalization movement represented a first step towards developing alternatives to segregation. During the post-war period, some parents and families of people with physical and mental disabilities responded to residential institutions and other forms of social and economic exclusion by introducing new community-based services and discourse on the possibilities of community integration. While family advocates and rehabilitation professionals presented a progressive-minded approach to disability, they did not embody a civil rights movement rooted in an identity politics which arrived somewhat later in the 1970s with the disability rights movement. Disability rights activists powered an evolving discourse of disability by carving out a role for people with disabilities in existing social movements and labour institutions. This proved a vital development, as disabled people demonstrated their ability to make meaningful contributions to society in their own right rather than relying upon their allies who ostensibly spoke on their behalf. If people with disabilities truly wanted better access to paid employment, they would eventually have to take it upon themselves to promote this objective.

The federalist structure of Canadian politics meant that seemingly major advances in disability rights, such as the Accessibility for Ontarians with Disabilities Act (AODA), were ultimately restricted by jurisdictional limitations. Disability activists and scholars alike lamented the degree to which a federalist political system inhibited the coordinated advancement of changes to the political and economic landscape in Canada but continued to work within this system to produce effective change.[1] Modelled on the Americans with Disabilities Act (ADA), the introduction of the AODA was nationally significant in that it reflects the latest outcome of the state-led approach to policy reform by disability rights activism to address the economic "problem" of disability in Canada. The AODA could not have the same impact as its model, given it is a provincial statute, and it has been roundly criticized for failing to produce substantive improvement in employment rates. However, David Lepofsky and other activists have advocated for a similar Canadians with Disabilities Act.[2] Comprehensive disability rights legislation such as the AODA serve an important role in policy development by providing leadership in the cultivation of innovative policies and standards in the pursuit of integrated responses to barrier removal in the workplace and broader society. Recent developments, including the election of Justin Trudeau's Liberal government in 2015, have reinvigorated calls for a National Disabilities Act, and the appointment of MPs with physical disabilities to key cabinet posts bears some promise of sustained attention to these issues.

Repeated studies documented a pattern of under- and unemployment in the Canadian disability community. The World Health Organization's (WHO) first *World Report on Disability* investigated the global state of disability issues and provided recommendations to alleviate widespread social and economic dislocation.[3] The WHO found that only 56 per cent of working-age adults with disabilities in Canada were employed, although this employment rate was generally better than that of other developed and developing countries around the globe.[4] The WHO also concluded that labour market outcomes for disabled people are contingent on a constellation of factors, noting, "Given the right environment, most PWD [persons with disabilities] can be productive."[5] In 2013 Human Resources and Skills Development Canada (HRSDC) published a report titled *Rethinking Disability in the Private Sector*, based on extensive consultations with private sector employers in Canada.[6] Echoing conclusions reached in previous reports on the attitudes and practices of employers discussed in chapter 5, the HRSDC report documented the persistence of a prejudicial mythology of disability among employers that discouraged the employment of disabled people. Even more disturbing is the use of language and strategies devised *more than seventy years ago*, such as "Hiring people with disabilities is good for business," signalling a return to antiquated "Hire the Handicapped" campaigns.

One explanation for the lack of change in attitudes about employability points to the potential failure of a younger generation of disability activists to step forward to replace an older generation by taking the disability rights movement to new spheres of influence. Key disability activists and organizations of the late 1970s and early 1980s continued to form the leadership of the disability rights movement in the early 2000s, suggesting that a younger generation of disability rights activists has not yet fully emerged to continue the fight. Some early activists that emerged from this period earned law degrees that enabled them to focus their energies on advancing the pursuit of precedent-setting disability rights legislation; yet many of these early leaders continued to lead disability movements into the twenty-first century. What happened to a subsequent generation of disability rights leaders? There were many more forms of activism than the activities organized by disability rights organizations spearheading awareness campaigns and lobbying for legislative changes.[7] However, many important developments in the advancement of legal rights for people with disabilities continued to accrue through the work of disability organizations led by a generation of activists who came of age during the emergence of civil rights activism.

In the face of tremendous political and economic change, disability organizations held fast to established patterns of activism that enabled them to exert political influence on the national stage in the past. The Council of Canadians with Disabilities (CCD; formerly COPOH) continues to be a leader in shaping national disability policy and influencing policymakers through its committees and provincial affiliates. Access to high-ranking government officials living with visible physical disabilities, such as Conservative MP Steven Fletcher and Ontario

Lieutenant-Governor David Onley, encouraged a degree of sustained attention to disability rights issues in political spheres. Faced with continued widespread poverty and unemployment in the disability community, the CCD's Social Policy committee initiated a major research project in 2008 called Disabling Poverty/Enabling Citizenship, which examines the impact of various political institutions and programs on the economic opportunities of people with disabilities.[8] One of the principal goals of the project centred around "economic independence," which the CCD defined as "the participation of persons with disabilities of working age (15 to 64) in the paid labour force, as self-employed and waged workers (real pay for real work), providing a degree of financial security and reducing dependence on income programs, such as social assistance."[9] The project spawned an annual community forum and rally called End Exclusion, which builds on long-standing efforts by disability activists to address poverty and unemployment in the disability community as the effect of prejudice and discrimination. As a result, disability rights activists' continued focus on this front indicates that important ideological work is far from over.

Amid the rise and fall of disability organizations, political initiatives, and social movement alliances, generations of people with disabilities sought to live and work free from social and physical barriers. They had seen many developments: the establishment of consumer-controlled disability organizations and advisory councils, new government bureaus dedicated to helping them find jobs, new legislative protections in the Charter of Rights and Freedoms and other statutes, employment equity legislation at the national and provincial levels, and new alliances between disability activists and labour leaders. They also watched as attention to disability issues ascended and fell according to waves of awareness. Despite evolving political and economic conditions over time, many people with disabilities ensconced themselves in mainstream workplaces, cultivating circles of awareness as they confronted established and emerging barriers to full participation. While individual workers with disabilities may not identify with disability organizations, their work struggles and achievements constitute acts of disability activism and were intimately connected with the goals of the disability rights movement. Similar to the unionized worker who eschews unionization but reaps the benefits of union wages, individual work experiences in the labour market were inseparable from collective action, as both shaped the identity politics of disability during the late twentieth century.

It was within the sphere of labour that disability movements and individual actions ultimately converged. While disability activists lamented the fact that decades of "Hire the Handicapped" campaigns had produced little statistical change in unemployment rates, as discussed in chapter 2, many people with disabilities found their way into the workforce partly on account of employability awareness-building and accessibility projects. With each new addition of disabled people to the workplace, ripples of awareness were created that reverberated back to the collective vision of the disability movements to break down social barriers to meaningful inclusion. As specialized employment counsellors at The World of One in Seven employment agency discovered (see chapter 5), attitudinal change was best achieved through personal interaction with disabled people rather than passive acknowledgment of disability issues articulated by disability organizations. The World of One in Seven cultivated a roster of employers willing to hire people with disabilities, thus engineering local or regional conditions favourable to economic integration. Here, the employment of people with disabilities was intimately connected with the goals of disability activism, whether or not individual participants understood their crucial role in the larger scheme of things.

As this book has emphatically argued, disability activism was not restricted to one political voice, organizing strategy, or group of people. Instead, disability movements on Canada involved a shared undertaking across a broad spectrum of institutions surrounding the labour market. As a result, accountability for change and the lack thereof must be distributed equally. Employers were culpable of failing to hire disabled people in numbers significant enough to alter the fortunes of many working-age adults with disabilities seeking employment. Governments, regardless of party distinctions, were similarly responsible in their role as public sector employers but also in terms of their progressive retreat from the sphere of labour. The transition towards a neoliberal style of politics from the 1980s onward undermined the state's ability to effect change in the labour market through policy and program mechanisms, upon which many disabled people had relied for access to job opportunities.[10] Labour organizations could have chosen to engage disability groups more emphatically, despite their conceptual dilemmas. Disabled people and their allies in various disability organizations and service agencies could also have worked harder to collaborate with a unified voice rather than be distracted by ideological differences, professional hubris, and organizational insularity.

Despite a larger story of disappointment about disabled people's participation in the Canadian labour market, significant steps towards employment integration were made during this period. Many employers did hire disabled people and shared their experiences with their peers in business associations and employment conferences. Governments funded many initiatives to raise awareness of disability issues, introduced legislative advances such as employment equity and new human rights protections, and promoted a progressive model of employment practices to a much larger private sector. Labour leaders and some unions forged temporary alliances with disability rights activists in response to mutually beneficial objectives, such as a shared opposition to sheltered workshops. Disability rights activists, family advocates, and rehabilitation professionals even collaborated in the context of identity politics and consumer control to reach a new consensus on the promotion of supported employment for people with disabilities seeking independent living.

However, cooperation between major labour market players and influences on the employment of disabled people remained tenuous at best and required constant maintenance. This was particularly the case regarding the relationship between disability rights activists and the labour movement. Alliances between disability activists and labour leaders suffered from neglect and fundamental differences in priority and benign neglect. Disability activists similarly found that productive working relations with federal cabinet ministers, members of provincial parliament, and city councillors that took years to mature could be erased suddenly with the installation of new officials and political parties. Relationships between disability activists and centres of power in the labour market were continually being renegotiated by political and managerial "changes of the guard" that interrupted sustained attention to barriers to economic participation. A devastating example flowed from the 1995 election of the Progressive Conservatives in Ontario, which deeply scarred provincial social policy and radically departed from decades of advancements in disability policy and programming. An increasingly hostile political and economic environment forced disability activists across Canada to redouble their efforts and regroup to confront new challenges.

Circumstances unfolded differently on the national, provincial, and local stages, as responses to disability activism were shaped by particular political configurations and histories. Certainly, future studies of local and provincial responses to disability activism will help to clarify the ways in which activists' relationships with policymakers affected employment opportunity structures for people with disabilities. As chapter 3 emphasized, individual activists, such as Scarborough's Beryl Potter, played a critical role in influencing the course of events at the local and regional levels. Activists watched for developments in disability policy and accessibility in other parts of the country and attempted to implement them locally. This was particularly so in the sphere of labour, where vocational rehabilitation, assistive devices, and other social programming that shaped the employability of disabled people fell largely within the jurisdiction of the provinces. While the federal government looked to the provinces for disability policy development, municipalities were dependent on provincial funding for the implementation of social and vocational programs at the local level. The Ontario Handicapped Employment Program, discussed in chapter 5, was a creature of the provincial government even though its promotional activities held national significance and awareness-building work with employers helped disabled workers on the ground in Toronto and elsewhere. The dynamic interplay of federal, provincial, and local authorities thus had a distinctly local and regional flavour, a theme that requires further study.

Disability activism during the late twentieth century in Canada was driven by the individual and collective pursuit of labour: from sheltered workshops to debates between rehabilitation organizations and disability rights activists over the meaning of consumer control, to differences between organized and unemployed disabled people, and to questions of self-identity and the role of identity politics in the workplace. The refusal by a generation of parents to accept that disability was equated with exclusion and marginalization opened the door to an entirely new paradigm that empowered people with disabilities to question and challenge obstacles in their life's path rather than begrudgingly accepting them as commensurate with the realities of impairment. The relocation of disability outside oneself to the surrounding environment created enormous potential for a revised way of thinking about causes and solutions to the social and economic dislocation of disabled people. The articulation and creative application of social constructionist philosophies during this period demonstrated that the categories "disabled" and "able-bodied" represented a continuum in the human experience and that living and working arrangements could (and should) be adapted to meet our changing needs rather than the other way around. Widespread poverty and unemployment in the disability community was a shared problem that crossed jurisdictional and ideological boundaries and it was here that disability rights activists, advocates, and allies found a common platform on which to pursue a collaborative agenda.

As a younger generation of people with disabilities come of age in a climate of economic instability and declining labour standards, prospective disability activists must be able to sort out meaningful action from rhetoric in their analyses and responses to policymakers, employers, and allies. Potential strategies and logistical pitfalls may be avoided by understanding the history and lessons learned from previous experiences of disability activism. This is particularly important if an older generation of activists is indeed failing to be replaced by a younger cohort of people with disabilities averse to identity politics and collective action. The prioritization of paid work by disability rights activists and their allies as a conduit to social integration was never meant to separate disabled people from the moral accountability of others in the community. If people with disabilities and their allies continue to seek full participation in the work and life of the community, they need to have a solid understanding of their own histories in order to recognize new developments in social and economic policy that threaten to roll back historic victories earned by disability activists. Nothing is sacred in the realm of labour, as union leaders can certainly attest, and the preservation of past successes requires constant vigilance by a well-informed population.

As disability history continues to evolve within Canadian and international historiography and disability gains traction as an essential category of analysis in contemporary and historical studies, there is a pressing need to ensure the field retains its roots as an emancipatory field of research while continuing to be relevant to a broader audience. The example set by a feminist historiography may offer a way forward. Gender history similarly emerged from second-wave women's rights movements during the 1960s and 1970s that sought to provide a revisionist perspective in the historiographical record.[11] Women's and gender historians incisively demonstrated ways in which gender could be used as a category of historical analysis and thus integrated into existing scholarship in order to deepen our knowledge of new and conventional historical themes. Disability historians can learn much from this approach, but we must also make our own case for "another 'Other.'"[12] Uncovering the hidden labour history of people with disabilities reflects a methodology that seeks to synthesize disability studies scholarship with other analytical tools and fields of historical inquiry in order to highlight the ways in which historians can use disability in the broader practice of social and cultural history. Through the incorporation of disability into the existing historiography we are forced to revisit past assessments of historical events and approaches in order to arrive at a fuller understanding of the individual and social experience of cultural and economic systems of work.

This book has shown how work was a fundamental component of the lived experience of disability in Canada during the late twentieth and early twenty-first centuries. Socially constructed barriers to labour market participation prevented many people with disabilities from exercising their full citizenship and formed the basis upon which a variety of social movements of disabled people and advocates emerged. The politics of disability was divided by differences over consumer control, rehabilitation models, day programs and sheltered workshops, the desirability of wage subsidies, and the relationship between unions and disability rights organizations. But progressive leaders within groups of parents, rehabilitation professionals, consumers, employers, policymakers, and unionists advanced a shared agenda for the social and economic integration of disabled people. Work and employment provided a common language in which disability activists, employers, labour institutions, and the state could communicate about the exercise of full citizenship and application of a broader platform of disability rights. As disability identity politics developed in the 1970s and 1980s, in large part owing to widespread experiences of poverty and unemployment, the discourse of economic integration proved particularly useful in attempting to resolve strongly contested perspectives of disability. Disabled people attempted – sometimes successfully – to break down social and physical barriers in Canadian society to provide people with disabilities access to greater opportunities in society. The presentation of an entirely new way of thinking about disability – one that proposed sweeping changes to Canadian social, political, and economic institutions – is perhaps the greatest contribution of disability activists and their allies during this period.

Appendix

Profiles of Interview Participants

The following profiles document some of the representative working experiences of thirty interview participants in Toronto during the 1950s–60s, 1970s, 1980s, and 1990s–2000s as they struggled against the prospect of lifelong unemployment and poverty that awaited many people with disabilities. While not necessarily statistically representative of the broader disabled population in Canada, individual narratives and collective experiences collected as part of this study document lived experiences of barriers and opportunities that reflect major changes in infrastructure and the discourse of disability in the late twentieth century. Individual and generational profiles give way to broader conclusions about how work consistently constituted a primary feature in disabled people's personal identities as they struggled to make ends meet or prospered during a period of extensive change in Toronto's labour market.

Participant employment trajectories illustrating temporal timelines for workforce entry and exit and age at time of interview

Participant*	Year started working	Age started working	Year stopped working/last in workforce	Age stopped working/last in workforce	Age at time of interview
Grace	1953	11	2001	59	69
Sofia	1957	19	1990	52	73
Robert	1960	13	2009	62	64
William	1965	23	1997	55	69
Dan	1967	14	2008	59	62

Participant employment trajectories illustrating temporal timelines for workforce
entry and exit and age at time of interview (*cont.*)

Participant*	Year started working	Age started working	Year stopped working/last in workforce	Age stopped working/last in workforce	Age at time of interview
Isabelle	1968	16	– -**	– -	59
Jacob	1969	12	– -	– -	52
Nathan	1970	13	– -	– -	54
Lisa	1970	24	– -	– -	65
Paul	1972	16	– -	– -	55
Lucy	1972	21	– -	– -	60
Alex	1974	20	– -	– -	57
Emily	1974	20	– -	– -	57
David	1975	26	2005	56	62
Ashley	1975	19	– -	– -	55
Mary	1981	17	2009	39	47
Lily	1981	29	– -	– -	59
Ruby	1981	23	– -	– -	53
Olivia	1981	23	– -	– -	53
Rachel	1982	16	– -	– -	45
Katie	1983	14	– -	– -	41
Danielle	1983	20	– -	– -	48
Linda	1984	15	– -	– -	42
Michael	1984	18	– -	– -	45
Richard	1986	18	– -	– -	43
Charlotte	1988	16	– -	– -	39
Sarah	1991	24	– -	– -	44
Leanne	1998	19	– -	– -	32
Thomas	2005	20	– -	– -	26
Marge	n/a***	n/a	n/a	n/a	47

* All participants were randomly assigned pseudonyms with no bearing on the actual identities of interviewees. Participant identities were protected by a University of Toronto Office of Research Ethics-sanctioned informed consent agreement, which prohibited the disclosure of participant information.

** "– -" denotes a participant who had not permanently left the workforce.

*** "n/a" denotes information not disclosed or otherwise unavailable.

Cluster 1: 1950s–1960s

Six participants (or 20 per cent) – Sofia, Grace, William, Dan, Robert, and Isabelle – began their working lives during the 1950s and 1960s, mostly as teenagers and young adults whose families expected participation in the paid workforce or whose financial circumstances demanded work as a necessity. Most participants experienced some form of institution-based treatment or rehabilitation for visual impairment, spinal cord injury, poliomyelitis, or fibromyalgia. Yet nearly all participants maintained that institutional education or treatment did not fundamentally disrupt their personal goal of finding paid work or pursuing a career. Half of the participants found their way into a booming public sector as civil servants at all levels of government, while the remainder found jobs in the private and non-profit sectors. Despite growing up with the belief that paid work was a natural part of the life cycle, participants in this eldest generation faced long-standing negative stereotypes about disability among employers and the broader public that manifested in the pervasive inaccessibility of Toronto's local communities and workplaces. Nevertheless, participants confronted sets of barriers with the determination to forge careers for themselves, maximizing their abilities and downplaying the needs that accompanied their disabilities.

Growing up during the 1940s and 1950s, "Sofia" learned that surviving the polio virus as a young child and the resulting scoliosis and mobility impairment that required her to use arm crutches and a wheelchair did not exempt her from personal and family expectations to find paid employment. "Sofia" described herself as belonging to a unique cohort of polio survivors whose entrance into young adulthood and labour market participation engendered a level of widespread acceptance of physical disability, so that as long as "you could do the job you got the job." While she understood that significant attitudinal and architectural barriers existed in the community and most workplaces, she managed to find a job at age nineteen working for a major retailer in Toronto in their telephone catalogue department. With employment options during the 1950s and 1960s already highly circumscribed for women, Sofia nevertheless quit her retail job to attend a local business college and took various jobs in the non-profit sector before becoming a teacher and librarian. At one school where she worked the principal advised her, "I don't care how you do the job as long as you do it" – an ideology of work that Sofia in fact shared. While some informal accommodations were made, such as exemption from outside duties during recess, she was expected to access and move about the school on her own. Sofia described how most schools where she worked in Toronto during the 1960s were inaccessible and children in wheelchairs would have to be carried up and down the stairs. Despite her mobility impairment and not wishing to be treated differently from others, Sofia often worked in second-floor classrooms – a situation that required her to take her lunch breaks in her classroom in order to avoid the physical energy and pain of joining her colleagues in the downstairs lunchroom.

"Grace" was born in the early 1940s and secured her first job – at age eleven – shining shoes for $2.00 a month at the Brantford School for the Blind. A testament to the cultivation of a strong work ethic at an early age, she spent her summers through the remainder of the 1950s working for the Canadian National Institute for the Blind (CNIB) in a variety of age- and gender-appropriate jobs, caring for younger students at the Brantford School, as a camp counsellor, and as a vendor at CNIB's Caterplan operations. As a young woman with her high school diploma in hand, she taught Braille reading and life skills to CNIB clients at the Bayview Avenue centre in Toronto. Eager to expand her horizons, she returned to school to earn undergraduate and graduate degrees, which enabled her to secure a highly competitive position with the provincial government where she began the steady climb up the career ladder. With limited access to assistive technology that would enable her to function effectively and competitively in the labour market, Grace purchased her own expensive equipment, including a Perkins Brailler, a specialized typewriter, and a talking calculator to supplement the services of a reader hired by the government to relay vast amounts of paperwork that was otherwise inaccessible to her.

"William," also born in the early 1940s, grew up as an able-bodied boy working during summer vacations as a farm labourer until, at age sixteen, he sustained a spinal cord injury in a diving accident and spent the next two years in Lyndhurst Rehabilitation Hospital in midtown Toronto, where he regained partial use of his arms and hands. Back at home and two years behind his peers academically, he quickly finished high school before moving on to pursue a university education. As a student in downtown Toronto, William confronted widespread lack of accessible sidewalks, transportation, and limited housing options, with the assistance of social workers at Lyndhurst, who helped bridge the gap between rehabilitation and community living. However, upon graduating in the mid-1960s William set out into the workforce, surviving on jobs below his competency level while attending countless interviews and receiving few call-backs. William described physical and attitudinal barriers as compounding issues that likely prevented him from landing a job. "Finding somebody who would hire me, and then to work in a building I could get into in the first place was not an easy thing." Unwilling to pursue a job that was literally inaccessible, he restricted his applications to workplaces in accessible buildings, eventually landing a job with the provincial government where he held a series of progressively responsible managerial positions.

Born in the late 1940s, "Dan" lost most of his sight when a common medical practice at the time for premature infants resulted in overexposure to oxygen, which irreparably damaged his eyesight. By age fourteen, Dan was working in an industrial workplace but soon found it was too dangerous, given his visual impairment. He completed his high school years working during summers at the CNIB's Caterplan tuck shops in various places throughout Toronto for $60 a week. After a stint at a machine shop, he began a contract position with the provincial government that led into permanent full-time employment for the following five years. He returned to the non-profit sector where he acquired managerial experience that eventually led him to find various management positions in the federal government where he stayed for the remainder of his career. While Dan qualified as having a Bachelor of Arts, it was the result of an equivalency rating based on his extensive work experience and in-house training to which he attributed years of hard work and professional advancement.

"Robert," a baby boomer of the late 1940s with a visual impairment, got his first job in 1960 at age thirteen working during weekends and summers at the counter at one of the CNIB's confectionary stands. Unable to find a job elsewhere, Robert knew he could get some extra money and work experience through the CNIB's Caterplan business, but soon learned he had an aptitude as a manager. This discovery was buoyed by the understanding that other opportunities for advancement within the organization at the services and administrative levels – opportunities that he understands existed only for a short time at the CNIB during the 1960s and early 1970s for his age cohort. Determined to become a working professional and confident of his competitive ability to access information through various assistive devices, Robert earned a university degree and returned to the CNIB as a supervisor while he progressively worked his way into upper management.

"Isabelle" entered the labour market in the late 1960s as an ablebodied teenage girl working the cash register at a local grocery store.

An early high school graduate, she completed additional college business courses and immediately set to work in various research, secretarial, and writing jobs – all of which involved her skills as a typist. Isabelle discovered she had an affinity for technology and word processing, a career choice that demanded extensive typing that would eventually cause her excruciating chronic pain aggravated by the onset of fibromyalgia. Unable to function in her chosen career path, Isabelle was forced into self-employment while pursuing a human rights complaint against her former employer.

Cluster 2: 1970s

Nine participants – Jacob, Nathan, Lisa, Paul, Lucy, Alex, Emily, David, and Ashley – who grew up during the 1960s entered the workforce during the 1970s within a context of tremendous changes affecting the labour market in Toronto. In contrast to experiences in previous decades, fewer participants found work in a shrinking public service and more found themselves working in the non-profit sector, owing largely to an expanding rehabilitation industry that handled the influx of people with disabilities expecting to live and work in the community. As the infrastructure of Toronto became more accessible with the advent of new policies and building projects, public awareness of disability resulted from the activities of family advocates, rehabilitation professionals, and disability rights activists. The initiation of a public discourse on disability issues during the 1970s promised future improvements in access to jobs, but such changes were slow or non-existent in the eyes of many participants who began working during this decade.

Despite having a degenerative visual impairment from an early age, "Jacob" found he was able to "pass" as fully sighted. As a late baby boomer he had trouble obtaining employment but found work at the local YMCA, where he gained enough experience to qualify for a full-time job as a childcare worker at a residential youth treatment centre. As the decade wore on, Jacob's visual impairment worsened and he found it increasingly difficult to hide his disability from his employer and co-workers, which caused him to apply for Canada Pension Plan Disability (CPP-D) benefits and quit his job. Jacob described how the process of becoming legally blind negatively affected his ability to find a suitable job in the private sector and caused him to seek frontline work with the CNIB, assured that his needs would be accommodated.

"Nathan" started working at age thirteen relabelling paint cans to comply with the recent introduction of regulations requiring products sold in Canada to display both official languages. A variety of industrial and service jobs eventually led him become an apprentice in a growing trade, where he eventually expected to earn good wages as a skilled worker. Before completing his apprenticeship, however, Nathan sustained various physical injuries from an accident that forced him to abandon his trade and highly competitive wages when his employer refused to accommodate him. As a result, Nathan returned to school to pursue a career in the legal profession where his physical injuries would not act as a barrier in his work. After some time in his new career, Nathan discovered he was experiencing a number of mental health issues that frustrated his ability to meet the demands of working in the legal sector. Eventually finding a degree of equilibrium, Nathan was unwilling to disclose his mental health issues to his employer or colleagues, fearing negative consequences for his career.

As a baby boomer, "Lisa" did not join the workforce until her mid-twenties, owing partly to a visual impairment and cerebral palsy. Not content to accept a future of unemployment and reliance on welfare benefits, Lisa attempted various jobs in the retail and services sectors. Many of these jobs did not work out on account of both the demands of the job exceeding the limitations presented by her disability in a largely inaccessible environment and a general disregard of accommodations. Unable to find a job that suited her interests and abilities, Lisa returned to school and eventually found employment with the public sector in the early 1970s in an entry-level position. Despite the advantages of a competitive salary and pension, Lisa found herself effectively working longer days than her peers because of transportation difficulties, limited access within the building in which she worked, continuous struggles to access assistive technology, and pervasive attitudinal barriers of co-workers and managers that created a poisonous workplace culture.

"Paul" began his work life as a teenager in a sheltered workshop operated by the CNIB, where he remained for "all of a week," packaging pipe filters for approximately $1.60 per day. Disgruntled by the lack of employment options, he waited two years until being provided with the opportunity to work on a special employment project producing Braille textbooks for $90 per week, which he described as "Fabulous money. The first time I actually earned money, so to speak." The experience had a transformative effect on young Paul, stimulating his enthusiasm to advance himself in the workforce. Working during summers at the CNIB while attending university, he acquired experience in the technological aspects of converting transcribed materials to tape that led him to further education and employment in the public sector, where he acquired various skills and confidence working with assistive technology for people with visual impairments. Disappointed with the lack of internal advancement in the public sector, he opted for self-employment in the technology sector, where he found that his skills, experience, and interests provided the foundation for a successful and rewarding career.

Fresh out of college in the early 1970s and looking for work, "Lucy" attempted to find entry-level positions in the private sector. As a person with a visual impairment, she described how "at that time I used a cane but I could fake it and roam around with my cane folded up and I didn't appear to be visually impaired." Lucy described being cautioned "not to put in our résumé or cover letter that we had a disability because your résumé was pretty certain to go in the garbage." Despite her ability to hide her visual impairment, she consistently found that interviews ended abruptly when she disclosed that she lived with vision loss. Unable to find a job elsewhere, she found work with the CNIB and as a counsellor in a local sheltered workshop and for the next few years moved between the private sector and what she described as the "safety net" of the non-profit sector while attending university. In retrospect, Lucy believes that "had it been later I would have had a lot more options open." However, with her university degree, employment experience, and renewed confidence, Lucy finally secured a career as a professional in the private sector, where she held a series of progressively responsible positions.

Like other young blind Canadians in the early 1970s, "Alex" began his employment history as a twenty-year-old, working during summer vacations at the CNIB's Caterplan business. But focused on forging his own path, he found work as a technician in the private sector. When the factory where he was working closed, Alex decided to return to school, where he earned a college diploma and shortly thereafter found work in the banking industry. The degenerative nature of his visual impairment meant that Alex encountered fewer difficulties in obtaining a job than in maintaining employment as his condition worsened and financial support for expensive assistive technology waned. Alex also described a shifting set of expectations from his employer following the provision of assistive equipment. "Lots of time their particular systems are not usable out of the box. There has to be scripting – which can be extremely costly, in the thousands of dollars that were spent over the years to set me up and be competitive. There tends to be that mindset, well we've already spent X number of dollars on him/her so they have a job. What more do they want?"

A young woman in the early 1970s, "Emily" was determined to "get out in the workforce" as soon as possible, having been raised and educated in mainstream environments all her life. As a Braille reader and user of assistive technologies from a young age due to a congenital visual impairment, Emily became interested in the technical aspects of producing Braille and other accessible information prior to the proliferation of computer technology. She adopted a philosophy regarding employment accommodations to "ask for as little as I need and get the most out of it" as a personal challenge and to avoid presenting employers with too many demands. Emily began working during her early twenties at various summer projects for employers in the education sector before moving into full-time employment with the CNIB, where she held a series of positions that used her skills and training.

Inspired by the growing disability rights movement in the United States, "David" entered the workforce in the mid-1970s in the area of non-profit community services, where he became involved in various aspects of disability activism. As a person with a visual impairment, David collaborated with others in the blind community and helped to establish coalitions with other disability activists motivated to forge an effective discourse on disability rights in Ontario. As a young activist, David poured his energy and talent into organizational development and cultivating networks of activists to improve the social and economic integration of disabled people. Ironically, but like many other activists in North America, David caught the attention of public sector employers. Encouraged by the deinstitutionalization movement, disability activism, and international developments in disability rights, various levels of government hired many disability activists to supply expertise in the area of disability issues. David explained that being a disability activist and public servant was "not the easiest ... because the movement's goal was to lobby external aid for changes in legislation programs and policies and I, as a civil servant, was expected and actually succeeded in delivering programs to the best of my ability as a non-biased civil servant." Nonetheless, David spent the remainder of his career balancing disability and labour activism with public service.

"Ashley" got her first job as a teenager during a period of techno-logical innovation as computer technology revolutionized library sci-ence and other information technology. As a member of the Deaf com-munity, Ashley found the language and communication barriers she encountered while attending post-secondary school caused her to re-main in an entry-level job below her level of competency and ambi-tion. Ashley learned that the lack of accommodation for sign language interpretation in her workplace and in other jobs limited her ability to advance within the labour market. When a physical injury forced her to leave her job, she encountered a labour market of underpaid contract work in the non-profit sector that encouraged her to return to work with the Deaf community, where her linguistic abilities and life experiences were valued.

Cluster 3: 1980s

The largest cohort of participants (eleven) – Mary, Ruby, Lily, Olivia, Rachel, Katie, Danielle, Linda, Michael, Richard, and Charlotte – en-tered the workforce during the 1980s, a decade in which disability rights, awareness of disability issues, and rapid technological change transformed the expectations of disabled people seeking labour market integration. Most participants found work in the private sector, encour-aged by the belief that an increasing number of companies had declared themselves "equal opportunity employers" and that many federally regulated businesses were subject to the (voluntary) provisions of em-ployment equity legislation. Successive media campaigns that followed the International Year of Disabled Persons (IYDP) in 1981 were coordi-nated by service agencies and new provincial and federal departments focused on highlighting the needs of disabled people in employment matters. The prospect that technological innovation would erase most employment barriers for disabled people, particularly with the advent of computerized workstations, meant that many people who might have avoided the mainstream labour market sought greater indepen-dence in the community through paid work.

Introduced to paid work as a teenage camp counsellor in the early 1980s, "Mary" worked during summers while completing her high school and college education in technical arts. Although her parents en-couraged her to attend university, she had "had enough of the school system and trying to get accessible course material. It was just driv-ing me nuts!" As a young, blind woman, Mary perceived a wealth of opportunities in technical services where, with the help of computerized workstations, she could compete on a level playing field with her colleagues. However, just as sidewalks and transportation systems could be inaccessible, computer systems were often constructed so that people with visual impairments and physical disabilities required special software and equipment to gain access. Hired by a major cable company, she liaised with a new accessible technology company in Toronto to install and train her on software calibrated to communicate with the company's settings. While Mary was indeed able to work on a par with others in her department, she described how repeated changes in software packages used by the company frustrated her ability to do her job until one day the company switched to an entirely new (and inaccessible) computer system. Reassigned to various "make work" projects, Mary eventually found employment elsewhere in the technology sector.

"Lily" entered the workforce at the height of public awareness during the early 1980s as a post-secondary student on a placement in the public sector. As a woman living with quadriplegia, she faced "a lot of scepticism as to whether I could do all the job duties satisfactorily and [I] had to demonstrate I could do that through an unpaid position." With an obvious physical impairment and incumbent accommodations, Lily believed, "I don't think if I just applied I would have gotten the job." Determined not to let her physical impairments impede her ability to excel in her new job, Lily confronted barriers in virtually every facet of her employment. An inflexible work schedule, an unreliable parallel transit system known as Wheel-Trans, inaccessible buildings and washrooms, inaccessible computer systems and workstations, and an unaccepting workplace culture all presented potential barriers for her. Fortunately, most of Lily's needs were met through formal and informal accommodations that she believed were the result of a culture of change in the public sector, where people with disabilities were increasingly seen as competent workers.

"Ruby" got her first job in the early 1980s working as a secretary and filing clerk. As a person with a learning disability, memory problems, and fibromyalgia, she concealed her non-visible disabilities from her private sector employer for fear of losing her job. Ruby described being in a workplace culture where disability was not accepted and employees were never encouraged to come forward with accommodations should they require them. While Ruby constantly struggled with information overload, miscommunication, fatigue, and time management, she understood that her employer and co-workers believed she was "not trying hard enough" or "couldn't be that stupid" when she would make mistakes or ask for extra time. Unable to continue in her job, she returned to school but had difficulty finding subsequent employment that accommodated her disabilities.

Growing up in a residential institution, "Olivia" defied low expectations of her by others as a result of her muscular dystrophy and enrolled in a local university. Working during summers as a student to build an employment history denied her as a result of her institutionalization, she landed a job in the public sector after finishing school, despite intense competition during a time of government downsizing. Olivia described entering the workforce during a unique period, "At the time in the 1980s there was a lot of interest in trying to hire people with disability … If you had a visible disability, employers seemed welcoming and more interested in hiring you so they could show off that they were more welcoming of people with disabilities." Confident, competent and presentable, Olivia enjoyed upward advancement in her career, owing to an increasingly acceptable workplace culture, fewer physical barriers, and a greater accommodation as her mobility and dexterity needs shifted.

"Rachel" entered the workforce as a seemingly able-bodied teenager in the early 1980s working at a variety of service sector jobs. She learned the value of paid employment at an early age when her father's physical disability removed him from the workforce and her family lived below the poverty line. An intelligent young woman, she attended university and completed a series of internships that qualified her to work in a traditionally male-dominated field. Determined to succeed, she devoted all her mental and physical energy to advancing herself within her field, taking on increasingly responsible and stressful jobs that caused long-standing mental health issues to escalate. Aware of her employer's duty to accommodate but afraid of jeopardizing her career, Rachel declined to disclose her disability to her employer until she reached a point of climax and was eventually fired. Forced to change career directions, Rachel returned to school and pursued various jobs in the non-profit sector, where her mental health issues were accommodated.

"Katie" grew up in "a working-class family" during the 1980s, always cognizant of the need to "work hard." As a result, she always held multiple jobs as a teenager and aspired to become a working professional. Shortly into her freshman year in university, Katie sustained a spinal cord injury that "messed up my goals as to what I was going to do and how." During rehabilitation, where she learned to live with paraple-gia, Katie was "approached to do some modelling and commercials be-cause there was an awareness wave going on." The experience sparked a new passion that led her to return to school and begin a career in the media industry. Despite infrastructural barriers that occasionally lim-ited her access within various workplaces, such as accessible parking, ramps, and accessible doors, Katie found her disability rarely presented an obstacle to her career goals and enabled her to pursue most of her personal and professional objectives.

"Danielle" started working in the early 1980s in the financial services industry. She described having always worked while living with chron-ic depression. "I was always the employee that had the most sick time. I always lost one or two days a month to depression." As a professional with experience in leading companies, she confidently advanced herself in various management positions until she was finally diagnosed with a central nervous system disorder. Danielle described a series of events that led her employer to fire her and deny compensation. Confident that she was the victim of discrimination on the basis of disability, Danielle lodged a complaint with the relevant Human Rights Commission. De-spite ample evidence in her favour, she suffered a lengthy and ultimate-ly under-compensated process while her disability progressed. Unable to earn much beyond her limited welfare benefits, Danielle pursued self-employment where her disability could be self-accommodated.

"Linda" grew up in a family environment where she was taught to have low expectations of her ability to be productive and independent as a result of her cerebral palsy and learning disability. Linda described how "significant people" in her life taught her to feel "inadequate" about her prospects in the workforce. Despite her upbringing and dis-satisfied with the prospect of living on welfare benefits, Linda attended university, where she earned a degree in social services. Upon gradu-ation, however, Linda encountered multiple barriers in the workforce that forced her to hold a series of paid and unpaid jobs. She explained how her learning disability frustrated her capacity to maintain employ-ment. In one example, where she was being trained in the banking in-dustry, she recalled "I just couldn't learn fast enough. It depends on the patience level of the person teaching me. If a person is frustrated and angry, nobody is going to take in what they're learning. It made my learning disability more heightened when I knew they were frustrat-ed." As a result, Linda found herself working in the non-profit sector, where she felt workplace cultures are often more accepting.

"Michael" found work in the service industry as a teenager fresh out of high school in the early 1980s as he saved money to attend university. During university he held a number of jobs, building an employment history while living with "the experience of schizophrenia." While he originally refrained from seeking accommodations in various jobs he has held, Michael has found that he is more willing to disclose his mental health issues since his hospitalization and recovery. Despite qualifying for work in a variety of industries, Michael found that the necessity for flexibility in employment scheduling and work organization was more readily acceptable in the mental health field than other areas of the private sector. One entry-level position he held in the private sector while completing a vocational rehabilitation program following his recovery demanded long hours and repetitive tasks that he described as "intense" and ultimately inappropriate. While numerous applications in the private sector failed at the interview stage, which he suspected was due to his mental health issue, Michael found a satisfying (albeit underpaid) career in the non-profit sector.

"Richard" entered the workforce in the mid-1980s as an able-bodied teenager delivering pizzas in his neighbourhood before attending college to work in the Information Technology sector. As part of his post-secondary training, Richard held several internships in the public and private sectors as he accumulated experience and contacts to build his work history. As an adult, however, Richard experienced the onset of muscular dystrophy and he eventually required the full-time use of a wheelchair. While never directly encountering discrimination, Richard believed that his disability prevented him from obtaining employment. He described how, since his disability became visible, he would go to many interviews but rarely "second interviews," indicating to him that the visibility of his disability removed him from the competition. In the workplace where he eventually found employment, Richard noted that, despite thousands of employees, he was the only person who used a wheelchair.

"Charlotte" began working in the retail sector during the late 1980s to save money in order to attend university. Born with cerebral palsy that limited her mobility, she earned a university degree and sought work in the social services sector. Despite having "all the good qualities of a good employee" and with a personal strategy not to go to an employer with a "list of demands" outlining accommodation needs, Charlotte encountered difficulty securing a full-time position, finding only contract work. Regardless of her difficulties, Charlotte stated, "Thank goodness I was born when I was because if I was born earlier my life could have been very different ... I'm not saying there's not a struggle now, but that was very limited."

Cluster 4: 1990s–2000s

Four participants – Sarah, Marge, Leanne, and Thomas – entered the labour market during the 1990s and 2000s when disability rights and growing awareness of disability issues were met by enormous changes in the labour market, government restructuring, and accessible infrastructure. People with disabilities entering the workforce during this period encountered unprecedented levels of awareness about disability, owing partly to years of awareness campaigns designed to sensitize employers and the broader public. Employment equity and "equal opportunity" provisions in various sectors of the economy coupled with the rise in access to assistive technologies and duty-to-accommodate jurisprudence created pathways into an otherwise inaccessible job market. However, widespread government restructuring at the federal and provincial levels and regulations guiding the construction of accessible environments resulted in shifting access to employment for people with mental and physical disabilities as some existing barriers receded and new barriers emerged.

"Sarah" started working in the early 1990s in the social services sector after completing vocational rehabilitation programs that prepared her to work in the mainstream labour market. As a person living with cerebral palsy, Sarah was supplied with and trained on various assistive devices provided through benefit programs that enabled her to function effectively in the competitive workforce. Despite her university education, Sarah encountered barriers in the application and interview process. "When I was searching for jobs I would call the organization before I actually started working on a résumé and cover letter to send off to them and find out if the building was even wheelchair accessible and I found that ... in most cases the buildings are not." Like other job applicants with visible disabilities, Sarah found herself going to many interviews but very few job offers. Once she finally landed a job in the non-profit sector, she found that she needed to advocate for herself. "When I first came on the job nothing was accessible. There was just an elevator and a lift to get in the building. When you go into the office space a lot of improvements needed to be made and I was very vocal about that."

"Marge" began working in the 1990s in a variety of industrial and service sector jobs. Although she possessed a university degree, Marge was able to find employment in entry level positions and was forced to leave when managers became frustrated with the manner in which she performed her work. As a person living with an acquired brain injury, Marge felt that her employers "tend to forget the limitations because my disability is non-visible," which caused them to become frustrated and angry when she did not work as expected.

"Leanne" got her first job as a teenager in the service industry in order to save money for university. As a young Deaf woman, Leanne discovered a passion for teaching others in the Deaf community and alternated between post-secondary education and employment in the public sector. Despite always achieving a "good reputation" in each workplace, Leanne described a litany of barriers revolving around employers' attitudes about her ability and competency level. She described how general bias against her method of communication was often augmented by the fact that most employers were not willing to pay for sign language interpretation services. As a result, Leanne found herself working with the Deaf community and in self-employment, where she could manage her own accommodations.

"Thomas" began his working life in the early 2000s in the service industry, where he had consistently worked while attending post-secondary school. As a young man with Autism Spectrum Disorder at the beginning of his employment history, Thomas demonstrated an adept awareness of the human rights protections available to him but admitted he would disclose his disability to an employer only if he felt "safe enough" to do so. Never having been accommodated or requesting accommodation, Thomas believed that his disability was a personal matter and that he had become very good at masking or hiding his condition "when necessary."

Notes

Introduction

1 Fiona Kumari Campbell, "Legislating Disability: Negative Ontologies and the Government of Legal Identities," in *Foucault, Governmentality, and Critical Disability Theory*, ed. Shelley Tremain (Ann Arbor: University of Michigan Press, 2005), 108–32.

2 Everett Hughes, "Dilemmas and Contradictions of Status," *American Journal of Sociology* 50:5 (1945): 353–9.

3 Douglas Baynton, "Disability and the Justification of Inequality in American History," in *The New Disability History: American Perspectives*, ed. Lauri Umansky and Paul Longmore (New York: New York University Press, 2000), 30.

4 Catherine Kudlick, "Disability History: Why We Need Another 'Other,'" *American Historical Review* 108:3 (2003): 768.

5 Sally Chivers, "Barrier by Barrier: The Canadian Disability Movement and the Fight for Equal Rights," in *Group Politics and Social Movements in Canada*, ed. Miriam Catherine Smith (Peterborough, ON: Broadview Press, 2008), 312.

6 Ava Baron and Eileen Boris demonstrate how disability can be integrated into historical studies of the working-class and of working bodies, arguing that a critical analysis of disability can reveal new insights about social roles and structures such as gender, race, and sexuality which surround corporeal and signified worker bodies; Baron and Boris, "'The Body' As a Useful Category for Working-Class History," *Labor: Studies in Working-Class History of the Americas* 4:2 (2007): 23–43. See also Edward Slavishak, *Bodies of Work: Civic Display and Labor in Industrial Pittsburgh* (Durham, NC, and London: Duke University Press, 2008); Daniel Bender, *Sweated*

Work, Weak Bodies: Anti-Sweatshop Campaigns and Languages of Labour (New Brunswick, NJ: Rutgers University Press, 2004); Janet Zandy, *Hands: Physical Labour, Class, and Cultural Work* (New Brunswick, N.J.: Rutgers University Press, 2004); Rosemarie Garland-Thomson, "Aberrant Bodies: Making the Corporeal Other in Nineteenth- and Twentieth-Century American Cultural Representations" (PhD diss., Brandeis University, 1993); Sarah Rose, "'Crippled' Hands: Disability and Labor in Working-Class History," *Labor: Studies in Working-Class History of the Americas* 2:1 (2005): 27–54.

7 Kudlick, "Why We Need Another 'Other,'" 766. Recent contributions to the historiography of the body, including Paul Lawrie's examination of the proletarianization of African-American workers during the onset of industrialization, further our understanding of the body as a category of analysis during this period; Lawrie, "'To Make the Negro Anew': The African American Worker in the Progressive Imagination, 1896–1928" (PhD diss., University of Toronto, 2011. See also Irina Metzler, *A Social History of Disability in the Middle Ages: Cultural Considerations of Physical Impairment* (London: Routledge, 2013).

8 Colin Barnes and Geof Mercer, "Disability, Work, and Welfare: Challenging the Social Exclusion of Disabled People," *Work, Employment & Society* 19:3 (2005): 527, accessed 16 August 2013, doi: 10.1177/0950017005055669; Kudlick, "Why We Need Another 'Other,'" 766.

9 Diane Driedger provided a landmark account in *The Last Civil Rights Movement*, which highlighted the contributions Canadians made to the development of the international disability rights movement through the organization Disabled Peoples International. Other accounts, such as *In Pursuit of Equality Participation* by Aldred Neufeldt and Henry Enns, provide a historical recounting of the development of organized disability activism in Canada based on firsthand experience. Works such as *Absent Citizens* by Michael Prince are written in the tradition of political history by documenting how disability rights influenced the course of Canadian policy development. See Neufeldt and Enns, eds, *In Pursuit of Equal Participation: Canada and Disability at Home and Abroad* (Concord, ON: Captus Press, 2003); Prince, *Absent Citizens: Disability Politics and Policy in Canada* (Toronto: University of Toronto Press, 2009); Diane Driedger, *The Last Civil Rights Movement: Disabled People's International* (New York: St Martin's Press, 1989); Deborah Stienstra and Aileen Wight-Felske with Colleen Watters, *Making Equality: History of Advocacy and Persons with Disabilities in Canada* (Concord, ON: Captus Press, 2003); Marcia Rioux and Michael Prince, "The Canadian Political Landscape of Disability:

Policy Perspectives, Social Status, Interest Groups and the Rights Move-
ment," in *Federalism, Democracy and Disability Policy in Canada*, ed. Allan
Puttee (Montreal: McGill-Queen's University Press, 2002), 11–28; Marcia
Rioux and Fraser Valentine, "Does Theory Matter: Exploring the Nexus
Between Disability, Human Rights, and Public Policy," in *Critical Disability
Theory: Essays in Philosophy, Politics, Policy and Law*, ed. Diane Pothier
and Robert Devlin (Vancouver: UBC Press, 2006), 47–69.

10 Christine Kelly, "Towards Renewed Descriptions of Canadian Disability
   Movements: Disability Activism Outside of the Non-Profit Sector,"
   Canadian Journal of Disability Studies, 2:1 (2013), accessed 17 August 2013,
   http://cjds.uwaterloo.ca/index.php/cjds/article/view/68.

11 See Donna Lero, Carolyn Pletsch, and Margo Hilbrecht, "Introduction
   to the Special Issue on Disability and Work: Toward Re-conceptualizing
   the 'Burden' of Disability," *Disability Studies Quarterly*, 32:3 (2012), ac-
   cessed 16 August 2013, http://dsq-sds.org/article/view/3275/3108;
   Tim Weinkauf, "Employer Attitudes and the Employment of People with
   Disabilities: An Exploratory Study Using the Ambivalence Amplification
   Theory," (PhD diss., University of Alberta, 2010); Robert Storey, "'Their
   Only Power Was Moral': The Injured Workers' Movement in Toronto,
   1970–1985," *Histoire Sociale / Social History* 41:81 (2009): 99–131; Robert
   Storey, "Social Assistance or a Worker's Right: Workmen's Compensation
   and the Struggle of Injured Workers in Ontario, 1970–1985," *Studies in
   Political Economy* 78 (2006): 67–91; Mary Grimley Mason, *Working Against
   Odds: Stories of Disabled Women's Work Lives* (Boston: Northeastern University
   Press, 2004); Sarah Rose, "No Right to Be Idle: The Invention of Disability,
   1850–1930" (PhD diss., University of Illinois at Chicago, 2008).

12 Derek Hum and Wayne Simpson, "Canadians with Disabilities and the
   Labour Market," *Canadian Public Policy* 22:3 (1996): 287.

13 Rioux and Prince, "The Canadian Political Landscape of Disability," 20;
   Ted Wannell and Nathalie Caron, "A Look at Employment-Equity Groups
   Among Recent Postsecondary Graduates: Visible Minorities, Aboriginal
   Peoples and the Activity Limited," *Business and Labour Market Analysis
   Group* 69 (Statistics Canada: 1992).

14 Mary Bunch and Cameron Crawford, "Persons with Disabilities: Literature
   Review of the Factors Affecting Employment and Labour Force Transitions,"
   Applied Research Branch Strategic Policy, Human Resources Development
   Canada (1998); Rioux and Prince, "The Canadian Political Landscape
   of Disability."

15 Ravi Malhotra, "The Politics of the Disability Rights Movements," *New
   Politics* 8:3 (Summer 2001), accessed 17 August 2013, http://nova.wpunj

.edu/newpolitics/issue31/malhot31.htm; Sarah Armstrong, "Disability Advocacy in the Charter Era," *Journal of Law & Equality* 2:1 (Spring 2003): 33–91; Gail Fawcett, "Living with Disability in Canada: An Economic Portrait," Human Resources Development Canada, 1996; Roeher Institute, "Factors Affecting the Employment of People with Disabilities: A Review of the Literature," Canadian Bankers Association, 2001.

16 Cameron Crawford, "Looking into Poverty: Income Sources of Poor People with Disabilities in Canada," Council of Canadians with Disabilities, Institute for Research on Inclusion and Society, 2013, available at http://www.ccdonline.ca/media/socialpolicy/Income%20Sources%20Report%20IRIS%20CCD.pdf.

17 Hum and Simpson, "Canadians with Disabilities and the Labour Market"; Emile Tompa et al., "Precarious Employment and People with Disabilities," in *Precarious Employment: Understanding Labour Market Insecurity in Canada*, ed. Leah Vosko (Montreal: McGill-Queen's University Press, 2006), 113.

18 Crawford, "Looking into Poverty."

19 Ibid.; Diane Galarneau & Marian Radelescu, "Employment Among the Disabled," Statistics Canada, *Perspectives* (May 2009); Roeher Institute, "On Target? Canada's Employment-Related Programs for Persons with Disabilities," 1993; Statistics Canada, *Adults with Disabilities, their Employment and Education Characteristics* (Ottawa: Queen's Printer, 1993); Statistics Canada, *Persons with Disabilities in Canada: 1986 Statistics and Bibliography*, 1993.

20 Cameron Crawford, *How Persons with Disabilities Are Faring in the Canadian Labour Market and Economy: Considerations for Ongoing Monitoring and Reporting* (Toronto: Roeher Institute, 1998); Gary Annable, "Unemployment Statistics: Let's Be Honest," *Ability & Enterprise* 6:1 (March 1993).

21 Gail Fawcett, *Bringing Down the Barriers: The Labour Market and Women with Disabilities in Ontario* (Canadian Council on Social Development, 2000), 4–18.

22 Marta Russell, *Beyond Ramps: Disability at the End of the Social Contract: A Warning from an Uppity Crip* (Monroe, ME: Common Courage Press, 1998), 61.

23 Frank Overboe, "'Difference in Itself': Validating Disabled People's Lived Experience," in *Rethinking Normalcy: A Disability Studies Reader*, ed. Tanya Titchkosky and Rod Michalko (Toronto: Canadian Scholars' Press, 2009), 82.

24 Peter Blanck, "Right to Live in the World: Disability Yesterday, Today, and Tomorrow: The Jacobus tenBroek Law Symposium," *Texas Journal on Civil*

Liberties & Civil Rights 13 (2007): 370; Barbara Wolfe and Robert Haveman, "Trends in the Prevalence of Work Disability from 1962 to 1984 and Their Correlates," *Milbank Quarterly* 68:1 (1990): 74; Ian Morris, "Technology and Disabled People: A Global View" in *The Future of Work for Disabled People: Employment and the New Technology*, ed. American Foundation for the Blind (Washington, DC: President's Committee on the Employment of the Handicapped, 1986), 12.

25 World Health Organization, *International Classification of Impairments, Disabilities, and Handicaps* (Geneva: General Assembly, 1980); Jerome Bickenbach, *Physical Disability and Social Policy* (Toronto: University of Toronto Press, 1993), 59–60.

26 Mary Johnson, *Make Them Go Away: Clint Eastwood, Christopher Reeve and the Case Against Disability Rights* (Louisville, KY: Advocado Press, 2003), 54.

27 Coalition of Provincial Organizations of the Handicapped (COPOH), *Improving Employment Opportunities for Disabled Canadians* (28 September 1983): 1.

28 Colin Barnes, *Disabling Imagery and the Media: An Exploration of the Principles for Media Representations of Disabled People* (Halifax, UK: Ryburn Publishing Services, 1992): 20, available at http://disability-studies.leeds.ac.uk/files/library/Barnes-disabling-imagery.pdf.

29 Disability studies scholars argue that the medicalization of disability, or "medical model," reflected a broader "individual model" of disability. See Tom Shakespeare, *Disability Rights and Wrongs* (New York: Routledge, 2006), 32; Michael Oliver, "The Social Model in Context," in *Rethinking Normalcy: A Disability Studies Reader*, ed. Tanya Titchkosky and Rod Michalko (Toronto: Canadian Scholars' Press, 2009).

30 Metzler, *A Social History of Disability*, 4.

31 Wolfe and Haveman, "Trends in the Prevalence of Work Disability," 57.

32 James Charlton, *Nothing About Us Without Us* (Berkeley, CA: University of California Press, 1998).

33 Snowball sampling techniques involve using existing study participants to recruit additional participants through personal networks.

1 Disability, Activism, Work, and Identity

1 Pat McKee, *Look Beyond*, © 1981 by Greenview Publishing; song, written and recorded by Pat McKee and arranged by John Hudson.

2 Cameron Crawford, "Disabling Poverty and Enabling Citizenship: Understanding the Poverty and Exclusion of Canadians with Disabilities" paper, Researched and written for the Community–University Research Alliance

between the CCD and University of Victoria,2010, accessed 22 May
2012, http://www.ccdonline.ca/en/socialpolicy/poverty-citizenship/
demographic-profile/understanding-poverty-exclusion; World Health
Organization and World Bank, *World Report on Disability* (Geneva, 2011).

3 "Robert," interview with author, 20 June 2011.

4 J.W. Budd, *The Thought of Work* (Ithaca, NY: ILR Press, 2011), 143.

5 Ibid., 90–102.

6 Ibid.

7 N. Watson, "Well, I Know This Is Going to Sound Very Strange to You, but
I Don't See Myself as a Disabled Person: Identity and Disability," *Disability
& Society* 17:5 (2002): 509.

8 Ibid.

9 Marta Russell, "What Disability Civil Rights Cannot Do: Employment
and Political Economy," *Disability & Society* 17:2 (2002): 128.

10 Slavishak, *Bodies of Work* (2008); Zandy, *Hands*, 2004; Sandra Bartrip,
The Wounded Soldiers of Industry: Industrial Compensation Policy, 1833–1897
(Cambridge: Cambridge University Press, 1983).

11 Paul Longmore, "Conspicuous Contribution and American Cultural
Dilemmas: Telethon Rituals of Cleansing and Renewal," in *Rethinking
Normalcy: A Disability Studies Reader*, ed. Rod Michalko and Tanya
Titchkosky (Toronto: Canadian Scholars' Press, 2009): 137–57.

12 Kathy Charmaz, "The Body, Identity, and Self: Adapting to Impairment,"
Sociological Quarterly 36:4 (1995): 657–80; Tanya Titchkosky, *Disability, Self,
and Society* (Toronto: University of Toronto Press, 2003).

13 C.J. Gill, "Four Types of Integration in Disability Identity Development,"
Journal of Vocational Rehabilitation 9:1 (1997): 39–46; S.F. Gilson, A. Tusler, and
C.J. Gill, "Ethnographic Research in Disability Identity: Self-Determination
and Community," *Journal of Vocational Rehabilitation* 9:1 (1997): 7–17.

14 Michelle Driedger, Valorie Crooks, and David Bennett, "Engaging in
the Disablement Process Over Space and Time: Narratives of Persons with
Multiple Sclerosis in Ottawa, Canada," *Canadian Geographer* 48:2 (2004):
119–36.; Vicki Schultz, "Life's Work," *Columbia Law Review* 100:7 (2000).

15 Karen Hirsch "From Colonization to Civil Rights: People with Disabilities
and Gainful Employment," in *Employment, Disability, and the Americans
with Disabilities Act: Issues in Law, Public Policy and Research*, ed. Peter
Blanck (Evanston, IL: North Western University Press, 2000), 429.

16 Following Research Ethics Board approval, thirty people with disabilities
were recruited through various advertisements and word of mouth to
conduct semi-structured oral interviews about how work and employment
shaped their lived experience of disability. Interview transcripts were

processed and coded using NVivo 9.0 and participants were given full control over the content of their testimonies. See the Appendix for a more detailed explanation of the oral history component used in this study.

17 See chapter 2.

18 "William," interview with author, 19 December 2011.

19 "Grace," interview with author, 28 July 2011.

20 "Grace."

21 "William."

22 "William."

23 "William."

24 See chapters 5 and 6.

25 "William."

26 "Grace."

27 "Nathan," interview with author, 16 June 2011.

28 "Nathan."

29 "Nathan."

30 "Michael," interview with author, 27 July 2011.

31 "Michael."

32 "Michael."

33 "Michael."

34 "Nathan."

35 See chapter 5.

36 "Mary," interview with author, 22 June 2011.

37 See chapter 6.

38 "Danielle," interview with author, 30 June 2011.

39 "Danielle."

40 "Danielle."

41 Microsoft Corporation, "A History of Windows," accessed 21 June 2013, http://windows.microsoft.com/en-CA/windows/history. Although Microsoft had developed and released Windows 1.0 in 1985 as an extension of DOS, it was not until the introduction of Windows 3.1 in May 1992, with add-on features such as Windows for Workgroups that enabled businesses to use key networking features, that a graphic user interface achieved widespread popularity as a viable alternative to the text-based DOS. Unprecedented success followed from the introduction of Windows 95 in August 1995, which was incompatible on DOS-only computers, and it signalled the rapid decline of accessible technologies on a primarily text-based operating system.

42 David Lepofsky, *The Disability Network* (Toronto: CBC Television, 1 February 1997).

43 Irwin Kaplan and Norman Hammond, "Projects with Industry: The Concept and the Realization," *American Rehabilitation* (December 1982).
44 "Mary."
44 "Mary."
45 "Mary."

2 Family Advocacy and Economic Integration

1 "Charlotte," interview with author, 27 June 2011.
2 "Grace," interview with author, 28 July 2011.
3 Melanie Panitch, *Disability, Mothers, and Organization: Accidental Activists* (New York: Routledge, 2008), 3; March of Dimes Canada, "Ellen Fairclough: Chief Marching Mother," accessed 4 April 2013, http://www.marchofdimes .ca/EN/AboutUs/history/Pages/EllenFairclough.aspx.
4 The March of Dimes was initially an American organization whose "Marching Mothers" campaigns engaged other charitable organizations. The Ontario-based Canadian Foundation for Poliomyelitis participated in the campaign but retained their name until 1973, when it was changed to the Ontario March of Dimes (OMOD). By 2006 the OMOD had created March of Dimes Canada to reflect the fact that its services had expanded beyond the province of Ontario. March of Dimes Canada, "Who We Are," accessed 25 September 2012, http://www.marchofdimes.ca/EN/ AboutUs/about%20modc/Pages/WhoWeAre.aspx.
5 March of Dimes Canada, "Our History," accessed 21 June 2013, http:// www.marchofdimes.ca/EN/AboutUs/history/Pages/marchingmothers .aspx.
6 Stienstra and Wight-Felske with Watters, *Making Equality*, 3.
7 Paul Longmore, "Conspicuous Contribution and American Cultural Dilemmas: Telethon Rituals of Cleansing and Renewal," in *Rethinking Normalcy: A Disability Studies Reader*, ed. Tanya Titchkosky and Rod Michalko (Toronto: Canadian Scholars' Press, 2009), 147.
8 Tracy Odell, "Not Your Average Childhood: Lived Experience of Children with Physical Disabilities Raised in Bloorview Hospital, Home and School from 1960 to 1989," *Disability & Society* 26:1 (2011): 60. For further discussion of the relationship between medical supports and discourses of denied or relinquished citizenship see Esther Ignagni, "Disabled Young People, Support and the Dialogical Work of Accomplishing Citizenship" (PhD diss., University of Toronto, 2011).
9 Panitch, *Accidental Activists*, 2.

10 "Sofia," interview with author, 12 January 2012.
11 "William," interview with author, 19 December 2011.
12 Pierre Berton, "What's Wrong at Orillia: Out of Sight – Out of Mind," *Toronto Star*, 6 January 1960; Community Living Ontario (CLO), "Betty Anglin Was 'Ahead of Her Time,'" accessed 30 September 2012, http://www.communitylivingontario.ca/news-events/news/betty-anglin-was-ahead-her-time.
13 CLO, "Betty Anglin."
14 *Willowbrook: The Last Great Disgrace*, directed by Albert Primo (New York: WABC-TV, 1972), VHS.
15 CLO, "Betty Anglin."
16 City of Toronto Archives (TA), SC 607, File 36, Report, Toronto Association for Community Living, 2000.
17 Archives of Ontario (AO), RG 7-148, Box B217563, File "Professional Outreach," Paper, Ontario Federation for the Physically Handicapped, *Affirmative Action: Public Education: 7th Annual General Meeting and Conference*, 23 October 1978. The OFPH was subsequently established as a federation of twenty-six local, provincial, and federal organizations. Although it included members from consumer and rehabilitation groups, its president in 1981 was Lee Rullman of the Ontario March of Dimes and it appeared that rehabilitation groups dominated the organization.
18 "Michael," interview with author, 27 July 2011.
19 "Grace."
20 "William."
21 Panitch, *Accidental Activists*, 2.
22 Ibid.
23 Ibid.
24 *Lorenzo's Oil*, directed by George Miller (Universal City, CA: Universal Pictures, 1992), DVD.
25 Donna Thomson, *Four Walls of My Freedom* (Toronto: McArthur, 2010), 130.
26 *Thursday's Child*, produced by Community Living Society (Vancouver, BC: Yaletown Productions, 1985), VHS.
27 *Hurry Tomorrow*, directed by Richard Cohen (Los Angeles, CA: Halfway House Partnership, 1975), DVD.
28 LAC, RG 29, Box 238, File 4302-3-9, Film Proposal, 21 July 1983; Community Living Society, "Woodlands Parents' Group, CLS History," accessed 9 October 2012, http://www.communitylivingsociety.ca/about-us/history/woodlands-parents-group.
29 "Woodlands Parents' Group."

30 Ibid.
31 Patricia Sealy and Paul Whitehead, "Forty Years of Deinstitutionalization of Psychiatric Services in Canada: An Empirical Assessment," *Canadian Journal of Psychiatry* 49:4 (2004): 251; AO, RG 7-148, Box B217563, File "Publications General 1981–82," Article, Canadian Association of Rehabilitation Personnel, "The Case for and against the Closing of the Lakeshore Psychiatric Hospital," *Chronicle* 1:1 (1979).
32 Steven Marwaha and Sonia Johnson, "Schizophrenia and Employment," *Social Psychiatry and Psychiatric Epidemiology* 39:5 (2004): 337–49.
33 *Moving On*, Season 1, Episode 14, first broadcast 20 June 1998 by the Canadian Broadcasting Corporation.
34 Panitch, *Accidental Activists*, 5.
35 Thomson, *Four Walls of My Freedom*, 152.
36 AO, RG 7-148, Box B217564, File "Agencies, Councils and Committees," Memo, Handicapped Employment Program, "Goodwill Demonstration Housing/Employment," 14 November 1980.
37 Aldred Neufeldt, "Growth and Evolution of Disability Advocacy in Canada," in *Making Equality: History of Advocacy and Persons with Disabilities in Canada*, ed. Deborah Stienstra and Aileen Wight-Felske with Colleen Watters (Concord, ON: Captus Press, 2003), 14–33.
38 Ibid.
39 Shakespeare, *Disability Rights and Wrongs*, 165. For further discussion on the debates between the social and medical models of disability see Alison Sheldon et al., "Disability Rights and Wrongs?" *Disability & Society* 22:2 (2007): 209–32.
40 Susan Peters, "From Charity to Equality: Canadians with Disabilities Take Their Rightful Place in Canada's Constitution," in *Making Equality: History of Advocacy and Persons with Disabilities in Canada*, ed. Deborah Stienstra and Aileen Wight-Felske with Colleen Watters (Concord, ON: Captus Press, 2003), 24.
41 M. Russell, *Beyond Ramps*, 86.
42 AO, RG 7-149, Box B363026, File "Publications," Article, Muscular Dystrophy Association, "Audience Pledges $31M to Combat Muscular Dystrophy," *Reporter* (Summer/Fall 1980).For further discussion on the representation of disability in telethons see Longmore, "Conspicuous Contribution," 2009; see also Beth Haller, *Representing Disability in an Ableist World: Essays on Mass Media* (Louisville, KY: Advocado Press, 2010).
43 Barbara Turnbull, *Looking in the Mirror* (Toronto: Toronto Star, 1997), 46.
44 Ibid.

45 Ibid.

46 United Nations, *Declaration on the Rights of Mentally Retarded Persons* (Geneva: General Assembly, 20 December 1971), Resolution 2856; United Nations, *Declaration on the Rights of Disabled Persons* (Geneva: General Assembly, 9 December 1975), Resolution 3447.

47 United Nations, World Programme of Action Concerning Disabled Persons (Geneva: General Assembly, 3 December 1982), Resolution 37/52.

48 LAC, RG-29, Box 238, File 4302-3-9, Film Proposal, 21 July 1983.

49 Woodlands Parents' Group, c.1984.

50 *The Disability Myth: Segregation*, directed by Alan Aylward (Toronto: Lauron Productions, 1981), 16 mm film.

51 AO, RG 7-148, Box B100558, File "Current Issues," Newsletter, OMOD, *Advocate* (July/August 1981).

52 *The Littlest Hobo*, Episode 2, "Boys on Wheels," first broadcast in 1979 by Canadian Television Networks.

53 Barnes and Mercer, "Disability Work and Welfare," 536; Barnes, *Disabling Imagery*, 451; Tom Shakespeare, "Cultural Representation of Disabled People: Dustbins for Disavowal?" *Disability & Society* 9:3 (1994): 292–3; Mark Priestly, "Constructions and Creations: Idealism, Materialism and Disability Theory," *Disability & Society*, 13:1 (1998): 87.

54 Archives of Manitoba (MA), Council of Canadians with Disabilities Fonds (hereafter CCD Fonds), Box P5365, File 19, Paper, Coalition of Provincial Organizations of the Handicapped (hereafter COPOH), "COPOH Prospective Why/Whereto," 1978.

55 Kathy Martinez, "Independent Living in the US and Canada," Independent Living Institute, 2003.

56 Chivers, "Barrier by Barrier," 329–30.

57 M. Russell, *Beyond Ramps*, 86; Parin Dossa, "Creating Alternative and Demedicalized Spaces: Testimonial Narrative on Disability, Culture, and Racialization," *Journal of International Women's Studies* 9:3 (2008): 95; Tania Burchardt, "Capabilities and Disability: The Capabilities Framework and the Social Model of Disability," *Disability & Society* 19:7 (2004): 737.

58 Neil Matheson, *Daddy Bent-Legs: The 40-Year-Old Musings of a Physically Disabled Man, Husband, and Father* (Winnipeg: WordAlive Press, 2009), 91.

59 Turnbull, *Looking in the Mirror*, 46; Graeme McCreath, *The Politics of Blindness* (Vancouver: Granville Island Publishing, 2011), 111.

60 Fred Pelka, *What We Have Done: An Oral History of the Disability Rights Movement* (Cambridge: University of Massachusetts Press, 2012), 324.

61 MA, CCD Fonds, Box P5364, File 9, Paper, Job Corps Proposal, 1979.

3 Rehabilitation, Awareness Campaigns, and Employability

1 Harold Remmes, *A Consumer's Guide to Organizing the Handicapped* (Newton, MA: Massachusetts Council of Organizations of the Handicapped, 1976), 12.
2 Bickenbach, *Physical Disability and Social Policy*, 105; Cameron and Valentine, "Comparing Policy Making," 95.
3 Paul Wright, "The Status of Disabled Persons in Canada: A Historical Analysis of the Evolution of Social Policy to Develop Effective Change Strategies Directed toward Achieving Equality" (MA thesis, Carleton University, 1990), 78.
4 Pelka, *What We Have Done*, 131.
5 Neufeldt, "Growth and Evolution of Disability Advocacy in Canada," 19; War Amps of Canada, "The War Amps History," accessed 24 October 2012, http://www.waramps.ca/history.html. For more information on the history of how fraternal associations worked to improve the lives of people with disabilities see Dustin Galer, "A Friend in Need or a Business Indeed: Disabled Bodies and Fraternalism in Victorian Ontario," *Labour / Le Travail* 66:1 (Fall 2010): 9–36.
6 Serge Durflinger, *Veterans with a Vision: Canada's War Blinded in Peace and War* (Vancouver: UBC Press, 2010), 250.
7 Mary Tremblay, Audrey Campbell, and Geoffrey Hudson, "When Elevators Were for Pianos: An Oral History Account of the Civilian Experience of Using Wheelchairs in Canadian Society: The First Twenty-Five Years: 1945–1970," *Disability & Society* 20:2 (2005): 103–16.
8 Blanck, *Right to Live in the World*, 375–6. For more information on the relationship between the Great War and disability see Nic Clarke, "'You Will Not Be Going To This War': The Rejected Volunteers of the First Contingent of the Canadian Expeditionary Force," *First World War Studies* 1:2 (2010): 161–83.
9 Tremblay, Campbell, and Hudson, "When Elevators Were for Pianos," 108.
10 Ibid.
11 Blanck, *Right to Live in the World*, 316; Cyril Greenland, *Vision Canada: The Unmet Needs of Blind Canadians* (Toronto: Canadian National Institute for the Blind, 1976), 3.
12 McCreath, *The Politics of Blindness*, 16.
13 Tremblay, Campbell, and Hudson, "When Elevators Were For Pianos," 107.
14 Michael Prince, "Designing Disability Policy in Canada," in *Federalism, Democracy and Disability Policy in Canada*, ed. Alan Puttee (Montreal: Institute of Intergovernmental Relations, 2002), 31–43; Peter Graefe and

Mario Levesque, "Accountability and Funding as Impediments to Social Policy Innovation: Lessons from the Labour Market Agreements for Persons with Disabilities," *Canadian Public Policy* 36:1 (2010): 50; Michele Campolieti and John Lavis, "Disability Expenditures in Canada, 1970–1996: Trends, Reform Efforts and a Path for the Future," *Canadian Public Policy* 26:2 (2000): 241–64.

15 Campolieti and Lavis, "Disability Expenditures in Canada," 246.
16 Tremblay, Campbell, and Hudson, "When Elevators Were for Pianos," 107.
17 Carey, Allison. *On the Margins of Citizenship: Intellectual Disability and Civil Rights in Twentieth-Century America* (Philadelphia: Temple University Press, 2009), 95.
18 Ibid.
19 War Amps, "The War Amps of Canada – Key Tag Service," accessed 29 October 2012, http://www.waramps.ca/keytags.html.
20 John Rae, Anne Musgrave, and Mike Yale, *Selfhelp and Government Commitment: A Call to Action. A Report from the Project Developing Alternative Service Models* (Toronto: Blind Organization of Ontario with Self-Help Tactics [BOOST], 1980), 34; Greenland, *Vision Canada*, 44.
21 McCreath, *The Politics of Blindness*, 27.
22 "Robert," interview with author, 20 June 2011.
23 "Dan," interview with author, 10 June 2011; "Grace," interview with author, 28 July 2011.
24 Euclid Herie, *Journey to Independence: Blindness – The Canadian Story* (Toronto: Dundurn Press, 2005), 115–16; figures based on calculations of sighted (S) and blind (B) workforce ratios reported by Euclid Herie (for 1968: 275[B], 2100[S]) and BOOST (for 1975: 125[B], 650[S]). See also Greenland, *Vision Canada*; BOOST, *The Third Eye* 11 (10 February 1977); Durflinger, *Veterans with a Vision*, 45.
25 Rae, Musgrave, and Yale, *Selfhelp and Government Commitment*, 214.
26 Handicapped Communications Society, *The Spokesman* (9 September 1979).
27 MA, CCD Fonds, Box P5365, File 19, Paper, Canadian Rehabilitation Council for the Disabled, Paper, "COPOH Prospective Why/Whereto," 1978.
28 Tremblay, Campbell, and Hudson, "When Elevators Were for Pianos," 103–16.
29 Ibid.
30 Geoffrey Reaume, *Lyndhurst : Canada's First Rehabilitation Centre for People with Spinal Cord Injuries, 1945–1998* (Montreal: McGill-Queen's University Press, 2007): 86.
31 Ibid.
32 Ibid.

33 AO, RG 7-148, Box B100660, File "General," Mark Lukasiewicz, "U of T's Handicapped Students," *The Varsity* (28 September 1977).

34 Tremblay, Campbell, and Hudson, "When Elevators Were for Pianos," 108.

35 "William," interview with author, 19 December 2011.

36 Reaume, *Lyndhurst*, 117.

37 "William."

38 Rene Gadacz, *Re-Thinking Dis-Ability: New Structures, New Relationships* (Edmonton: University of Alberta Press, 1994), 68.

39 Marta Russell and Ravi Malhotra, "Capitalism and Disability," *Socialist Register* 38 (2002): 216.

40 Charlton, *Nothing About Us Without Us* (Berkeley: University of California Press, 1998), 46–7.

41 Russell and Malhotra, "Capitalism and Disability," 214.

42 Gadacz, *Re-Thinking Dis-Ability*, 64.

43 Claire Liachowitz, *Disability as a Social Construct: Legislative Roots* (Philadelphia: University of Pennsylvania Press, 1988), 60; Doris Fleischer and Frieda Zames, *The Disability Rights Movement: From Charity to Confrontation* (Philadelphia: Temple University Press, 2011), 34.

44 Ruth O'Brien, "From a Doctor's to a Judge's Gaze: Epistemic Communities and the History of Disability Rights Policy in the Workplace," *Polity* 35:3 (2003): 325–46.

45 Ibid.

46 Barnes and Mercer, "Disability, Work and Welfare," 531; Liachowitz, *Disability as a Social Construct*, 107.

47 Fraser Valentine and Jill Vickers, "Released from the Yoke of Paternalism and 'Charity': Citizenship and the Rights of Canadians with Disabilities," *International Journal of Canadian Studies* 14 (1996): 158–9.

48 MA, CCD Fonds, Box P5365, File 22, Paper, Canadian Rehabilitation Council for the Disabled, "CRCD Public Awareness Campaign – Focus on Attitudes," 1981.

49 Anne Finger, *Elegy for a Disease: A Personal and Cultural History of Polio* (New York: St Martin's Press, 2006).

50 AO, RG 7-148, Box B217563, File "Publications," Newsletter, Canadian Rehabilitation Council for the Disabled, *Access: A Quarterly Newsletter for Members and Associates of CRCD* 3:2 (February 1981).

51 Colin Barnes, *Cabbage Syndrome: The Social Construction of Dependence* (New York: Falmer Press, 1990), 155; Sarah Lock et al, "Work After Stroke: Focusing on Barriers and Enablers," *Disability and Society* 20:1 (2005): 33.

52 Harold Russell, *The Best Years of My Life* (Middlebury, VT: P.S. Eriksson, 1981), 155.

53 Ibid.

54 Ibid., 158.

55 AO, RG 7-148, Box B353847, File "Mayor's Task Force," Report, Toronto Mayor's Task Force on the Disabled and Elderly, *This City Is for All Its Citizens*, June 1976.

56 AO, RG 7-148, Box B100558, File "Speeches/TV," Newsletter, *Goodwill Quarterly* (Spring 1978).

57 Ontario Human Rights Commission, *Life Together: A Report on Human Rights in Ontario*, 1978.

58 AO, RG 7-148, Box 100615, File "Speeches/TV," Conference Proceedings, Handicapped Employment Program, "A Conference on Education Now – Employment Later: The Hearing Impaired Job Candidate and the Changing Employment Scene," 10–11 November 1980.

59 AO, RG 7-149, Box B363026, File "Public Relations," Letter, Vocational Rehabilitation Advisory Committee to Handicapped Employment Program, 26 March 1980.

60 *The Littlest Hobo*, Season 6, Episode 5, "One Door Closes," first broadcast 11 October 1984 by Canadian Television Networks.

61 Robert McRuer, *Crip Theory: Cultural Signs of Queerness and Disability* (New York: New York University Press, 2006), 111.

62 Ontario Human Rights Commission, *Life Together*.

63 Frank Bowe, *Handicapping America: Barriers to Disabled People* (New York: Harper & Row, 1978), 181.

64 AO, RG 7-149, Box B367312, File "Dr Stephenson's Speech," Speech, 26 November 1976.

65 James Sears, "The Able Disabled," *Journal of Rehabilitation* (March/April, 1975): 19–22.

66 E.I. DuPont de Nemours and Company, *Equal to the Task*, 1982.

67 Anonymous, "Hiring the Handicapped: Why More Companies Are Beginning to Look into It," *Management* (30 March 1981); AO, RG 7-148, Box B100660, File "News Clippings," Article, Personnel Association of Toronto, "Hiring the Handicapped," 3–4 December 1981.

68 "A Conference on Education Now – Employment Later" (see n58).

69 Canadian Rehabilitation Council for the Disabled, "IYDP Display Tour in Ontario," *Access* 3:4 (August 1981); Ontario March of Dimes, "IYDP in Ontario," *Advocate* (September/October 1981); AO, RG 74-30, Box B173677, File "DDP," Letter, Minister Responsible for Disabled Persons to Ontario Legislature, 18 June 1986.

70 "Jeweller Honored for Hiring Disabled," *Globe and Mail* (2 July 1982).

71 Kirk Makin, "Label Us Able – But Legibly," *Globe and Mail* (1 July 1981).

72 University of Toronto, "Queen's Park Says 'They're Able!'" *The Varsity: Supplement on Disabled Persons* (9 November 1981).

73 AO, RG 7-148, Box B100558, File "General Series," Newsletter, *Momentum*, 3 (Winter 1981).

74 Makin, "Label Us Able."

75 Ibid.

76 Canadian Council for Rehabilitation and Work, "Who's Driving the System?" *Ability & Enterprise* (November/December 1986).

77 Ibid.

78 Ibid.

79 Ibid.

80 Ibid.

81 David Cameron and Fraser Valentine, "Comparing Policy-Making in Federal Systems: The Case of Disability Policy and Programs," in *Disability and Federalism: Comparing Different Approaches to Full Participation*, ed. David Cameron and Fraser Valentine (Montreal: Institute of Intergovernmental Relations, 2001), 5–6; Valentine and Vickers, "Released from the Yoke of Paternalism," 156.

82 Renée Anspach, "From Stigma to Identity Politics: Political Activism Among the Physically Disabled and Former Mental Patients," *Social Science and Medicine, Part A Medical: Psychology and Medical Sociology* 13 (1979): 771.

83 Susan Peters, "Is There a Disability Culture? A Syncretisation of Three Possible Worldviews," *Disability & Society* 15:4 (2000): 595.

84 Oliver, "The Social Model in Context," 19.

85 Ruth Enns, *A Voice Unheard: The Latimer Case and People with Disabilities* (Halifax, NS: Fernwood Publishing, 1999), 85.

86 Valentine and Vickers, "Released from the Yoke of Paternalism," 162.

87 Ibid.

88 Ibid., 86.

89 Ibid.

90 Ibid.

91 MA, CCD Fonds, Box P5364, File 1, Memo, COPOH Development, 1978.

92 Ibid.

93 AO, RG 7-149, File "Rehab Digest," Canadian Rehabilitation Council for the Disabled, "Guide information for exhibitors," 1979.

94 MA, Hugh Allan Fonds, Collection of the Society for Manitobans with Disabilities.

95 MA, CCD Fonds, Box P5364, File 1, Paper, COPOH, "COPOH: 1980 World Rehab Congress," 1978.

96 Ibid., Box P5365, File 23, Letter, Rehabilitation International to COPOH, 2 August 1978.
97 Ibid., Box P5364, File 1, Paper, COPOH, "COPOH: 1980 World Rehab Congress," 1978.
98 Ibid., Box P5365, File 23, Telefax, COPOH to ACCD, 1978.
99 John Lord, *Impact: Changing the Way we View Disability: The History, Perspective, and Vision of the Independent Living Movement in Canada* (Ottawa: Creative Bound International, 2010).
100 Gadacz, *Re-Thinking Dis-Ability*, 81.
101 Lord, *Impact*.

4 "A Voice of Our Own"

1 "Katie," interview with author, 25 July 2011.
2 "Rachel," interview with author, 27 November 2011.
3 April D'Aubin, "We Will Ride: A Showcase of CCD Advocacy Strategies in Support of Accessible Transportation," in *Making Equality: History of Advocacy and Persons with Disabilities in Canada*, ed. Deborah Stienstra and Aileen Wight-Felske with Colleen Watters (Concord, ON: Captus Press, 2003), 113.
4 AO, RG 7-148, Box B335968, File "Employment Practices," Article, Department of National Health and Welfare, "Action Group – The Disabled," c.1975.
5 Anspach, "From Stigma to Identity Politics," 766.
6 Michael Oliver, *The Politics of Disablement* (Basingstoke, UK: Macmillan, 1990).
7 Ian Milligan, "Rebel Youth: Young Workers, New Leftists, and Labour in English Canada, 1964–1973" (PhD diss., York University, 2011); Bryan Palmer, *Canada's 1960s: The Ironies of Identity in a Rebellious Era* (Toronto: University of Toronto Press, 2009).
8 Milligan, "Rebel Youth," iv.
9 Ibid., 1–2.
10 Dominique Clement, *Canada's Rights Revolution: Social Movements and Social Change, 1937–82* (Vancouver: UBC Press, 2008), 200.
11 Ibid., 56–60
12 Jennifer Ruth Hosek, "The Canadian National Security War on Queers and the Left," in *New World Coming: The Sixties and the Shaping of Global Consciousness*, ed. Karen Dubinsky (Toronto: Between the Lines, 2009).
13 MA, CCD Fonds, Box P5360, File 1, Letter, COPOH to Credit Union Central, 9 January 1979.

14 Ibid., File 2, Paper, COPOH, "Challenge for the 80's: Partners in Planning and Independent Living," c. 1979.
15 Ibid., File 1, Memo, COPOH, 1979.
16 Sharon Barnartt analysed 177 Canadian and 1,215 American protests that occurred between 1970 and 2005, concluding that there were "substantial, and statistically significant, differences between the US and Canada." Barnartt, "Social Movement Diffusion? The Case of Disability Protests in the US and Canada," *Disability Studies Quarterly*, 28:1 (2008), accessed 16 August 2013, http://dsq-sds.org/article/view/70/70.
17 Ibid.
18 Chivers, "Barrier by Barrier," 308.
19 Ibid.
20 Peters, "From Charity to Equality," 24.
21 MA, CCD Fonds, Box P5364, File 2, Letter, COPOH to Secretary of State, 16 May 1978.
22 Chivers, "Barrier by Barrier," 308.
23 MA, CCD Fonds, Box P5367, File 2, Paper, COPOH, "Statement,"1978.
24 Ibid., File 1, Letter, COPOH to Canadian Labour Congress, 20 April 1978.
25 Ibid., File 1, Paper, COPOH, "National Employment Conference Outline," 1978.
26 Ibid., File 1, Press Release, COPOH, 25 June 1978.
27 Ibid., File 1, COPOH, "National Employment Conference Reviews," 1978.
28 MA, CCD Fonds, Box P5364, File 21, Report, Ontario Ministry of Labour, *It's Up to You ... Disabled People Can Work! Job Hunting Hints for the Handicapped*, 1979.
29 Ibid., Box P5367, File 1, Letter, Canadian Human Rights Commission to COPOH, 27 June 1978.
30 Ibid., Box P5360, File "Letters Patent," COPOH Letter of Incorporation, 27 Oct 1978; ibid., Box P5367, File 2, Report, COPOH, "Coordinator's Report From Washington, DC," 13 July 1978.
31 Michael Prince, "Canadian Disability Activism and Political Ideas: In and Between Neo-Liberalism and Social Liberalism," *Canadian Journal of Disability Studies*, 1:2 (2012), accessed 17 August 2013, http://cjds .uwaterloo.ca/index.php/cjds/article/view/16.
32 Lord, *Impact*, 13.
33 Greenland, *Vision Canada*, 43.
34 Ibid., 42.
35 Ibid., 3.
36 Ibid., 43.
37 Rae, Musgrave, and Yale, *Selfhelp and Government Commitment*.

38 Ibid.
39 Ibid., 30.
40 Ibid., 15.
41 Greenland, *Vision Canada*, 6–12.
42 McCreath, *The Politics of Blindness*, 67.
43 MA, CCD Fonds, Box P5367, File 30, Newsletter, Handicapped Communications Society, *The Spokesman* (9 September 1979).
44 See chapter 7 for further discussion of the CNIB strike.
45 "Ontario Blind Picket CNIB Demanding Access to Own Files," *Our Future: Ontario's Independent Newspaper By and For Handicapped Persons and Their Community* 6:3 (Spring 1979).
46 *The World of One in Seven*, directed by Michael Steele (Kingston, ON: Quarry Films, 1975), VHS.
47 Ibid.
48 "Finding Jobs for Area Handicapped," *Kingston Whig-Standard* (16 July 1977).
49 *The World of One in Seven*.
50 "The Best Thing That Ever Happened ... and His Employers Agree," *Kingston Whig-Standard* (16 July 1977).
51 "Handicapped Placement Service Transferred to Canada Manpower," *Kingston Whig-Standard* (3 May 1979).
52 MA, CCD Fonds, Box P5364, File 5, Minutes, COPOH, "Employment Meeting," 7 November 1981.
53 Ibid., Box P5360, File 2, Paper, COPOH, "Emergence of the Consumer Movement of the Handicapped in Canada," 1979.
54 "Handicapped Unemployed," *Globe and Mail* (25 May 1979).
55 Ibid.
56 MA, CCD Fonds, Box P5360, File 1, Memo, COPOH, 1978.
57 "Peterborough Is Nerve Centre for Province-Wide Disabled Movement," *Kawartha Sun* (10 July 1979).
58 "UHGO Gets Federal Aid," *Our Future: Ontario's Independent Newspaper By and For Handicapped Persons and Their Community* 6:3 (Spring 1979); Bank of Canada, "Inflation Calculator," accessed 4 May 2013, http://www.bankofcanada.ca/rates/related/inflation-calculator/.
59 MA, CCD Fonds, Box P5364, File 13, Letter, Secretary of State to COPOH Ontario Job Corps Project Leader, 17 May 1979.
60 Ibid., Letter, Secretary of State to COPOH Ontario Job Corps Project Leader, 17 May 1979.
61 Ibid., Letter, UHGO to COPOH, 18 May 1979.
62 Ibid., Minutes, "UHGO/March of Dimes Meeting re Relationship under YJC Project," 13 August 1979.

63 Ibid., Letter, OMOD to UHGO, 5 December 1979.

64 "Disabled Demand Equality and Integration, Not Favors," *Toronto Star* (15 December 1979).

65 Ibid.

66 Peggy Hutchison et al., "The Impact of Independent Living Resource Centres in Canada on People with Disabilities," *Canadian Journal of Rehabilitation* 10:2 (1997): 99–112.

67 Gerben DeJong, "Independent Living: From Social Movement to Analytic Paradigm," *Archives of Physical and Medical Rehabilitation* 60 (1979): 435–46.

68 Ibid. Independent living became a reality for many people with disabilities in Canada during the early 1980s following the precedent-setting experience of Judith Snow, who was granted a special Order in Council for the necessary supports and attendant services she required to function independently in the community. See Jack Pearpoint, *From Behind the Piano: The Building of Judith Snow's Unique Circle of Friends* (Toronto: Inclusion Press, 1991).

69 Minister of Supply and Services Canada. *Obstacles: Report of the Parliamentary Special Committee on the Disabled and the Handicapped* (Ottawa: Queen's Printer, February 1981).

70 "Scarborough Prepares for Year of Disabled," *Scarborough Mirror* (7 January 1981).

71 Mark Bromfield, "TV Film Stars Triple Amputee," *Toronto Star* (15 September 1981), E11.

72 Ibid.

73 "Disabled Welcome Committee's Report," *Toronto Star* (17 February 1981).

74 AO, RG 7-148, Box B100558, File "Publications," Poster, Handicapped Employment Program, 1 June 1981.

75 AO, RG 74-30, Box B392871, File "Films," Hamilton-Brown & AVCOMM Productions, *Life Another Way*, 1982.

76 LAC, RG 29, Box 24, File 18, Paper, Centre for Independent Living Toronto, "CILT: Empowerment and Independent Living," 1990.

77 Paul Longmore, *Why I Burned My Book and Other Essays on Disability* (Philadelphia: Temple University Press, 2003), 103; Carey, *On the Margins of Citizenship*, 176; Fleischer and Zames, *The Disability Rights Movement*, 46.

78 "CILT: Empowerment and Independent Living" (see n76).

79 MA, CCD Fonds, Box T1288, File 23, Paper, COPOH, "Training: A New Partnership for People with Disabilities," 1993; ibid., File 1, Minutes, COPOH Employment Committee, 17 December 1991.

80 AO, RG 74-30, Box B181135, File "CILT," Memo, Office for Disabled Persons, "Minister's Visit to the CILT," 31 January 1991; ibid., Box B165810,

File "CILT," Paper, Office for Disabled Persons, "The Radio Connection," 1988.

81 Ibid., Box B162586, File "Employment Equity," Letter, Canadian Broadcasting Corporation to Office for Disabled Persons, "The Disability Network: A Unique Opportunity for Corporate Involvement in the Community," January 1990.

82 Ibid., Box B186697, File "TILAC," Paper, Toronto Independent Living Advisory Committee (TILAC), 11 January 1990.

83 Members of TILAC included ALS Society, Lyndhurst Hospital, Bloorview Children's Hospital, Easter Seals, Bellwoods Park House, Muscular Dystrophy Association of Canada, COTA, Gage Transitional Living Centre, Ministry of Community and Social Services, and Participation Apartments Toronto.

84 AO, RG 74-30, Box B186697, File "TILAC," Letter, Minister Responsible for Disabled Persons to TILAC, 11 December 1989.

85 Ibid., Box B167563, File "Labour study (1)," Paper, Ontario Advisory Council for the Handicapped (OACPH), "Background Information," 1985.

86 "150 Disabled Travel to Ottawa to Protest Job Bill with 'No Teeth,'" *Toronto Star* (15 April 1986); "Disabled Protest Hits House," *Montreal Gazette* (15 April 1986).

87 "150 Disabled Travel to Ottawa."

88 AO, RG 74-49, Box B299294, File "Beryl Potter," Ontario Action Awareness, "Work Plan," 1991; Minutes of the Council of the City of Toronto 712 (13 May 1998), 865–6. Potter subsequently ran an awareness program during the late 1980s and early 1990s that toured Ontario, establishing connections with local schools, policymakers, media, consumer groups, and other disability organizations. For these and other activities Potter's profile as a leading activist also earned her an Order of Canada medal and formal recognition by the City of Toronto Council upon her death on 1 May 1998 for her contribution to the promotion of disability rights in the city.

89 "150 Disabled Travel to Ottawa" (see n86).

90 DisAbled Women's Network (DAWN), "Our History," accessed 10 July 2015, http://www.dawncanada.net/about/about/our-history/.

91 DAWN, *Different Therefore Unequal: Employment and Women with Disabilities* (Winnipeg: DAWN, 1989).

92 AMEIPH, "Publications," accessed 13 July 2015, http://www.ameiph.com/; see also AMEIPH, "20 ans d'action," March 2002.

93 MA, CCD fonds, Box T1288, File 1, Memo, COPOH to Steering Committee on Employment and Disability, 21 November 1990.

94 ERDCO, "About Us," accessed 13 July 2015, http://www.erdco.ca/.

95 "Lily," interview with author, 27 June 2011.
96 "David," interview with author, 27 June 2011.
97 "Michael," interview with author, 27 July 2011.
98 "Michael."
99 "Lily."
100 "Lily."
101 "Charlotte," interview with author, 27 June 2011.

5 Sheltered Workshops

1 Wayne Roberts, "A Little Hong Kong: Sheltered Workshops in Ontario," *Rank and File*, Canadian Broadcasting Corporation Radio, first broadcast in 1982. The quotation is an excerpt from an interview Roberts conducted with Ebar Brione, a former supervisor at a sheltered workshop in Toronto, Ontario, regarding his experiences and thoughts on the state of sheltered employment in the city.

2 MA, CCD Fonds, Box P5367, File 2, Conference Proceedings, COPOH National Employment Conference, 1978.

3 Geoffrey Reaume, *Remembrance of Patients Past: Patient Life at the Toronto Hospital for the Insane, 1870–1940* (Toronto: University of Toronto Press, 2009), 134.

4 Ibid.

5 Judith Friedland, *Restoring the Spirit: The Beginnings of Occupational Therapy in Canada, 1890–1930* (Montreal: McGill-Queen's University Press, 2011), 155; AO, RG 7-148, Box B335962, File "Workshops," Paper, Ontario Ministry of Community and Social Services (MCSS), "1978 Workshop Survey: Research and Statistics Section," 20 April 1979.

6 Durflinger, *Veterans with a Vision*, 186; Fleischer and Zames, *The Disability Rights Movement*, 19; Greenland, *Vision Canada*, 103–4.

7 Friedland, *Restoring the Spirit*, 147.

8 Ibid.

9 Ibid., 155.

10 Rosemarie Garland-Thomson, *Extraordinary Bodies: Figuring Physical Disability in American Culture and Literature* (New York: Columbia University Press, 1997), 146; Geoffrey Reaume, "Patients at Work: Insane Asylum Inmates' Labour in Ontario, 1841–1900," in *Rethinking Normalcy: A Disability Studies Reader*, ed. Tanya Titchkosky and Rod Michalko (Toronto: Canadian Scholars' Press, 2009), 158.

11 "Rachel," interview with author, 27 November 2011.

12 "David," interview with author, 27 June 2011.

13 Pelka, *What We Have Done*, 186.
14 Mayor's Task Force on the Disabled and Elderly, Report, *This City Is for All Its Citizens* (Toronto: City of Toronto, 1973); Greenland, *Vision Canada*, 47.
15 Mayor's Task Force, *This City Is for All Its Citizens*.
16 Enns, *A Voice Unheard*, 83; Prince, *Absent Citizens*, 182.
17 "Paul," interview with author, 23 June 2011.
18 "Lucy," Interview with author, 28 July 2011.
19 Mary Tremblay, "Going Back to Main Street: The Development and Impact of Casualty Rehabilitation for Veterans with Disabilities, 1945–1948," in *The Veterans Charter and Post-World War II Canada*, ed. Peter Neary and J.L. Granatstein (Montreal: McGill-Queen's University Press, 1998), 161, 173–4; Reaume, *Lyndhurst*, 68; Tremblay, Campbell, and Hudson, "When Elevators Were for Pianos," 104, 111–12; Durflinger, *Veterans with a Vision*, 283.
20 Neufeldt, "Growth and Evolution of Disability Advocacy," 19–21.
21 O'Brien, "From a Doctor's to a Judge's Gaze," 325–46.
22 MA, CCD Fonds, Box P5364, File 5, Paper, COPOH, "A Proposal: COPOH Employment Policy," 1982; ibid., Box Q012249, File 14, Brief, COPOH, "Fact Sheet," 1983.
23 Friedland, *Restoring the Spirit*.
24 TA, Alexandra Studio Fonds 1257, SC 1057, Item 369.
25 Judith Sandys, "'It Does My Heart Good': The Perceptions of Employers Who Have Hired People with Intellectual Disabilities through Supported Employment Programs" (PhD diss., University of Toronto, 1993), 55.
26 Reaume, *Remembrance of Patients Past*, 144.
27 Robert Grimm, "Working with Handicaps: Americans with Disabilities, Goodwill Industries and Employment, 1920s–1970s" (PhD diss., Indiana University, 2002), 179.
28 Norman Acton, "Employment of Disabled Persons: Where Are We Going?" *International Labour Review* 120:1 (1981): 5; MA, CCD Fonds, Box Q01225, File "DPU," Paper, Disabled Persons Unit, "Status Report on the Integration of Adult Persons with Disabilities into the Regular Labour Market," 3 July 1992; AO, RG 7-148, Box B100615, File "ABT Associates Wage Permit Study #2," Report, ABT Associates, "Wage Permits for Handicapped Employees," 7 November 1980.
29 John Alexander, *Capabilities and Social Justice: The Political Philosophy of Amartya Sen and Martha Nussbaum* (Burlington, VT: Ashgate, 2008).
30 Panitch, *Accidental Activists*, 2.
31 Canadian Council on Rehabilitation and Work, "Who We Are," accessed 20 September 2012, http://web.archive.org/web/20000816033544/http://www.ccrw.org/ccrw/en/mission.htm.

32   Martinez, "Independent Living in the U.S. and Canada."
33   Sealy and Whitehead, "Forty Years of Deinstitutionalization," 251.
34   Ibid.
35   Sandys, "'It Does My Heart Good,'" 55.
36   AO, RG 7-148, Box B217563, File "Publications General, 1981–82," Canadian Association of Rehabilitation Personnel, "The Case For and Against the Closing of the Lakeshore Psychiatric Hospital," *The Chronicle* 1:1 (1979).
37   Welsh, *Tales from a Human Warehouse*, 13.
38   Ibid.
39   Ontario Disability Employment Network, "A Brief History of Employment Services in Ontario for People Who Have a Disability: The Pendulum Swings," accessed 16 August 2012, https://odenetwork.com/tag/sheltered-workshops/.
40   "1978 Workshop Survey" (see n5).
41   Janalee Morris, "Working for Equity: Issues of Employment for Youth with Disabilities" (MA thesis, University of Manitoba, 2000), 20.
42   AO, RG 7-148, Box B100558, File "Current Issues 1980-81," Article, OMOD, *The Advocate* (July/April 1981); File "Current Issues 1980–81," Article, Handicapped Action Committee, *HACing Away* 2:2 (February 1982).
43   Ibid., File "Speeches/TV," Newsletter, *Goodwill Quarterly* (Spring 1978).
44   MCSS, "The Shift to Community Living: The 1970s," accessed 16 August 2012, http://www.mcss.gov.on.ca/en/dshistory/community/1970s. aspx; ARCH Disability Law Centre, "Enforcing the Rights of People with Disabilities in Ontario's Developmental Services System" (Toronto: Law Commission of Ontario, 2010), 19.
45   "1978 Workshop Survey."
46   Ibid.
47   Alberto Migliore, "Sheltered Workshops and Individual Employment: Perspectives of Consumers, Families, and Staff Members" (PhD diss., Indiana University, 2006), 5; Pelka, *What We Have Done*, 574.
48   "1978 Workshop Survey"; "MR shops" were defined in the 1978 MCSS study as "those which predominantly served persons who were developmentally handicapped." "Non-MR shops" were either mixed shops or those dedicated solely to people with physical disabilities.
49   Pelka, *What We Have Done*, 574.
50   *The Disability Myth, Part II: Employment: Beggars Can't Be Choosers*, directed by Alan Aylward (Toronto: Lauron Productions, 1982) 16 mm.
51   Arthur O'Reilly, *The Right to Decent Work of Persons with Disabilities* (Geneva: International Labour Office, 2003), 133, 147; Vera Chouinard and Valorie Crooks, "Negotiating Neoliberal Environments in British

Columbia and Ontario, Canada: Restructuring of State-Voluntary
Sector Relations and Disability Organizations' Struggles to Survive,"
Environment & Planning 26 (2008): 187–8; Robert Wilton and Stephanie
Schuer, "Towards Socio-Spatial Inclusion? Disabled People, Neoliberalism
and the Contemporary Labour Market," *Area* 32:2 (2006): 186–95; Robert
Wilton, "Working at the Margins: Disabled People in Precarious Employ-
ment," in *Critical Disability Theory*, ed. Robert Devlin and Diane Pothier
(Vancouver: UBC Press, 2005).

52 Michael Bach, *Achieving Social and Economic Inclusion: From Segregation
to 'Employment First*, Law Reform and Public Policy Series (Toronto:
Canadian Association for Community Living, 2001), Foreword.

53 "1978 Workshop Survey," 11–20.

54 MA, CCD Fonds, Box Q012250, File 45, Letter, Anonymous Concerned
Citizen to COPOH, 5 March 1984.

55 Longmore, *Why I Burned My Book*, 111.

56 AO RG 7-148, Box B335968, CMHA Ontario, "Community Mental Health
Alternatives," 1981.

57 LAC, RG 29, Box 210, File 4314-4-2, Press Release, Bureau on
Rehabilitation, 13 August 1979.

58 MA, CCD Fonds, Box P5364, File 19, Brief, CCRW, "Business Industrial
Development Strategies," 1980.

59 "1978 Workshop Survey."

60 MA, CCD Fonds, Box P5364, File 19, Letter, Bureau on Rehabilitation to
COPOH, 27 April 1979.

61 LAC, RG 29, Box 238, File 4314-3-1 9(1), Paper, Bureau on Rehabilitation,
"Potential Incentives to Employment of the Handicapped," May 1979.

62 Ibid., Paper, Bureau on Rehabilitation, "Projects Relating to Employment
of the Disabled," 1 April 1979; CCRW also held a special conference to
clarify roles around the marketing, contract procurement, and manufacturing business of workshops. MA, CCD Fonds, Box P5364, File 19,
Conference Program, CCRW, "Implementing Industrial Strategies for
Workshops," 19–21 June 1980.

63 "At Butler Centre: Clients Begin Recovery Program," *Truro Daily News*
(15 January 1980).

64 LAC, RG 29, Box 238, File 4314-3-1, Press Release, Bureau on
Rehabilitation, "Policy on Employment of the Handicapped Announced,"
21 March 1978; ibid., Box 210, File 4314-4-3, Letter, Bureau on Rehabilitation
to Department of Supply and Services, 27 April 1979; ibid., File 4314-4-2,
Letter, Department of Supply and Services to Bureau on Rehabilitation,
14 March 1983.

65 MA, CCD Fonds, Box P5364, File 19, Letter, Bureau on Rehabilitation to COPOH, Undated.

66 LAC, RG 29, Box 210, File 4314-4-3, Report, Bureau on Rehabilitation, "Organization, Implementation and Assessment of Opportunities for Canadian Sheltered Workshops in the Recycling Industries: Follow-up Report," October 1982.

67 Ibid., SPAR Systems for Department of National Health and Welfare Social Services Programs Branch, "Organization, Implementation and Assessment of Opportunities for Canadian Sheltered Workshops in the Recycling Industry: Executive Summary and Overview," January 1981.

68 Ibid., Report, Bureau on Rehabilitation, "Organization, Implementation and Assessment of Opportunities for Canadian Sheltered Workshops in the Recycling Industry: Implementation – Fort Erie, Ontario," January 1981.

69 Ibid., Bureau on Rehabilitation, "Organization, Implementation … Follow-up Report," October 1982.

70 Ibid., File 4314-4-2, Report, Bureau on Rehabilitation, "Analysis of Project BIDS: Phase II Report and Phase III Proposal," October 1982.

71 MA, CCD Fonds, Box P5364, File 19, Letter, CCRW to COPOH, 30 March 1979.

72 Ibid., Box P5360, File 1, Letter, COPOH to BIOS Committee, 1980.

73 Ibid., Box P5364, File 19, Paper, COPOH, "Project BIDS: Federal Government Sponsored Study of Canadian Rehabilitation Workshops: A COPOH Critique," 1980.

74 Ibid., Box P5367, File 8, Conference Proceedings, COPOH, "Vancouver Conference Resolutions," 1980.

75 David Cooney, "A Second View of Workshops," *Ability & Enterprise* (May/June 1987).

76 AO, RG 7-149, Box B363026, File "Speeches/TV," Memo, Handicapped Employment Program, 1 April 1982. In April 1982 an internal memo at the Ontario Ministry of Labour pointed to "renewed media interest in sheltered workshops," including a fifteen-minute segment on CBC Radio's *Metro Morning*, with similar features on CTV's program *W5*, as well as on CFTO. Other news articles included Roona Maloney, "Hearing People Are Outsiders at Centre for the Deaf," *Globe and Mail* (9 September 1981), A14; Arthur Moses, "Not Paid Minimum Wage, Cerebral Palsy Victim Suing Ontario," *Globe and Mail* (12 October 1981), A10; "Group Rejects Union Scheme for Disabled," *Globe and Mail* (16 October 1981), A10; OMOD, *Advocate* (July/April 1981); Handicapped Action Committee, *HACing Away* 2:2 (February 1982); OMOD, "Awareness Theme of Employment Conference," *The Advocate* (November/December 1981).

77 MA, CCD Fonds, Box P5364, File 18, Paper, Lola Freeman, "Why Does Rehabilitation Have to Hurt So Much? Sheltered Workshops in Ontario," January 1983.
78 "Clients or Employees: No Minimum Wage for Disabled Workers," *Hamilton Spectator* (22 October 1983); "'Disability Myth' Hard-Hitting Documentary on Plight of Disabled," *Montreal Gazette* (10 September 1982); *The Disability Myth, Part II: Employment: Beggars Can't Be Choosers*, 1982.
79 "Unions Vow Fight for Disabled," *Toronto Star* (9 October 1981), A17.
80 Bowe, *Handicapping America*, 165; Fred Pelka, *The ABC-CLIO Companion to the Disability Rights Movement* (Santa Barbara, CA: ABC-CLIO, 1997).
81 MA, CCD Fonds, Box P5364, File 5, Letter, CCRW to COPOH, 8 January 1981.
82 Ontario Ministry of Labour (OML), "Wage Permits for Handicapped Employees."
83 AO, RG 74-30, Box B162583, File "Rehabilitation," Paper, Ontario Rehabilitation Workshops Council, "The Disabled Persons' Fair Wages Act," 1989.
84 Ibid., ORWC, "The Disabled Persons' Fair Wages Act: Concerns and Suggestions," 1989.
85 Geoffrey Reaume, "No Profits, Just a Pittance: Work, Compensation, and People Defined as Mentally Disabled in Ontario, 1964–1990," in *Mental Retardation in America*, ed. S. Noll and J. Trent (New York: New York University Press, 2004), 466–93.
86 MA, CCD Fonds, Box Q012240, File 19, Brief, Lauron Productions, "Disability Myth," 1982.
87 The *Disability Myth Part I: Segregation* was financed primarily by Suncor Corp., while subsequent films secured funding from a variety of federal ministries and provincial departments of social services.
88 *The Disability Myth, Part I: Segregation*, 1981.
89 *The Disability Myth, Part II: Employment*, 1982.
90 OML, "Wage Permits for Handicapped Employees."
91 MA, CCD Fonds, Box Q012254, File "COPOH, CAP and VRDP," Paper, CCRW, "Submission to the Consultation Regarding the Fiscal Arrangements Affecting Persons with Disabilities," 3 November 1987.
92 Sandys, "'It Does My Heart Good,'" 1993.
93 Royal Commission on Equality in Employment, *Report* (Ottawa: Queen's Printer, 1984), Recommendation 114.
94 Jonathan Oldman et al., "A Case Report of the Conversion of Sheltered Employment to Evidence-Based Supported Employment in Canada," *Psychiatric Services* 56:11 (2005): 1437; D. Mank, "The Underachievement of Supported Employment: A Call for Reinvestment," *Journal of Disability*

Policy Studies 5:2 (1994): 1–24; P. Wehman and J. Kregel, "At the Cross-roads: Supported Employment a Decade Later," *Journal of the Association of Persons with Severe Handicaps* 20 (1995): 286–99.

95 OML, "Wage Permits for Handicapped Employees."

96 Valerie Duffy, "The Canadian Council on Rehabilitation and Work," *Abilities Magazine* (Summer 1995).

97 MA, CCD Fonds, Box Q012249, File 14, Letter, CCRW to COPOH, 4 January 1983.

98 Duffy, "The Canadian Council on Rehabilitation and Work."

99 Robert E. Drake, Gary R. Bond, and Deborah R. Becker, *Individual Placement and Support: An Evidence-Based Approach to Supported Employment* (New York: Oxford University Press, 2012); David Hagner and Dale DiLeo, *Working Together: Workplace Culture, Supported Employment, and Persons with Disabilities* (Cambridge, MA: Brookline Books, 1993).

100 *Moving On*, Season 1, Episode 6, 11 April 1998, Canadian Broadcasting Corporation.

101 Hagner and DiLeo, *Working Together*.

102 "Retarded People Placed in Jobs," *Kingston Whig-Standard* (30 September 1976).

103 Ibid.

104 MA, CCD Fonds, Box P5364, File 5, Paper, The World of One in Seven, "The World of One in Seven Inc.: A Brief History," 11 December 1979; *The World of One in Seven*, 16 mm film, directed by Michael Steele (Kingston, ON: Quarry Films, 1975).

105 Mona Winberg, "A 'Step' in the Right Direction," *Toronto Star*, 17 July 1988.

106 MA, CCD Fonds, Box Q012254, File "COPOH, CAP and VRDP," Paper, CCRW, "Submission to the Consultation Regarding the Fiscal Arrangements Affecting Persons with Disabilities," 3 November 1987.

107 CCRW, "An Emerging Workforce: Strategies to Employ Persons with Disabilities," Conference proceedings, 1990.

108 MA, CCD Fonds, Box P5364, File 19, Paper, COPOH, "Project BIDS: Federal Government Sponsored Study of Canadian Rehabilitation Workshops: A COPOH Critique," 1980.

6 Employers and the Workplace

1 Peter Silverman, "Hire Handicapped for Ability, Not Disability," *Financial Post* (20 June 1981).

2 "Ibid.

3 "Untapped Resource," *Financial Post* (2 May 1981).
4 Doyle, *Disability, Discrimination and Equal Opportunities*, 174.
5 Weinkauf, "Employer Attitudes," 12.
6 Ibid.
7 Susan Peters, "The Politics of Disability Identity," in *Disability and Society: Emerging Issues and Insights*, ed. Len Barton (New York: Longman, 1996), 220.
8 "Rachel," interview with author, 27 November 2011.
9 Garland-Thomson, *Extraordinary Bodies*, 69.
10 "Olivia," interview with author, 5 July 2011.
11 Carolyn Vash, "What's Behind Employer Resistance to Hiring Disabled!" *Accent on Living* (Fall 1973): 92.
12 MA, Box P5364, File 21, Pamphlet, Program for Employment of the Disadvantaged, *It's Up To You: Disabled People Can Work! Job Hunting Hints for the Handicapped*, 1981.
13 "Many Handicapped People Wallow in Self Pity Rather Than Learn Skills, Group President Says," *Kingston Whig-Standard* (23 September 1981).
14 Ibid.
15 "Lisa," interview with author, 17 June 2011.
16 "Dan," interview with author, 10 June 2011.
17 "Richard," interview with author, 13 September 2011.
18 Ibid.
19 LAC, RG-29, Box 238, File 4314-3-1-9 (1), Brief, Canadian Chamber of Commerce, "The CCC and Its Relationship to Health and Welfare Canada," 1979.
20 Ibid., Canadian Chamber of Commerce and Health and Welfare Canada, "Employability of the Handicapped," (Ottawa: Queen's Printer, 1975).
21 Ibid., Paper, Canadian Chamber of Commerce, Ottawa Liaison Committee, "Role and Initiatives of the Federal Government Regarding Rehabilitation and Employment of the Handicapped," 31 May 1979.
22 AO, RG 7-148, Box B100558, File "Publications," Newsletter, BOOST, *The Third Eye* 10 (10 December 1976), "A Letter to the Premier."
23 AO, RG 7-149, Box B367312, File "Dr Stephenson's Speech," Speech, 26 November 1976.
24 AO, RG 7-148, Box B100558, File "Public Relations General," *Metropolitan Toronto Business Journal* 69:1 (January 1979).
25 Ibid., Box 217563, File "Professional Outreach," Report, OACPH, "3rd Annual Report," 31 March 1978.
26 Ibid., Box B100558, File "Publications," Newsletter, BOOST, *The Third Eye* (25 May 1977).

27　MA, CCD Fonds, P5364, File 23, Paper, Canadian Human Rights Commission, "Employ-Ability: A Guide to the Employment of Persons with Physical Disabilities," 1982.
28　Ibid., Article, *International Rehabilitation Review* 3 (1980).
29　Rae, Musgrave, and Yale, *Selfhelp and Government Commitment*.
30　Canada Works grants were originally introduced in 1976 to replace Local Initiatives Programs and were intended to further stimulate the development of innovative social programs, such as those proposed by BOOST.
31　Rae, Musgrave, and Yale, *Selfhelp and Government Commitment*.
32　Minister of Supply and Services Canada, *Obstacles*.
33　Ibid.
34　Canadian Employment and Immigration Commission, *Employ-Ability: A Guide to the Employment of Persons with Physical Disabilities*, 1982.
35　Ontario Task Force on Employers and Disabled Persons, *Linking for Employment: Report of the Task Force on Employers and Disabled Persons* (Toronto: Queen's Printer, 1983).
36　Ibid.
37　Ibid.
38　Royal Commission on Equality in Employment, *Report*.
39　Ibid.
40　Rosalie Silberman Abella, "A Generation of Human Rights: Looking Back to the Future," *Osgoode Hall Law Journal* 36:3 (1998): 597–616.
41　Ravi Malhotra, "The Legal Genealogy of the Duty to Accommodate American and Canadian Workers with Disabilities: A Comparative Perspective," *Washington University Journal of Law and Policy* 1 (2007): 1–32.
42　Canadian Council on Rehabilitation and Work, *Focus on Ability: An Employer's Handbook on Employment and Disability* (Winnipeg: CCRW, 1991).
43　Patricia Thornton and Neil Lunt, "Employment for Disabled People: Social Obligation or Individual Responsibility," *Social Policy Reports* 2 (Toronto: York University Social Policy Research Unit, 1995).
44　Ibid.
45　MA, CCD Fonds, Box T1282, File 22, Submission, COPOH, "Request for Qualifications Canadian Sponsorship Job Accommodation Network," 1990/91.
46　Ontario Human Rights Commission, *Guidelines for Assessing Accommodation Requirements for Persons with Disabilities* (Toronto: Queen's Printer, 1993).
47　Standing Committee on Human Rights and the Status of Disabled Persons, *A Consensus for Action: The Economic Integration of Disabled Persons* (Ottawa: Queen's Printer, 1990).

48 MA, CCD Fonds, Box Q012253,File "DPU," Report, National Welfare Grants Division, "Status Report on the Integration of Adult Persons with Disabilities into the Regular Labour Market," 3 July 1992.

49 Rae, Musgrave, and Yale, *Selfhelp and Government Commitment*; MA, CCD Fonds, Box P4360, File 2, Open Letter, COPOH, "Our Challenge: To All Candidates, Political Parties and the General Public in the Forthcoming Federal Election of 1979," 1979.

50 MA, CCD Fonds, Box P5360, File 18, Report, Jim Derksen, "Progress Report to COPOH National Council Concerning Federal Government Responses to Obstacles Report Recommendations," 23 February 1982, Recommendation 25.

51 AO, RG 7-148, Box B217563, File "Publications," Report, Metro Toronto Human Resources Development, "Employment of Physically Handicapped People," 22 March 1979.

52 Charles Lammam, Milagros Palacios, Feixue Ren, and Jason Clemens, "Comparing Public and Private Sector Compensation in Canada: Studies in Labour Markets," *Fraser Institute Bulletin* (December 2013), 9–10.

53 Ontario Ministry of Labour, *The Hamilton Affirmative Action Project for the Physically Disabled*.

54 Ibid.

55 Ibid.

56 AO, RG 7-148, Box 217563, File "Professional Outreach," Ontario Association for the Mentally Retarded and MCSS, "Understanding the Mentally Retarded," c. 1979; Marc Gold and Associates, "About Marc Gold," accessed 23 May 2013, https://www.marcgold.com. The assembly demonstration was performed by students of Marc Gold, whose "Try Another Way" workshops toured Canada and the United States during the 1970s, presenting to audiences of disability professionals and employers. The distillation of this approach was reproduced as part of a joint project between the Ontario Association for the Mentally Retarded and the Ontario Ministry of Community and Social Services and reflected a typical promotional pamphlet that encouraged employers to rethink their prejudicial attitudes regarding the employment of disabled people.

57 AO, RG 7-148, Box 217563, File "Agencies," Pamphlet, Personnel Association of Toronto, "Hiring the Handicapped," 3–4 December 1980.

58 Ibid., Paper, Personnel Association of Toronto and Handicapped Employment Program, "Employing People with Handicaps," 1981/82.

59 LAC, RG 29, Box 210, File 4315-06-91 001, Brief, CCRW, "Richard Pimentel," 1991.

60 CCRW, "An Emerging Workforce: Strategies to Employ Persons with Disabilities," Conference proceedings, 1990.

61 Ed Jackson, "Metro Votes for Equal Opportunity but Refuses to Say Who's Equal," *Body Politic* (1 October 1980).

62 MA, CCD Fonds, File 21, Pamphlet, Handicapped Employment Program, "Introduction to Employing the Handicapped," 1980.

63 Metropolitan Toronto Equal Employment Opportunity Division, *Equal Employment Opportunity: First Report* (Toronto, 1985).

64 Ibid.

65 Metropolitan Toronto Equal Employment Opportunity Division, *Equal Employment Opportunity: A Strategy for the 90s* (Toronto, 1989).

66 Ibid.

67 LAC, RG 29, Box 210, File 35, Letter, CILT to NHWC, 15 January 1992.

68 AO, RG 74-30, Box B162586, File "Employment Equity," Paper, Ontario Public Service, "Accommodation in Employment for Persons with Disabilities: Policy Framework," 10 April 1990.

69 Turnbull, *Looking in the Mirror*, 151.

70 Wilton, "Working at the Margins," 132.

71 Ibid.

72 AO, RG 7-148, Box B377723, File "General Series Computers," Paper, Ontario Ministry of Labour, "Computers and the Handicapped: Pilot Employment Project: Proposal," 1980. For further discussion of the impact of technology on the experiences of work for people with disabilities see Alan Roulstone, "Employment Barriers and Inclusive Futures?" in *Disabling Barriers, Enabling Environments*, ed. John Swain, Sally French, Colin Barnes, and Carol Thomas (London: SAGE, 2004; 2nd ed.); Roulstone, "Disabling Pasts, Enabling Futures? How Does the Changing Nature of Capitalism Impact on the Disabled Worker and Jobseeker?" *Disability & Society* 17:6 (2002): 627; Roulstone, *Enabling Technology: Disabled People, Work, and New Technology* (Philadelphia: Open University Press, 1998).

73 AO, RG 7-148, Box B100558, File "Speeches/TV," Article, CNIB, *Employment Services NEWS* 2:2 (May 1979).

74 Ibid., Box B377723, File "Employment Practices Accessibility," Paper, IBM, "Removing a Barrier …," c.1981; and File "Employment Practices Accessibility," Article, IBM, "'Unhandicapping' Blind Office Workers with a Speaking Typewriter," *Solutions* 8:1 (1981).

75 Valentine and Vickers, "Released from the Yoke of Paternalism," 1996.

76 Roulstone, "Disabling Pasts, Enabling Futures?" 636–7.

77 Dimitris Michailakis, "Information and Communication Technologies and the Opportunities of Disabled Persons in the Swedish Labour Market,"

Disability & Society 16:4 (2001): 496; Richard Scotch and Kay Schriner, "Disability as Human Variation: Implications for Policy," *Annals of the American Academy of Political and Social Science* 549 (1997): 155.

78 Wilton, "Working at the Margins," 190; O'Brien, "From a Doctor's to a Judge's Gaze," 345.

79 Wilton, "Working at the Margins," 132.

80 CRCD, "Attitude Overhaul," *Rehabilitation Digest* 10:2 (1979).

81 Ibid.

82 AO, RG 7-149, Box B367312, File "Assistive Devices," Letter, OMOD to Study Committee on Assistive Devices, 10 April 1981.

83 "Paul," interview with author, 23 June 2011.

84 "Alex," interview with author, 24 June 2011.

85 "Mary," interview with author, 22 June 2011.

86 "Emily," interview with author, 28 June 2011.

87 "Ashley," interview with author, 20 February 2012.

88 "Paul."

89 "Lily," interview with author, 27 June 2011.

90 "Mary."

7 Rise and Decline of the Activist Canadian State

1 Bruce Ackerman, "Foreword: Law in an Activist State," *Yale Law Journal* 92:7 (1983): 1083.

2 Valentine and Vickers, "Released from the Yoke of Paternalism," 169.

3 United Nations, Declaration on the Rights of Disabled Persons (Geneva: General Assembly, 1975), Resolution 3447.

4 Ibid.

5 MA, CCD Fonds, Box P5364, File 2, Paper, COPOH, "Government Plans for Increasing Opportunities for Employment of the Physically and Mentally Handicapped in the Federal Public Service," 21 March 1978.

6 Richard Gwyn, *The Northern Magus: Pierre Trudeau and Canadians* (Toronto: McClelland & Stewart, 1980), 130.

7 Pierre Elliott Trudeau, "The Values of a Just Society," in *Towards A Just Society: The Trudeau Years*, ed. Pierre Elliott Trudeau and Lloyd Axworthy (Toronto: Penguin, 1990), 358–61.

8 Ibid., 358

9 Ibid., 360.

10 Valentine and Vickers, "Released from the Yoke of Paternalism," 164.

11 United Nations, International Year of Disabled Persons (Geneva: General Assembly, 1976), Resolution 21/123.

12 The Canadian Human Rights Act was amended in 1980 to include people with "mental disabilities" in addition to people with physical disabilities; Canadian Human Rights Act, R.S.C. 1980.
13 Ontario Legislative Assembly, "An Act to Provide for the Employment of Disabled Persons," Bill 181, 31st Legislature, 2nd session, 1978. [Toronto]: The Assembly, 1978; Ontario Legislative Assembly, "An Act to Provide for the Employment of Disabled Persons," Bill 104, 31st Legislature, 4th session, 1980. [Toronto]: The Assembly, 1980; Ontario Legislative Assembly, "An Act to Provide for the Employment of Disabled Persons," Bill 44, 32nd Legislature, 1st session, [Toronto]: The Assembly, 1981; Ontario Legislative Assembly, "An Act to Provide for the Employment of Disabled Persons," 32nd Legislature, 2nd session, Bill 69, [Toronto]: The Assembly, 1982; Ontario Legislative Assembly, "An Act to Provide for the Employment of Disabled Persons," 33rd Legislature, 1st session, Bill 100, [Toronto]: The Assembly, 1986; Ontario Legislative Assembly, "An Act to Provide for the Employment of Disabled Persons," 33rd Legislature, 3rd session, Bill 37, [Toronto]: The Assembly, 1987; Ontario Legislative Assembly, "An Act to Provide for the Employment of Disabled Persons," 34th Legislature, 1st session, [Toronto]: The Assembly, 1987.
14 Ontario Legislative Assembly, "An Act to Provide for the Employment of Disabled Persons," Bill 181, 31st Legislature, 2nd session, 1978. [Toronto]: The Assembly, 1978.
15 Robert Mackenzie, "Disabled Persons Employment Act" in Ontario Legislative Assembly, Legislative Debates (Hansard), 32nd Legislature, 1st session (1 May 1981), accessed 17 August 2013, http://hansardindex.ontla.on.ca/hansardeissue/32-1/l009.htm.
16 Michael Cassidy, "Human Rights Code" in Ontario Legislative Assembly, Legislative Debates (Hansard), 32nd Legislature, 1st session (19 May 1981), accessed 17 August 2013, http://hansardindex.ontla.on.ca/hansarde issue/32-1/l022.htm.
17 United States Congress, 29, Rehabilitation Act, Washington, 1973: Section 501; Great Britain, Disabled Persons (Employment) Act, London, 1944.
18 Robert Mackenzie, "Throne Speech Debate," in Ontario Legislative Assembly, Legislative Debates (Hansard), 34th Legislature, 2nd session (8 May 1989), accessed 17 August 2013, http://hansardindex.ontla.on.ca/hansardeissue/34-2/l008.htm.
19 Minister of Supply and Services Canada, Obstacles.
20 Ibid, 5.
21 TA, SC 113, File 92, Letter, Federation of Canadian Municipalities to Special Parliamentary Committee on the Disabled and Handicapped, 8 January 1981.

22 Virtual Museum, "Disability Rights in Canada: A Virtual Museum,"
    accessed 28 May 2013, http://disabilityrights.freeculture.ca/exhibits_
    th_p_idc.php
23 David Lepofsky, "The *Charter's* Guarantee of Equality to People with
    Disabilities: How Well Is It Working?" *Windsor Yearbook of Access to Justice*
    16 (1998): 168; Chivers, "Barrier by Barrier," 318.
24 "Disabled Demand Rights," *Winnipeg Free Press* (22 October 1981).
25 United Nations, World Programme of Action Concerning Disabled Persons
    (Geneva: General Assembly, 1982), Resolution 37/52; United Nations,
    Decade of Disabled Persons (Geneva: General Assembly, 1982), Resolution
    37/52.
26 "PM Names Minister for Disabled," *Toronto Star* (1981); AO, RG 74-30, Box
    B162577, File "ODP," Article, Minister Responsible for Disabled Persons,
    "Introductory Statement: 1986/87 Estimates, ODP," 6 November 1986.
27 AO, RG 74-30, Box B165813, File "ODP," Paper, ODP, "Origins and Strategic
    Framework of the ODP," August 1990.
28 MA, CCD Fonds, Box T1282, File 5, Speech, Brian Mulroney, "On the
    Government's Strategy for Persons with Disabilities," Winnipeg, 6 Septem-
    ber 1991.
29 LAC, RG 29, Box 238, File 4304-1-4, Paper, "Bureau on Rehabilitation:
    NHWC," 1981.
30 Ibid., File 4314-3-19(1), Minutes, Bureau on Rehabilitation, "Deputy
    Minister's Meeting with the Ottawa Liaison Committee of Chamber
    of Commerce – Employment of the Handicapped," 20 May 1979.
31 LAC, Box 238, File 4312-4-1, Brief, "The Disability Myth," 8 December 1981.
32 Ibid., Letter, Bureau on Rehabilitation to Lauron Productions, 27 November
    1980.
33 Ibid., File 4314-4-4, Letter, CILT to DPU, 19 June 1989.
34 See chapter 1 for a discussion of the family advocacy background of
    the Toronto Mayor's Task Force on the Disabled and Elderly.
35 AO, RG 7-149, Box B363026, File "Publications," Article, Mayor's Task
    Force on the Disabled and Elderly, *Access* (1 May 1977).
36 Jon Caulfield, *The Tiny Perfect Mayor: David Crombie and Toronto's Reform
    Aldermen* (Toronto: Lorimer, 1974), ix, 20.
37 AO, RG 7-149, Box B363026, File "Publications," Article, Mayor's Task
    Force on the Disabled and Elderly, *Access* (1 May 1977).
38 John Ferri, "'Real Dynamo' to Police Metro Hiring," *Toronto Star* (1981).
39 Ibid.
40 MA, CCD Fonds, Box P5364, File 21, Brief, Handicapped Employment
    Program, "Employers' Questions and Answers: Specific Disabilities and
    How to Cope," 1980.

41 AO, RG 74-30, Box B391448, File "Mayor's Task Force," Letter, Working Committee of Mayor's Task Force on Disabled/Elderly to Neighbourhoods Committee, 30 November 1981.

42 Caulfield, *The Tiny Perfect Mayor*, 74.

43 AO, RG 7-148, Box B100616, File "HEP and OMOD Articles," Article, OACPH, "OACPH Column," *Advocate* (November/December 1981).

44 Ibid., Box B100558, File "HEP Activity Report," Report, Handicapped Employment Program, "Report on Activity From September 1978 to November 1979," 1979.

45 John Rae, interview with author, 27 June 2011.

46 Ibid.

47 LAC, RG 29, Box 210, File 44, Brief, "Access Connections: Media Connection Narrative Report," April 1990.

48 Liam Lacey, "Radio Show Is Voice for Disabled," *Globe and Mail* (20 February 1988) E3.

49 LAC, RG 29, Box 210, File 25, Submission, Centre for Independent Living Toronto to Health and Welfare Canada, "Application for Health and Welfare Canada Independent Living Centre Pilot Project Funding," 15 January 1992.

50 AO, RG 7-148, Box B100558, File "Publications Posters," Open Letter, Ministry of Labour, 1981.

51 AO, RG 7-149, Box B367312, File "Employer Awareness Posters," Brief, "Jonathan Milne," 1981.

52 Jonathan Milne, interview with author, 31 January 2013.

53 AO, RG 7-148, Box B100558, File "Publications Posters," Letter, Assistant Deputy Minister of Labour to Minister of Labour, 27 April 1981.

54 Ibid., Letter, Handicapped Employment Program to Minister of Labour, 11 May 1981.

55 "New Poster on Disabled Called 'In Poor Taste,'" *Toronto Star* (24 April 1981), A3 .

56 AO, RG 7-148, Box B100558, File "Publications Posters," Letter, Working Committee of the Mayor's Task Force on the Disabled and Elderly to Minister of Labour, 22 April 1981.

57 Jonathan Milne, interview.

58 John Stapleton and Catherine Laframboise, "Coming of Age in a Man's World: The Life, Times and Wisdom of Dorothea Crittenden, Canada's First Female Deputy Minister," unpublished paper, January 2007, accessed 12 June 2013, https://openpolicyontario.com.

59 Brian Howe, "The Evolution of Human Rights Policy in Ontario," *Canadian Journal of Political Science* 24:4 (1991): 798–802; Ontario Human Rights

Commission, *The Donna Young Report: The Handling of Race Complaints at the Ontario Human Rights Commission* (Toronto: Queen's Printer, 1992).

60 AO, RG 7-148, Box B100558, File "Publications Posters," Letter, Ontario Human Rights Commission to Minister of Labour, May 1981.

61 Ibid., Brief, Handicapped Employment Program, "HEP Posters," 1 June 1981.

62 Ibid., Box B217563, File "Professional Outreach," Report, OACPH, "3rd Annual Report," 31 March 1978.

63 Sidney Katz, "Disabled Don't Want Sympathy," *Toronto Star* (18 November 1978), C5.

64 AO, RG 74-30, Box B167563, File "Labour Study (1)," Letter, OACPH to SDP, 28 April 1986.

65 Ibid., File "Professional Outreach," Brief, OACPH, 15 December 1978.

66 Katz, "Disabled Don't Want Sympathy."

67 AO, RG 7-148, Box B217563, File "Professional Outreach," Paper, OACPH, "OACPH Holds Public Forum," 3 November 1978.

68 Katz, "Disabled Don't Want Sympathy."

69 AO, RG 7-148, Box B217563, File "Professional Outreach," Report, OACPH, "3rd Annual Report," 31 March 1978.

70 Ibid., Report, OACPH, "4th Annual Report," September 1979.

71 Ibid., File "Agencies," Report, OACPH, "5th Annual Report," 1980.

72 Ontario Legislative Assembly, "An Act to Provide for the Rights of Handicapped Persons," 31st session, 3rd session, 1979, [Toronto]: The Assembly, 1979.

73 Ontario Human Rights Commission, *Life Together*; AO, RG 7-149, Box B363026, File "Publications," Article, "Advocacy Research Centre for the Handicapped," *ARCH Type* 1:1 (January 1981).

74 Lepofsky, "The Long, Arduous Road," 135–6.

75 Ibid.

76 Ibid.

77 Ibid.; John Rae, "History of Human Rights Protection for Persons with Disabilities in Ontario," Alliance for Equality of Blind Canadians (2006), accessed 16 February 2013, http://www.blindcanadians.ca/publications/briefs/2006-flawed-process-flawed-bill.

78 AO, RG 74-31, Box B180996, File "Sunset Review," Report, OMOD, "Report Card on the OACPH," 17 May 1982.

79 Rae, "History of Human Rights Protection."

80 MA, CCD Fonds, Box T1272, File 5, Letter, Kim Campbell to COPOH, 7 September 1993.

81 Ibid., Box T1282, File 7, Letter, CCD to Prime Minister Jean Chrétien, "Changes to Federal Cabinet," 29 January 1996.

82 Ibid., Letter, CCD to Prime Minister Jean Chrétien, "Government of Canada Turns its Back on Canadians with Disabilities," 29 April 1996; CCD Fonds, Box T1282, File 7, Letter, CCD to Prime Minister Jean Chrétien, 22 April 1997.
83 Ontario Legislative Assembly, Employment Equity Act, S.O. (1993): Chapter 35. Repealed 14 December 1995, c.4, s.1(1).
84 Bob Rae, "Social Contract" in Ontario Legislative Assembly, *Legislative Debates (Hansard)*, 35th Legislature, 3rd Session (9 June 1993), accessed 17 August 2013, http://hansardindex.ontla.on.ca/hansardeissue/35-3/1030.htm.
85 LAC, Box 210, File 4315-06-91 001, pamphlet, Training Coordinating Group [TCG] for PwD, "Real Skills ... for Real Work," 1991.
86 Chouinard and Crooks, "Negotiating Neoliberal Environments," 176; Storey, "Social Assistance or a Worker's Right," 87; Lepofsky, "The Long, Arduous Road," 150.
87 Thomas Walkom, "MPPs' Failure to Help Disabled Makes No Sense," *Toronto Star* (18 May 1996), F5.
88 AO, RG 74-30, Box B419190, File "OPS Advisory Group," Open Draft Letter, Michael Harris, Leader, Ontario Progressive Conservative Party, 1993.
89 Ibid., Box B432612, File "Equal Opportunity," Speech, Minister of Citizenship, Culture and Recreation, "To the Toronto Employment Equity Practitioners' Association Conference," 8 February 1996.
90 "Untapped Resource," *Financial Post* (2 May 1981).
91 Ibid.
92 Lepofsky, "The Long, Arduous Road," 149; Ontarians with Disabilities Act Committee, "Promise Letter to the ODA Committee," accessed 13 June 2013, http://www.odacommittee.net/letters/promise.html
93 AO, RG 74-30, Box B419190, File "Undue Hardship," Brief, Disability Issues Group, "Proposed Questions and Answers for Minister's Visit to the Ontario Games for the Physically Disabled," 6 July 1995; Ibid., Box B432612, File "Equal Opportunity Orientation Package," Speech, Minister of Citizenship, Culture and Recreation, "To the Toronto Employment Equity Practitioners' Association Conference," 8 February 1996.
94 Lepofsky, "The Long, Arduous Road," 149; Ontarians with Disabilities Act Committee, "Promise Letter to the ODA Committee."
95 "The Long, Arduous Road."
96 AO, RG 74-30, Box B419190, File "Equal Opportunity," Disability Issues Group, "Joblink Ontario Innovations Fund: First Year of Operation," 1994–5.

97 Laurie Montebraaten, "Disabled Win Battle of the Barriers," *Toronto Star* (17 May 1996).
98 AO, RG 74-30, Box B419190, File "OPS Advisory Group," Letter, Advisory Group on Employment Equity for Persons with Disabilities to Deputy Minister of Labour, 17 October 1994.
99 Ibid., Letter, Centre for Disability and Work to David Lepofsky, 7 December 1994.
100 Ibid., Letter, Advisory Group on Employment Equity for Persons with Disabilities to Deputy Minister of Labour, 17 October 1994.
101 TA, SC 1089, File 275, Paper, Daily Bread Food Bank, "The Disabled and the Common Sense Revolution," 4 June 1997; AO, RG 74-30, Box B162585, File "Income," Submission, Income Maintenance for the Handicapped Co-ordinating Group to Standing Committee on Finance and Economic Affairs, "Pre-Budget Consultation, 1990–91," 16 January 1990.
102 David Crombie, *The Disability Network* (Toronto: CBC Television), 1 February 1997; Crombie, *CBC Evening News* (Toronto: CBC Television), 29 January 1997.
103 AO, RG 74-30, Box B834951, File "Who Does What," Paper, Ministry of Citizenship, Culture & Recreation, "Who Does What 'SWAT' Team," 1997; Ibid., "Who Does What Provincial/Municipal Transition Team," 1997.

8 Labour Organizations, Disability Rights, and the Limitations of Social Unionism

1 Derek Fudge and Patty Holmes, *Together for Social Change: Employing Disabled Canadians* (Ottawa: COPOH and the National Union of Provincial Government Employees, 1983).
2 *Challenging Attitudes*, Canadian Union of Public Employees, Video (Ottawa: CUPE National Equality Branch, 2007). Quotation from CUPE National President Paul Moist delivered to a meeting of CUPE's Working Group for Persons with Disabilities.
3 Craig Heron, *The Canadian Labour Movement* (Toronto: Lorimer, 1996), 95.
4 Ibid., 96.
5 Desmond Morton, "Government Worker Unions: A Review Article," *Labour / Le Travail* 35 (Spring 1995): 299.
6 Heron, *The Canadian Labour Movement*, 98; Morton, "Government Worker Unions," 298.
7 Canadian Union of Public Employees, "Topics," accessed 26 March 2013, https://cupe.ca/topics.
8 Heron, *The Canadian Labour Movement*, 147.

9 Diane Driedger, The Last Civil Rights Movement: Disabled People's International (New York: St Martin's Press, 1989); Paul Longmore and Lauri Umansky, "Disability History: From the Margins to the Mainstream," in The New Disability History: American Perspectives, ed. Paul Longmore and Lauri Umansky (New York: New York University Press, 2001); Charlton, Nothing About Us Without Us, 149.

10 TA, SC 1143, Item 2357, Paper, Metro EEO Division, "Equal Employment Opportunity: A Strategy for the 90s," June 1989.

11 David Rayside and Fraser Valentine, "Broadening the Labour Movement's Disability Agenda," in Equity, Diversity, and Canadian Labour, ed. Gerald Hunt and David Rayside (Toronto: University of Toronto Press, 2007), 178.

12 Canadian Union of Public Employees, Equal Opportunity at Work: A CUPE Affirmative Action Manual (Ottawa: CUPE Education Department 1976), 3.

13 MA, CCD Fonds, Box Q012249, File 3, Policy Statement, COPOH and Canadian Labour Congress, "Draft Policy Statement on the Disabled," 1980.

14 Patty Holmes, "CLC Action Plan for Disabled Persons," Canadian Labour 26:7 (September 1981).

15 Canadian Charter of Rights and Freedoms, Section 2, Part I of the Constitution Act, 1982. Section 15 of the Charter provided for the protection from discrimination of people with a mental or physical disability.

16 Ibid., Section 15(1).

17 Abella, "A Generation of Human Rights," 601.

18 Armstrong, "Disability Advocacy in the Charter Era," 38–40.

19 Lavigne v. Ontario Public Service Employees Union, [1991] 2 S.C.R. 211.

20 Ontario Federation of Labour, "Labour and the Charter," 29th Annual Convention (November 1985), 4.

21 Canadian Union of Public Employees, "Collective Rights," in Jeff Rose: Worth Fighting For: Selected Speeches and Articles, 1983–1991 (Ottawa: Canadian Union of Public Employees, 1991).

22 Judy Rebick, "The Political Impact of the Charter," Supreme Court Law Review 29 (2005): 85–91.

23 M. Kaye Joachim, "Conflicts Between the Accommodation of Disabled Workers and Seniority Rights" (MA thesis, University of Toronto, 1997), 67; Ravi Malhotra, "The Duty to Accommodate Unionized Workers with Disabilities in Canada and the United States: A Counter-Hegemonic Approach, "Journal of Law & Equality 2 (2003): 92–155.

24 Centre for Addiction and Mental Health (CAMH) Archives, Lakeshore Psychiatric Hospital (LPH) Fonds, File 2-12, Paper, Walther

Melamet-Vetter, "The Lakeshore Psychiatric Hospital: A World in Its Own, Another Coocoo's [*sic*] Nest in New Toronto," 1989.

25 Ibid., File 2-17, Brief, Ministry of Health, 17 February 1979.
26 Ibid., File 2-12, Paper, Ontario Public Service Employees Union, "The Closing of Lakeshore Psychiatric Hospital: The Case for Reconsideration," 1979.
27 Ibid., Paper, McKinsey & Co., "A Role Study of Lakeshore, Queen Street and Whitby Psychiatric Hospitals," Government of Ontario, 1978.
28 Paul McClellan, "Supplementary Estimates: Ministry of Health," Legislative Assembly of Ontario, *Parliamentary Debates (Hansard)*, 29 March 1982.
29 CAMH Archives, LPH Fonds, File 2-12, Paper, McKinsey & Co., "A Role Study."
30 Ibid., File 2-17, Speech, Minister of Health to Metro Toronto Mental Health Services, 22 January 1979.
31 The Queen Street Mental Health Centre was subsequently renamed the Centre for Addiction and Mental Health. For background on the facility and its role in the provincial public health system see Geoffrey Reaume, "999 Queen Street West: Patient Life at the Toronto Hospital for the Insane, 1870–1940" (PhD diss., University of Toronto, 1997).
32 CAMH Archives, LPH Fonds, File 2-12, Paper, OPSEU, 1979.
33 Ibid., File 2-17, Speech, Minister of Health, 1979.
34 Ibid., File 2-12, Paper, OPSEU, 1979.
35 AO, RG 7-148, Box B353794, File "Labour OFL," Paper, Ontario Federation of Labour, "Outline of Study of Handicapped Workers: Provisions in Collective Agreements," 1978.
36 MA, CCD Fonds, Box Q012242, File 11, Letter, COPOH to Treasury Board of Canada, 4 March 1986.
37 "Union Seniority Rules Have Shut Us Out, Delegates Say," *Kingston Whig-Standard* (28 May 1979), 2.
38 "Handicapped Unemployed," *Globe and Mail* (25 May 1979).
39 "Union Seniority Rules Have Shut Us Out."
40 AO, RG 7-148, Box B377723, File "General Series," Paper, Handicapped Employment Program, 15 January 1982.
41 Michael Lynk, "Accommodating Disabilities in the Canadian Workplace," *Canadian Blind Monitor* 183 (1999).
42 AO, RG 7-148, Box B217563, File "Agencies," Paper, Ontario Federation of Labour, 1982.
43 Lynk, "Accommodating Disabilities in the Canadian Workplace."

44 Ibid.
45 "David," interview with author, 27 June 2011.
46 "David."
47 "Lisa," interview with author, 17 June 2011.
48 "Lisa"; "David."
49 AO, RG, 7-148, Box B100558, File "Publications," Article, *Canadian Labour* 24:7 (29 June 1979).
50 AO, RG 7-149, Box B363026, File "Publications," Article, "Law Reform and Rehabilitation Themes of 12th Safety Conference," 1981; John Williams-Searle, "Broken Brothers and Soldiers of Capital: Disability, Manliness, and Safety on the Rails, 1863–1908" (PhD diss., University of Iowa, 2004).
51 "Law Reform and Rehabilitation Themes of 12th Safety Conference," *Canadian Labour* 26:9 (November/December 1981).
52 Oliver, "The Social Model in Context," 19–25; Michael Oliver and Colin Barnes, *The New Politics of Disablement* (New York: Palgrave Macmillan, 2012); Cameron and Valentine, "Comparing Policy-Making in Federal Systems," 4–8; Liachowitz, *Disability as a Social Construct.*
53 Oliver, "The Social Model in Context," 19–25.
54 Ontario Federation of Labour, "Persons with Disabilities: Labour's View," 2 December 2001: 5, 8. This policy statement from the OFL in 2001 spoke of the need to continue to develop close relationships with disability organizations and how the labour movement has been much more successful in developing formal institutional links with injured workers organizations such as the Canadian Injured Workers Alliance, Ontario Network of Injured Workers, and affiliate organizations than with disability rights organizations.
55 Storey, "Social Assistance or a Worker's Right," 73; Campolieti and Lavis, "Disability Expenditures in Canada," 261; Martha McClusky, "Reforming Insurance to Support Workers' Rights to Compensation," *American Journal of Industrial Medicine* 55 (2012): 545–59.
56 "Fair Compensation for Injured Workers," *Toronto Star* (22 December 1986), A12 .
57 Storey, "Their Only Power Was Moral," 128; Storey, "Social Assistance or a Worker's Right," 86.
58 Storey, "Their Only Power Was Moral," 120.
59 *A Right to Live: The Union of Injured Workers*, VHS (Toronto: Right Now Films, 1977).
60 Ibid.
61 O'Brien, "From a Doctor's to a Judge's Gaze," 328.
62 Storey, "Social Assistance or a Worker's Right," 72.

63 Ibid.

64 *A Right to Live.*

65 Advocacy Research Centre for the Handicapped, "ARCH – Celebrating 25 Years," accessed 24 November 2012, http://www.archdisabilitylaw. ca/?q=history.

66 MA, CCD Fonds, Box T1288, File 1, Minutes, Steering Committee for Study Group on Employment and Disability, 6 December 1990.

67 *Nova Scotia (Workers' Compensation Board) v. Martin* [2003] 2 S.C.R. 504; *Nova Scotia (Workers' Compensation Board) v. Laseur*, [2003] 2 S.C.R. 504; see also Ravi Malhotra and Morgan Rowe, "Justice Gonthier and Disability Rights: The Case of Nova Scotia (Workers' Compensation Board) v. Martin," *Supreme Court Law Review* 56 (2012).

68 *A Right to Live* (see n59).

69 CCRW, "Canadian Injured Workers Alliance," *Ability & Enterprise* 6:1 (March 1993).

70 Ibid.

71 LAC, RG 29, Box 210, File 4315-06-92/12, Report, Canadian Injured Workers Alliance (CIWA), "The Re-Employment of Injured Workers: Working Together for a Fair Deal," 1990.

72 Ibid., Brief, CIWA, "Strategic Plan," December 1991.

73 Ibid., Letter, CIWA to DPU, 6 July 1993.

74 "Lisa"; "David."

75 *A Right to Live.*

76 Storey, "Their Only Power Was Moral," 114.

77 *A Right to Live.*

78 MA, CCD Fonds, Box P5367, File 30, Newsletter, Handicapped Communications Society, *The Spokesman* (9 September 1979).

79 AO, RG 7-148, Box B100660, File "News Clippings," Article, National Union of Public and General Employees, "NUPGE Program to Assist Disabled Workers," *Canadian Labour* (October 1981).

80 LAC, RG 29, Box 210, File 4314-4-3, Report, Bureau on Rehabilitation, "Organization, Implementation and Assessment of Opportunities for Canadian Sheltered Workshops in the Recycling Industry: Implementation – Fort Erie, Ontario," January 1981.

81 "Group Rejects Union Scheme for Disabled," *Globe and Mail* (16 October 1981).

82 Ibid.

83 Ibid.

84 CCRW, "Labor's Awareness of Supported Employment," *Ability & Enterprise* 4:2 (Spring 1990).

85 MA, CCD Fonds, Box Q012249, File 3, Letter, COPOH to CLC, 23 September 1982.

86 Ibid., Letter, COPOH to CLC, 29 October 1982.

87 Ibid., Letter, CLC to COPOH, 29 April 1981.

88 Ibid., Submission, CLC, "For the Canadian Government Delegation Attending the 68th Session of the International Labour Conference, Geneva, Switzerland," 1982.

89 Canadian Labour Congress, *Policy Statement on the Disabled* (Ottawa: CLC, 1980).

90 Fudge and Holmes, *Together for Social Change.*

91 CCD, "Labour and Disability," *Abilities* (Fall 1994).

92 William Carroll and R.S. Ratner, "Old Unions and New Social Movements," *Labour / Le Travail* 35 (Spring 1995): 196.

93 Human Resources Development Canada, *Final Report on the Proceedings from the National Workplace Equity Symposium for Persons with Disabilities* (Ottawa, April 1998).

94 Carroll and Ratner, "Old Unions and New Social Movements," 218.

95 Ibid.

96 Ibid., 196.

97 Havi Echenberg, "Income Security and Support for Persons with Disabilities: Future Directions" Canadian Labour Congress, February 1998, 2.

98 Yvonne Peters, "Survey on People with Disabilities," CUPE Equality Branch, 1992, 2.

99 Canadian Labour Congress, *The MORE We Get Together: Disability Rights and Collective Bargaining Manual* (Ottawa: CLC, 2004).

100 Ibid., 16–32.

101 Ibid.

102 Rayside and Valentine, "Broadening the Labour Movement's Disability Agenda," 178–9.

Conclusion

1 Alan Puttee, ed., *Federalism, Democracy and Disability Policy in Canada* (Montreal: Institute of Intergovernmental Relations, 2002); Cameron and Valentine, "Comparing Policy-Making in Federal Systems," 1–44.

2 Mark Weber, "The Americans with Disabilities Act and Employment: A Non-Retrospective," *Alabama Law Review* 52:1 (2000): 375–418.

3 World Health Organization and World Bank, *World Report on Disability*, xxi.

4 Ibid., 238.

5 Ibid., 235.

6 Human Resources and Skills Development Canada, *Rethinking Disability in the Private Sector: We All Have Abilities. Some Are Just More Apparent Than Others. Report from the Panel on Labour Market Opportunities for Persons with Disabilities* (Ottawa: Human Resources and Skills Development Canada, 2013).

7 Kelly, "Towards Renewed Descriptions," 1–27.

8 CCD, "Disabling Poverty/Enabling Citizenship (CURA)," accessed 18 July 2013 http://www.ccdonline.ca/en/socialpolicy/poverty-citizenship.

9 Yvonne Peters & Michael J. Prince, "Disability, Poverty and Citizenship: A Short Note for The Community-University Research Alliance," Council of Canadians with Disabilities, February 2009.

10 Chouinard and Crooks, "Negotiating Neoliberal Environments," 173–90.

11 Linda Kealey, ed., *A Not Unreasonable Claim: Women and Reform in Canada, 1880s–1920s* (Toronto: The Women's Press, 1979); Joan Sangster, *Dreams of Equality: Women on the Canadian Left, 1920–1950* (Toronto: McClelland & Stewart, 1989); Marlene Epp, Franca Iacovetta, and Frances Swripa, eds, *Sisters or Strangers? Immigrant, Ethnic and Racialized Women in Canadian History* (Toronto: University of Toronto Press, 2004).

12 Kudlick, "Disability History," 763–93.

Bibliography

Primary Sources

Archives

ARCHIVES OF MANITOBA (MA)
Council of Canadians with Disabilities Fonds.

ARCHIVES OF ONTARIO (AO)
Handicapped Employment Program. RG 7-148.
Handicapped Employment Program – Operation Media Files. RG 7-149.
Office for Disability Issues. RG 74-30.
Secretariat for Disabled Persons. RG 74-49.

CENTRE FOR ADDICTION AND MENTAL HEALTH (CAMH) ARCHIVES
Lakeshore Psychiatric Hospital (LPH) Fonds.
999 News Periodical Collection.

CITY OF TORONTO ARCHIVES (TA)
Alexandra Studio Fonds. F 1257.
Bruce Sinclair Fonds. F 288.
City of Toronto Archives Collection. F 2.
Michele Landsberg Fonds. F 250.
Anne Johnston Fonds. F 1312.
David Hutcheon Fonds. F 1683.
C. Dennis Flynn Fonds. F 10.
Elizabeth Anglin Fonds. F 61.
Papers and Theses Collection. F 92.

Urban Alliance on Race Relations Fonds. F 40.
Municipality of Metropolitan Toronto Fonds. F 220.
Rochdale Community Forum Fonds. F 27.
City of North York Fonds. F 217.
Eric Hounsom Fonds. F 1248.
Barbara Hall Fonds. F 1684.
City of Etobicoke Fonds. F 213.
Michele Prue Fonds. F 285.
Jack Layton Fonds. F 1361.
Former City of Toronto Fonds. F 200.
Mario Silva Fonds. F 255.
Metropolitan Toronto Housing Company Limited Fonds. F 45.
Toronto Transit Commission Fonds. F 16.
Community Folk Art Council of Toronto Fonds. F 53.
Howard Moscoe Fonds. F 301.
Patrick Corrigan Fonds. F 69.
Larry Becker Fonds. F 70.
Arts Etobicoke Fonds. F 272.

LIBRARY AND ARCHIVES CANADA (LAC)
Disabled Persons Unit. RG 29.

ORAL INTERVIEWS
"Dan." Interview with author. 10 June 2011.
"Nathan." Interview with author. 16 June 2011.
"Lisa." Interview with author. 17 June 2011.
"Robert." Interview with author. 20 June 2011.
"Mary." Interview with author. 22 June 2011.
"Linda." Interview with author. 22 June 2011.
"Paul." Interview with author. 23 June 2011.
"Jacob." Interview with author. 23 June 2011.
"Alex." Interview with author. 24 June 2011.
"Marge." Interview with author. 26 June 2011.
"David." Interview with author. 27 June 2011.
"Charlotte." Interview with author. 27 June 2011.
"Lily." Interview with author. 27 June 2011.
"Emily." Interview with author. 28 June 2011.
"Danielle." Interview with author. 30 June 2011.
"Olivia." Interview with author. 5 July 2011.

"Ruby." Interview with author. 6 July 2011.
"Katie." Interview with author. 25 July 2011.
"Michael." Interview with author. 27 July 2011.
"Isabelle." Interview with author. 28 July 2011.
"Grace." Interview with author. 28 July 2011.
"Lucy." Interview with author. 28 July 2011.
"Sarah." Interview with author. 17 September 2011.
"Richard." Interview with author. 13 September 2011.
"Thomas." Interview with author. 27 September 2011.
"Leanne." Interview with author. 20 October 2011.
"Rachel." Interview with author. 27 November 2011.
"William." Interview with author. 19 December 2011.
"Sofia." Interview with author. 12 January 2012.
"Ashley." Interview with author. 20 February 2012.

Periodicals

999 News (Queen Street Mental Health Centre). Toronto, ON. 1963–94.
Abilities Magazine. 1990–2005.
Ability & Enterprise (Canadian Council for Rehabilitation and Work). Winnipeg, MB. 1986–1997.
Access (Canadian Rehabilitation Council for the Disabled). Ottawa, ON. 1979–85.
Access (Mayor's Task Force on the Disabled and Elderly). Toronto, ON. 1977–8.
Advocate (Ontario March of Dimes). Toronto, ON. Various dates.
Canadian Human Resources Reporter. Ottawa, ON. 1987.
Canadian Labour. Toronto, ON. 1979–81.
Canadian Manufacturer, The. Toronto, ON. 1987
Chronicle, The (Canadian Association of Rehabilitation Personnel). 1979.
Emerge (Canadian Council for Rehabilitation and Work). Winnipeg, MB. 1989.
Employment Services (Canadian National Institute for the Blind). Toronto, ON. 1981–2.
Financial Post. Toronto, ON. 1981.
Globe and Mail. Toronto, ON. Various dates.
Goodwill Quarterly. Toronto, ON. 1978–9.
Hamilton Spectator. Hamilton, ON. 1981.
Kawartha Sun. Peterborough, ON. 1979.
Kingston Whig-Standard. Kingston, ON. 1977–9.
Metro Toronto Business Journal. Toronto, ON. 1979.

Ottawa Citizen. Ottawa, ON. Various dates.
Our Future (United Handicapped Groups of Ontario). Kawartha Lakes, ON. 1979
Rehabilitation Digest (Canadian Rehabilitation Council for the Disabled). Ottawa, ON. 1979.
Rehabilitation Review (International Society for Rehabilitation of the Disabled). 1980.
Reporter (Personnel Association of Toronto). 1978.
Solutions (International Business Machines). 1981.
Spokesman, The (Handicapped Communications Society). Edmonton, AB. 1979.
Third Eye, The (Blind Organization of Ontario with Selfhelp Tactics). Toronto, ON. 1976–83.
Varsity, The (University of Toronto student newspaper). 1977–81.
Toronto Star. Toronto, ON. Various Dates.
Wheels of Progress (United Handicapped Groups of Ontario). Kawartha Lakes, ON.

PRIVATE COLLECTIONS
Rob McInnes.
Gary Annable.
Joanne Smith.

Reports

Rae, John, Anne Musgrave, and Mike Yale. *Selfhelp and Government Commitment: A Call to Action. A Report from the Project Developing Alternative Service Models* (1980) Toronto: Blind Organization of Ontario with Selfhelp Tactics.
Canadian Chamber of Commerce and Health and Welfare Canada. *Employability of the Handicapped*. Ottawa: Queen's Printer, 1975.
Canadian Employment and Immigration Commission. *Employ-Ability: A Guide to the Employment of Persons with Physical Disabilities*. Ottawa: Queen's Printer, 1982.
Coalition of Provincial Organizations of the Handicapped (COPOH). *Improving Employment Opportunities for Disabled Canadians*. 28 September 1983.
Echenberg, Havi. "Income Security and Support for Persons with Disabilities: Future Directions." Canadian Labour Congress, February 1998.
E.I. DuPont de Nemours and Company. *Equal to the Task*. 1982.

Fudge, Derek and Patty Holmes. *Together for Social Change: Employing Disabled Canadians*. Ottawa: COPOH and the National Union of Provincial Government Employees, 1983.

Health and Welfare Canada. *Organization, Implementation and Assessment of Opportunities for Canadian Sheltered Workshops in the Recycling Industries*. Ottawa: Queen's Printer, 1981.

Health and Welfare Canada. *Organization, Implementation and Assessment of Opportunities for Canadian Sheltered Workshops in the Recycling Industries: Follow-up Report*. Ottawa: Queen's Printer, 1982.

Human Resources Development Canada. *Persons with Disabilities: Literature Review of the Factors Affecting Employment and Labour Force Transitions*. Applied Research Branch Strategic Policy. Ottawa: Queen's Printer, 1998.

Human Resources Development Canada. *Living with Disability in Canada: An Economic Portrait*. Ottawa: Queen's Printer, 1996.

Human Resources Development Canada. *Final Report on the Proceedings from the National Workplace Equity Symposium for Persons with Disabilities*. Ottawa: Queen's Printer, 1998.

Human Resources and Skills Development Canada. *Rethinking Disability in the Private Sector – We All Have Abilities, Some Are Just More Apparent Than Others. Report from the Panel on Labour Market Opportunities for Persons with Disabilities*. Ottawa: Queen's Printer, 2013.

Martinez, Kathy. "Independent Living in the US and Canada." Independent Living Institute, 2003.

Mayor's Task Force on the Disabled and Elderly. *This City Is for All Its Citizens*. Toronto: City of Toronto, 1973.

Metropolitan Toronto Equal Employment Opportunity Division. *Equal Employment Opportunity: A Strategy for the 90s*. Toronto, 1989.

Metropolitan Toronto Equal Employment Opportunity Division. *Equal Employment Opportunity: First Report*. Toronto, 1985.

Metropolitan Toronto Human Resources Development. *Employment of Physically Handicapped People*. Toronto, 1979.

Minister of Supply and Services Canada. *Obstacles: Report of the Parliamentary Special Committee on the Disabled and the Handicapped*. Ottawa: Queen's Printer, 1981.

National Welfare Grants Division. *Status Report on the Integration of Adult Persons with Disabilities into the Regular Labour Market*. Ottawa: Queen's Printer, 1992.

Office for Disabled Persons. *A Model for the Introduction of an Employment Equity Program for Ontario*. Toronto: Queen's Printer, 1987.

Office for Disabled Persons. *Secretariat for Disabled Persons: Strategic Directions.* Toronto: Queen's Printer, 1986.

Ontario Advisory Council for Disabled Persons. *Workable: Fulfilling the Potential of People with Disabilities.* Toronto: Queen's Printer, 1990.

Ontario Advisory Council for Persons with Disabilities. *Government Advisory Councils: The "Other" Players in the Public Policy Process.* Toronto: Queen's Printer, 1989.

Ontario Advisory Council for the Physically Handicapped. *Eleventh Annual Report.* Toronto: Queen's Printer, 1986.

Ontario Advisory Council on the Physically Handicapped. *Geneva Park Seminar.* Toronto: Queen's Printer, 1982.

Ontario Advisory Council on the Physically Handicapped. *Position Paper on the Role and Future of the Ontario Advisory Council on the Physically Handicapped.* Toronto: Queen's Printer, 1982.

Ontario Disability Issues Group. *Joblink Ontario Innovations Fund: First Year of Operation.* Toronto: Queen's Printer, 1995.

Ontario Human Rights Commission. *Guidelines for Assessing Accommodation Requirements for Persons with Disabilities.* Toronto: Queen's Printer, 1993.

Ontario Human Rights Commission. *Life Together: A Report on Human Rights in Ontario.* Toronto: Queen's Printer, 1978.

Ontario Human Rights Commission. *The Donna Young Report: The Handling of Race Complaints at the Ontario Human Rights Commission.* Toronto: Queen's Printer, 1992.

Ontario Ministry of Citizenship, Culture and Recreation. *Who Does What: Provincial/Municipal Transition Team.* Toronto: Queen's Printer, 1997.

Ontario Ministry of Labour. *Employers' Questions & Answers: Specific Disabilities and How to Cope.* Toronto: Queen's Printer, 1980.

Ontario Ministry of Labour. *Handicapped Employment Program: Report on Activity from September 1978 to November 1979.* Toronto: Queen's Printer, 1979.

Ontario Ministry of Labour. *It's Up to You ... Disabled People Can Work! Job Hunting Hints for the Handicapped.* Toronto: Queen's Printer, 1979.

Ontario Ministry of Labour. *The Hamilton Affirmative Action Project for the Physically Disabled.* Toronto: Queen's Printer, 1980.

Ontario Public Service. *Accommodation in Employment for Persons with Disabilities: Policy Framework.* Toronto: Queen's Printer, 1990.

Ontario Task Force on Employers and Disabled Persons. *Linking for Employment: Report of the Task Force on Employers and Disabled Persons.* Toronto: Queen's Printer, 1983.

Royal Commission on Equality in Employment. *Report of the Royal Commission on Equality in Employment.* Ottawa: Queen's Printer, 1984.

Standing Committee on Human Rights and the Status of Disabled Persons. *A Consensus for Action: The Economic Integration of Disabled Persons*. Ottawa: Queen's Printer, 1990.

United Nations. Decade of Disabled Persons. Geneva: General Assembly, 1982. Resolution 37/52.

United Nations. *Declaration on the Rights of Disabled Persons*. Geneva: General Assembly, 1975. Resolution 3447.

United Nations. *Declaration on the Rights of Mentally Retarded Persons*. Geneva: General Assembly, 1971. Resolution 2856.

United Nations. International Year of Disabled Persons. Geneva: General Assembly, 1976. Resolution 21/123.

United Nations. World Programme of Action Concerning Disabled Persons. Geneva: General Assembly, 1982. Resolution 37/52.

Working Committee of the Mayor's Task Force on the Disabled and Elderly. *Final Report*. Toronto, 1981.

World Health Organization and World Bank. *World Report on Disability*. Geneva, 2011.

World Health Organization. *International Classification of Impairments, Disabilities, and Handicaps*. Geneva: General Assembly, 1980.

Radio and Television Shows

Moving On (Canadian Broadcasting Corporation TV). Toronto, ON. 1998–2005.

The Disability Network (Canadian Broadcasting Corporation TV). Toronto, ON. 1997.

The Radio Connection (Access Connections). CILT, University of Toronto, and Government of Ontario. Broadcast on CIUT-FM. Toronto, ON, 1987.

Documentaries

A Difference of Ability: Recruiting, Hiring and Employing People with Disabilities. VHS. Toronto: CERIC, 2007.

A Different Approach. DVD. South Bay, CA: South Bay Mayor's Committee for Employment of the Handicapped, 1978.

A Right to Live: The Union of Injured Workers. VHS. Toronto: Right Now Films, 1977.

Hurry Tomorrow. DVD. Directed by Richard Cohen. Los Angeles: Halfway House Partnership, 1975.

Making a Difference: A Celebration. VHS. Directed by Bruce Kappel. Toronto: G. Allan Roeher Institute, 1980.

The Disability Myth, Part I: Segregation. 16 mm film. Directed by Alan Aylward. Toronto: Lauron Productions, 1981.

The Disability Myth, Part II: Employment: Beggars Can't Be Choosers. 16 mm film. Directed by Alan Aylward. Toronto: Lauron Productions, 1982.

The World of One in Seven. VHS. Directed by Michael Steele. Kingston, ON: Quarry Films, 1975.

Thursday's Child. VHS. Vancouver: Yaletown Productions, 1985.

Movies

Lorenzo's Oil. DVD. Directed by George Miller. Universal City, CA: Universal Pictures, 1992.

Secondary Sources

Books

Alexander, John. *Capabilities and Social Justice: The Political Philosophy of Amartya Sen and Martha Nussbaum*. Burlington, VT: Ashgate, 2008.

Barnes, Colin. *Cabbage Syndrome: The Social Construction of Dependence* New York: Falmer Press, 1990.

Barnes, Colin. *Disabling Imagery and the Media: An Exploration of the Principles for Media Representations of Disabled People*. Halifax, UK: Ryburn Publishing Services, 1992.

Bartrip, Sandra. *The Wounded Soldiers of Industry: Industrial Compensation Policy, 1833–1897*. Cambridge: Cambridge University Press, 1983.

Bender, Daniel. *Sweated Work, Weak Bodies: Anti-Sweatshop Campaigns and Languages of Labour*. New Brunswick, NJ: Rutgers University Press, 2004.

Bickenbach, Jerome. *Physical Disability and Social Policy*. Toronto: University of Toronto Press, 1993.

Bowe, Frank. *Handicapping America: Barriers to Disabled People*. New York: Harper & Row, 1978.

Budd, J.W. *The Thought of Work*. Ithaca, NY: ILR Press, 2011.

Carey, Allison. *On the Margins of Citizenship: Intellectual Disability and Civil Rights in Twentieth-Century America*. Philadelphia: Temple University Press, 2009.

Caulfield, Jon. *The Tiny Perfect Mayor: David Crombie and Toronto's Reform Aldermen*. Toronto: Lorimer, 1974.

Charlton, James. *Nothing About Us Without Us*. Berkeley: University of California Press, 1998.

Christie, Nancy, and Michael Gauvreau. *A Full-Orbed Christianity: The Protestant Churches and Social Welfare in Canada, 1900–1940*. Montreal: McGill-Queen's University Press, 1996.

Clement, Dominique. *Canada's Rights Revolution: Social Movements and Social Change, 1937–82*. Vancouver: UBC Press, 2008.

Doyle, Brian. *Disability, Discrimination and Equal Opportunities: A Comparative Study of the Employment Rights of Disabled Persons*. New York: Mansell. 1995.

Drake, Robert, Gary R. Bond, and Deborah R. Becker. *Individual Placement and Support: An Evidence-Based Approach to Supported Employment*. New York: Oxford University Press, 2012.

Driedger, Diane. *The Last Civil Rights Movement: Disabled People's International*. New York: St Martin's Press, 1989.

Durflinger, Serge. *Veterans with a Vision: Canada's War Blinded in Peace and War*. Vancouver: UBC Press, 2010.

Engel, David, and Frank Munger. *Rights of Inclusion: Law and Identity in the Life Stories of Americans with Disabilities*. Chicago: University of Chicago Press, 2003.

Enns, Ruth. *A Voice Unheard: The Latimer Case and People with Disabilities*. Blackpoint, NS: Fernwood Publishing, 1999.

Epp, Marlene, Franca Iacovetta, and Frances Swripa, eds. *Sisters or Strangers? Immigrant, Ethnic and Racialized Women in Canadian History*. Toronto: University of Toronto Press, 2004.

Finger, Anne. *Elegy for a Disease: A Personal and Cultural History of Polio*. New York: St Martin's Press, 2006.

Fleischer, Doris, and Frieda Zames. *The Disability Rights Movement: From Charity to Confrontation*. Philadelphia: Temple University Press, 2011.

Friedland, Judith *Restoring the Spirit: The Beginnings of Occupational Therapy in Canada, 1890–1930*. Montreal: McGill-Queen's University Press, 2011.

Gadacz, Rene. *Re-Thinking Dis-Ability: New Structures, New Relationships*. Edmonton: University of Alberta Press, 1994.

Garland-Thomson, Rosemarie. *Extraordinary Bodies: Figuring Physical Disability in American Culture and Literature*. New York: Columbia University Press, 1997.

Greenland, Cyril. *Vision Canada: The Unmet Needs of Blind Canadians*. Toronto: Canadian National Institute for the Blind, 1976.

Grimley Mason, Mary. *Working Against Odds: Stories of Disabled Women's Work Lives*. Boston: Northeastern University Press, 2004.

Gwyn, Richard. *The Northern Magus: Pierre Trudeau and Canadians*. Toronto: McClelland & Stewart, 1980.

Hagner, David, and Dale DiLeo, *Working Together: Workplace Culture, Supported Employment, and Persons with Disabilities*. Cambridge, MA: Brookline Books, 1993.

Haller, Beth. *Representing Disability in an Ableist World: Essays on Mass Media.* Louisville, KY: Advocado Press, 2010.

Herie, Euclid. *Journey to Independence: Blindness – The Canadian Story.* Toronto: Dundurn Press, 2005.

Heron, Craig. *The Canadian Labour Movement.* Toronto: Lorimer, 1996.

Johnson, Mary. *Make Them Go Away: Clint Eastwood, Christopher Reeve and the Case Against Disability Rights.* Louisville, KY: Advocado Press, 2003.

Kealey, Linda, ed. *A Not Unreasonable Claim: Women and Reform in Canada, 1880s–1920s.* Toronto: Women's Press, 1979.

Keshen, Jeffery, and Serge Durflinger. *War and Society in Post-Confederation Canada.* Toronto: Nelson, 2007.

Liachowitz, Claire. *Disability as a Social Construct: Legislative Roots.* Philadelphia: University of Pennsylvania Press, 1988.

Longmore, Paul. *Why I Burned My Book and Other Essays on Disability.* Philadelphia: Temple University Press, 2003.

Lord, John. *Impact: Changing the Way We View Disability: The History, Perspective, and Vision of the Independent Living Movement in Canada.* Ottawa: Creative Bound International, 2010.

Malhotra, Ravi, and Morgan Rowe. *Exploring Disability Identity and Disability Rights through Narratives.* London: Routledge, 2013.

Marx, Karl. *Capital: A Critique of Political Economy.* Harmondsworth, UK: Penguin, 1981.

Matheson, Neil. *Daddy Bent-Legs: The 40-Year-Old Musings of a Physically Disabled Man, Husband, and Father.* Winnipeg: WordAlive Press, 2009.

McCreath, Graeme. *The Politics of Blindness.* Vancouver: Granville Island Publishing, 2011.

McRuer, Robert. *Crip Theory: Cultural Signs of Queerness and Disability.* New York: New York University Press, 2006.

Metzler, Irina. *A Social History of Disability in the Middle Ages: Cultural Considerations of Physical Impairment.* London: Routledge, 2013.

Miller, Ian. *Our Glory and Our Grief: Torontonians and the Great War.* Toronto: University of Toronto Press, 2002.

Morton, Desmond. *When Your Number's Up: The Canadian Soldier in the First World War.* Toronto: Random House, 1993.

Morton, Desmond, and Glenn Wright. *Winning the Second Battle: Canadian Veterans and the Return to Civilian Life, 1915–1930.* Toronto: University of Toronto Press, 1987.

Murphy, Robert. *The Body Silent: The Different World of the Disabled.* London: W.W. Norton, 2001.

O'Reilly, Arthur. *The Right to Decent Work of Persons with Disabilities*. Geneva: International Labour Office, 2003.

Oliver, Michael. *The Politics of Disablement*. Basingstoke, UK: Macmillan, 1990.

Oliver, Michael, and Colin Barnes. *The New Politics of Disablement*. New York: Palgrave Macmillan, 2012.

Palmer, Bryan. *Canada's 1960s: The Ironies of Identity in a Rebellious Era*. Toronto: University of Toronto Press, 2009.

Panitch, Melanie. *Disability, Mothers, and Organization: Accidental Activists*. New York: Routledge, 2008.

Pearpoint, Jack. *From Behind the Piano: The Building of Judith Snow's Unique Circle of Friends*. Toronto: Inclusion Press, 1991.

Pelka, Fred. *The ABC-CLIO Companion to the Disability Rights Movement*. Santa Barbara, CA: ABC-CLIO, 1997.

Pelka, Fred. *What We Have Done: An Oral History of the Disability Rights Movement*. Cambridge, MA: University of Massachusetts Press, 2012.

Prince, Michael. *Absent Citizens: Disability Politics and Policy in Canada*. Toronto: University of Toronto Press, 2009.

Puttee, Alan, ed. *Federalism, Democracy and Disability Policy in Canada*. Montreal: Institute of Intergovernmental Relations, 2002.

Reaume, Geoffrey. *Lyndhurst: Canada's First Rehabilitation Centre for People with Spinal Cord Injuries, 1945–1998*. Montreal: McGill-Queen's University Press, 2007.

Reaume, Geoffrey. *Remembrance of Patients Past: Patient Life at the Toronto Hospital for the Insane, 1870–1940*. Toronto: University of Toronto Press, 2009.

Remmes, Harold. *A Consumer's Guide to Organizing the Handicapped*. Newton, MA: Massachusetts Council of Organizations of the Handicapped, 1976.

Roulstone, Alan. *Enabling Technology: Disabled People, Work, and New Technology*. Philadelphia: Open University Press, 1998.

Russell, Harold. *The Best Years of My Life*. Middlebury, VT: P.S. Eriksson, 1981.

Russell, Marta. *Beyond Ramps: Disability at the End of the Social Contract: A Warning from an Uppity Crip*. Monroe, ME: Common Courage Press, 1998.

Sangster, Joan. *Dreams of Equality: Women on the Canadian Left, 1920–1950*. Toronto: McClelland & Stewart, 1989.

Shakespeare, Tom. *Disability Rights and Wrongs*. New York: Routledge, 2006.

Slavishak, Edward. *Bodies of Work: Civic Display and Labor in Industrial Pittsburgh*. Durham, NC: Duke University Press, 2008.

Snyder, Sharon, and David Mitchell. *Cultural Locations of Disability*. Chicago: University of Chicago Press, 2006.

Splane, Richard. *Social Welfare in Ontario, 1791–1893: A Study of Public Welfare Administration*. Toronto: University of Toronto Press, 1965.

Stienstra, Deborah, and Aileen Wight-Felske, with Colleen Watters, eds. *Making Equality: History of Advocacy and Persons with Disabilities in Canada*. Concord, ON: Captus Press, 2003.

Stiker, Henry. *A History of Disability*. Ann Arbor: University of Michigan Press, 1999.

Struthers, James. *No Fault of Their Own: Unemployment and the Canadian Welfare State, 1914–1941*. Toronto: University of Toronto Press, 1983.

Thomson, Donna. *Four Walls of My Freedom*. Toronto: McArthur, 2010.

Tillotson, Shirley. *Contributing Citizens: Modern Charitable Fundraising and the Making of the Welfare State, 1920–66*. Vancouver: UBC Press, 2008.

Titchkosky, Tanya. *Disability, Self, and Society*. Toronto: University of Toronto Press, 2003.

Tremain, Shelley. *Foucault, Governmentality, and Critical Disability Theory*. Ann Arbor: University of Michigan Press, 2005.

Turnbull, Barbara. *Looking in the Mirror*. Ebook, StarDispatches. Toronto: Toronto Star, 1997.

Vance, Jonathan. *Death So Noble: Memory, Meaning, and the First World War*. Vancouver: UBC Press, 1997.

Welsh, Marion. *Tales from a Human Warehouse: A Book about People with Special Needs* Boston: Branden Press, 1982.

Zandy, Janet. *Hands: Physical Labor, Class, and Cultural Work*. New Brunswick, NJ: Rutgers University Press, 2004.

Articles

Ackerman, Bruce. "Foreword: Law in an Activist State." *Yale Law Journal* 92:7 (1983): 1083–128.

Acton, Norman. "Employment of Disabled Persons: Where Are We Going?" *International Labour Review* 120:1 (1981): 1–14.

Allen, Richard. "The Social Gospel and the Reform Tradition in Canada." *Canadian Historical Review* 49:4 (1968): 381–99.

Anonymous, "Hiring the Handicapped: Why More Companies Are Beginning to Look into It," *Management* (30 March 1981).

Anspach, Renée. "From Stigma to Identity Politics: Political Activism among the Physically Disabled and Former Mental Patients." *Social Science and Medicine, Part A Medical: Psychology and Medical Sociology* 13 (1979): 765–73.

Armstrong, Sarah. "Disability Advocacy in the Charter Era." *Journal of Law & Equality* 2:1 (Spring 2003): 33–91.

Bach, Michael. *Achieving Social and Economic Inclusion: From Segregation to "Employment First."* Law Reform and Public Policy Series. Toronto: Canadian Association for Community Living, 2001.

Barnartt, Sharon. "Social Movement Diffusion? The Case of Disability Protests in the US and Canada." *Disability Studies Quarterly* 28:1 (2008). Accessed 16 August 2013. http://dsq-sds.org/article/view/70/70.

Barnes, Colin. "A Working Social Model? Disability, Work and Disability Politics in the 21st Century." *Critical Social Policy* 20:4 (2000): 441–57.

Barnes, Colin, and Geof Mercer. "Disability, Work, and Welfare: Challenging the Social Exclusion of Disabled People." *Work, Employment & Society* 19:3 (2005): 527–45. Accessed 16 August 2013. doi: 10.1177/0950017005055669.

Baron, Ava, and Eileen Boris. "'The Body' as a Useful Category for Working-Class History." *Labor: Studies in Working-Class History of the Americas* 4:2 (2007): 23–43.

Blanchard, Lyse. "Rachelle Halpenny: A Woman First, an Athlete Second, and Way at the Other End of the Scale, Disabled." *Canadian Woman Studies* 4:3 (1983): 66–7.

Blanck, Peter. "Right to Live in the World: Disability Yesterday, Today, and Tomorrow: The Jacobus tenBroek Law Symposium." *Texas Journal on Civil Liberties & Civil Rights* 13 (2007): 367–401.

Burchardt, Tania. "Capabilities and Disability: the Capabilities Framework and the Social Model of Disability." *Disability & Society* 19:7 (2004): 735–51.

Campolieti, Michele, and John Lavis. "Disability Expenditures in Canada, 1970–1996: Trends, Reform Efforts and a Path for the Future." *Canadian Public Policy* 26:2 (2000): 241–64.

Carroll, William, and R.S. Ratner. "Old Unions and New Social Movements." *Labour/Le Travail* 35 (Spring 1995): 195–221.

Charmaz, Kathy. "The Body, Identity, and Self: Adapting to Impairment." *Sociological Quarterly* 36:4 (1995): 657–80.

Chouinard, Vera. "Women with Disabilities' Experience of Government Employment Assistance in Canada." *Disability and Rehabilitation* 32:2 (2010): 148–58.

Chouinard, Vera, and Valorie Crooks. "Negotiating Neoliberal Environments in British Columbia and Ontario, Canada: Restructuring of State-Voluntary Sector Relations and Disability Organizations' Struggles to Survive." *Environment & Planning* 26 (2008): 173–90.

Clarke, Nic. "'You Will Not Be Going To This War': The Rejected Volunteers of the First Contingent of the Canadian Expeditionary Force." *First World War Studies* 1:2 (2010): 161–83.

Crooks, Valerie. "Women's Experiences of Developing Musculoskeletal Diseases: Employment Challenges and Policy Recommendations." *Disability & Rehabilitation* 29:14 (2007): 1107–16.

Deal, Mark. "Disabled People's Attitudes toward Other Impairment Groups: A Hierarchy of Impairments." *Disability & Society* 18:7 (2003): 897–910.

DeJong, Gerben. "Independent Living: From Social Movement to Analytic Paradigm." *Archives of Physical and Medical Rehabilitation* 60 (1979): 435–46.

Dews, Peter. "Power and Subjectivity in Foucault." *New Left Review* 144 (1984): 72–95.

Dossa, Parin. "Creating Alternative and Demedicalized Spaces: Testimonial Narrative on Disability, Culture, and Racialization." *Journal of International Women's Studies* 9:3 (2008): 79–98.

Driedger, Michelle, Valorie Crooks, and David Bennett. "Engaging in the Disablement Process over Space and Time: Narratives of Persons with Multiple Sclerosis in Ottawa, Canada." *Canadian Geographer* 48:2 (2004): 119–36.

Galer, Dustin. "A Friend in Need or a Business Indeed: Disabled Bodies and Fraternalism in Victorian Ontario." *Labour/Le Travail* 66:1 (Fall 2010): 9–36.

Galer, Dustin. "Disabled Capitalists: Exploring the Intersections of Disability and Identity Formation in the World of Work." *Disability Studies Quarterly* 32:3 (2012). Accessed 16 August 2013. http://dsq-sds.org/article/view/3277/3122.

Galvin, R. "A Genealogy of the Disabled Identity in Relation to Work and Sexuality." *Disability & Society* 21:5 (2006): 499–512.

Gill, C.J. "Four Types of Integration in Disability Identity Development." *Journal of Vocational Rehabilitation* 9:1 (1997): 39–46.

Gilson, S.F., A. Tusler, and C.J. Gill. "Ethnographic Research in Disability Identity: Self-Determination and Community." *Journal of Vocational Rehabilitation* 9:1 (1997): 7–17.

Graefe, Peter, and Mario Levesque. "Accountability and Funding as Impediments to Social Policy Innovation: Lessons from the Labour Market Agreements for Persons with Disabilities." *Canadian Public Policy* 36:1 (2010): 45–62.

Hernandez, Brigida, et al. "Employer Attitudes toward Workers with Disabilities and Their ADA Employment Rights: A Literature Review." *Journal of Rehabilitation* 66:4 (2000): 4–16.

Howe, Brian. "The Evolution of Human Rights Policy in Ontario." *Canadian Journal of Political Science* 24:4 (1991): 798–802.

Hughes, Everett. "Dilemmas and Contradictions of Status." *American Journal of Sociology* 50:5 (1945): 353–9.

Hum, Derek, and Wayne Simpson. "Canadians with Disabilities and the Labour Market." *Canadian Public Policy* 22:3 (1996): 285–99.

Hutchison, Peggy, Alison Pedlar, John Lord, Peter Dunn, Mary McGeown, Andrew Taylor, and C. Vanditelli. "The Impact of Independent Living Resource Centres in Canada on People with Disabilities." *Canadian Journal of Rehabilitation* 10:2 (1997): 99–112.

Jackson, Robert. "Sports for the Physically Disabled: The 1976 Olympiad (Toronto)," *American Journal of Sports Medicine* 7:5 (1979): 293–6.

Jackson, Robert. "What Did We Learn from the Torontolympiad?" *Canadian Family Physician* 23 (1977): 586–9.

Jackson, Ed. "Metro Votes for Equal Opportunity but Refuses to Say Who's Equal." *Body Politic* (1 October 1980).

Kayfetz, Ben. "The Development of the Toronto Jewish Community." *Tradition* 13:1 (1972): 5–17.

Kelly, Christine. "Towards Renewed Descriptions of Canadian Disability Movements: Disability Activism Outside of the Non-Profit Sector." *Canadian Journal of Disability Studies* 2:1 (2013). Accessed 17 August 2013. http://cjds.uwaterloo.ca/index.php/cjds/article/view/68.

Kudlick, Catherine. "Disability History: Why We Need Another 'Other.'" *American Historical Review* 108:3 (2003): 763–93.

Lammam, Charles, Milagros Palacios, Feixue Ren, and Jason Clemens. "Comparing Public and Private Sector Compensation in Canada: Studies in Labour Markets." *Fraser Institute Bulletin* (December 2013).

Lepofsky, David. "The *Charter's* Guarantee of Equality to People with Disabilities: How Well Is It Working?" *Windsor Yearbook of Access to Justice* 16 (1998): 155–296.

Lepofsky, David. "The Long, Arduous Road to a Barrier-Free Ontario for People with Disabilities: The *Ontarians with Disabilities Act* – The First Chapter." *National Journal of Constitutional Law* 15 (2004): 125–333.

Lero, Donna, Carolyn Pletsch, and Margo Hilbrecht. "Introduction to the Special Issue on Disability and Work: Toward Re-conceptualizing the 'Burden' of Disability." *Disability Studies Quarterly* 32:3 (2012). Accessed 16 August 2013. http://dsq-sds.org/article/view/3275/3108.

Lock, Sarah, Lesley Jordan, Karen Bryan, and Jane Maxim. "Work after Stroke: Focusing on Barriers and Enablers." *Disability and Society* 20:1 (2005): 33–47.

Lynk, Michael, "Accommodating Disabilities in the Canadian Workplace." *Canadian Blind Monitor* (1999): 183.

Malhotra, Ravi. "The Duty to Accommodate Unionized Workers with Disabilities in Canada and the United States: A Counter-Hegemonic Approach." *Journal of Law & Equality* 2 (2003): 92–155.

Malhotra, Ravi. "The Legal Genealogy of the Duty to Accommodate American and Canadian Workers with Disabilities: A Comparative Perspective." *Washington University Journal of Law and Policy* 1 (2007). Accessed 17 August 2013. https://ssrn.com/404.cfm?404;http://ssrn.com:80/abstract=2195100.

Malhotra, Ravi. "The Politics of the Disability Rights Movements." *New Politics* 8:3 (Summer 2001). Accessed 17 August 2013. http://nova.wpunj.edu/newpolitics/issue31/malhot31.htm.

Malhotra, Ravi, and Morgan Bronwyn Reid Rowe. "Justice Gonthier and Disability Rights: The Case of Nova Scotia (Workers' Compensation Board) v. Martin." *Supreme Court Law Review* 56 (2012): 509–40.

Mank, D. "The Underachievement of Supported Employment: A Call for Reinvestment." *Journal of Disability Policy Studies* 5:2 (1994): 1–24.

Marwaha, Steven, and Sonia Johnson. "Schizophrenia and Employment." *Social Psychiatry and Psychiatric Epidemiology* 39:5 (2004): 337–49.

McClusky, Martha. "Reforming Insurance to Support Workers' Rights to Compensation." *American Journal of Industrial Medicine* 55 (2012): 545–59.

Michailakis, Dimitris. "Information and Communication Technologies and the Opportunities of Disabled Persons in the Swedish Labour Market." *Disability & Society* 16:4 (2001): 477–500.

Morton, Desmond. "Government Worker Unions: A Review Article." *Labour / Le Travail* 35 (Spring 1995): 297–307.

Obel, Camilla, and Roslyn Kerr. "Athlete First: A History of the Paralympic Movement." *Leisure Studies* 28:4 (2009): 497–500.

O'Brien, Ruth. "From a Doctor's to a Judge's Gaze: Epistemic Communities and the History of Disability Rights Policy in the Workplace." *Polity* 35:3 (2003): 325–46.

Odell, Tracy. "Not Your Average Childhood: Lived Experience of Children with Physical Disabilities Raised in Bloorview Hospital, Home and School from 1960 to 1989." *Disability & Society* 26:1 (2011): 49–63.

Oldman, Jonathan, et al. "A Case Report of the Conversion of Sheltered Employment to Evidence-Based Supported Employment in Canada." *Psychiatric Services* 56:11 (2005). doi: 10.1176/appi.ps.56.11.1436

Ott, Katherine. "Disability and the Practice of Public History: An Introduction." *Public Historian* 27:2 (2005): 9–24.

Peters, Susan. "Is There a Disability Culture? A Syncretisation of Three Possible Worldviews." *Disability & Society* 15:4 (2000): 583–601.

Priestly, Mark. "Constructions and Creations: Idealism, Materialism and Disability Theory." *Disability & Society* 13:1 (1998): 75–94.

Prince, Michael. "Canadian Disability Activism and Political Ideas: In and Between Neo-Liberalism and Social Liberalism." *Canadian Journal of*

Disability Studies 1:2 (2012). Accessed 17 August 2013. http://cjds
.uwaterloo.ca/index.php/cjds/article/view/16.

Rebick, Judy. "The Political Impact of the Charter." *Supreme Court Law Review* 29 (2005): 85–91.

Rodgers, Daniel. "Worlds of Reform." *OAH Magazine of History* 20:5 (2006): 49–54.

Rose, Sarah. "'Crippled' Hands: Disability and Labor in Working-Class History." *Labor: Studies in Working-Class History of the Americas* 2:1 (2005): 27–54.

Roulstone, Alan. "Disabling Pasts, Enabling Futures? How Does the Changing Nature of Capitalism Impact on the Disabled Worker and Jobseeker?" *Disability & Society* 17:6 (2002): 627–42.

Russell, Marta. "What Disability Civil Rights Cannot Do: Employment and Political Economy." *Disability & Society* 17:2 (2002): 117–35.

Russell, Marta, and Ravi Malhotra. "Capitalism and Disability." *Socialist Register* 38 (2002): 212.

Schultz, Vicki. "Life's Work." *Columbia Law Review* 100:7 (2000). https://ssrn
.com/404.cfm?404;http://ssrn.com:80/abstract=250512.

Scotch, Richard, and Kay Schriner. "Disability as Human Variation: Implications for Policy." *Annals of the American Academy of Political and Social Science* 549 (1997): 148–59.

Sealy, Patricia, and Paul Whitehead. "Forty Years of Deinstitutionalization of Psychiatric Services in Canada: An Empirical Assessment." *Canadian Journal of Psychiatry* 49:4 (2004): 249–57.

Sears, James. "The Able Disabled." *Journal of Rehabilitation* (March/April, 1975): 19–22.

Shakespeare, Tom. "Cultural Representation of Disabled People: Dustbins for Disavowal?" *Disability & Society* 9:3 (1994): 283–99.

Sheldon, Alison, Rannveig Traustadóttir, Peter Beresford, Kathy Boxall, and Mike Oliver. "Disability Rights and Wrongs?" *Disability & Society* 22:2 (2007): 209–32.

Silberman Abella, Rosalie. "A Generation of Human Rights: Looking Back tothe Future." *Osgoode Hall Law Journal* 36:3 (1998): 597–616.

Storey, Robert. "'Their Only Power Was Moral': The Injured Workers' Movement in Toronto, 1970–1985." *Histoire Sociale / Social History* 41:81 (2009): 99–131.

Storey, Robert. "Social Assistance or a Worker's Right: Workmen's Compensation and the Struggle of Injured Workers in Ontario, 1970–1985." *Studies in Political Economy* 78 (2006): 67–91.

Taylor, Sunny. "The Right Not to Work: Power and Disability." *Monthly Review* 55 (2004): 36–7.

Thornton, Patricia, and Neil Lunt, "Employment for Disabled People: Social Obligation or Individual Responsibility." *Social Policy Reports* 2. Toronto: York University Social Policy Research Unit, 1995.

Titchkosky, Tanya. "Governing Embodiment: Technologies of Constituting Citizens with Disabilities." *Canadian Journal of Sociology* 28:4 (2003): 517–42.

Tremblay, Mary, Audrey Campbell, and Geoffrey Hudson. "When Elevators Were for Pianos: An Oral History Account of the Civilian Experience of Using Wheelchairs in Canadian Society. The First Twenty-Five Years: 1945–1970." *Disability & Society* 20:2 (2005): 103–16.

Valentine, Fraser, and Jill Vickers. "Released from the Yoke of Paternalism and 'Charity': Citizenship and the Rights of Canadians with Disabilities." *International Journal of Canadian Studies* 14 (1996): 155–77.

Vash, Carolyn. "What's Behind Employer Resistance to Hiring Disabled!" *Accent on Living* (Fall 1973): 92.

Watson, Nick. "Well, I Know This Is Going to Sound Very Strange to You, but I Don't See Myself as a Disabled Person: Identity and Disability." *Disability & Society* 17:5 (2002): 509–27.

Watson, Nick, and Brian Woods. "No Wheelchairs Beyond This Point: A Historical Examination of Wheelchair Access in the Twentieth Century in Britain and America." *Social Policy & Society* 4:1 (2005): 97–105.

Webborn, A.D. "Fifty Years of Competitive Sport for Athletes with Disabilities: 1948–1998." *British Journal of Sports Medicine* 33:2 (1999): 138.

Weber, Mark. "The Americans with Disabilities Act and Employment: A Non-Retrospective." *Alabama Law Review* 52:1 (2000): 375–418.

Wehman, P., and J. Kregel. "At the Crossroads: Supported Employment a Decade Later." *Journal of the Association of Persons with Severe Handicaps* 20 (1995): 286–99.

Wilton, Robert, and Stephanie Schuer. "Towards Socio-Spatial Inclusion? Disabled People, Neoliberalism and the Contemporary Labour Market." *Area* 32:2 (2006): 186–95.

Wolfe, Barbara, and Robert Haveman. "Trends in the Prevalence of Work Disability From 1962 to 1984 and Their Correlates." *Milbank Quarterly* 68:1 (1990): 53–80.

Book Chapters

Abberley, Paul. "The Spectre at the Feast: Disabled People and Social Theory." In *The Disability Reader: Social Science Perspectives*, ed. Tom Shakespeare. London: Cassell, 1998.

Baynton, Douglas. "Disability and the Justification of Inequality in American History." In *The New Disability History: American Perspectives*, ed. Lauri Umansky and Paul Longmore. New York: New York University Press, 2000.

Cameron, David, and Fraser Valentine. "Comparing Policy-Making in Federal Systems: The Case of Disability Policy and Programs." In *Disability and Federalism: Comparing Different Approaches to Full Participation*, ed. David Cameron and Fraser Valentine. Montreal: Institute of Intergovernmental Relations, 2001.

Campbell, Fiona Kumari. "Legislating Disability: Negative Ontologies and the Government of Legal Identities." In *Foucault, Governmentality, and Critical Disability Theory*, ed. Shelley Tremain. Ann Arbor: University of Michigan Press, 2005.

Chivers, Sally. "Barrier by Barrier: The Canadian Disability Movement and the Fight for Equal Rights." In *Group Politics and Social Movements in Canada*, ed. Miriam Catherine Smith. Peterborough, ON: Broadview Press, 2008.

D'Aubin, April. "We Will Ride: A Showcase of CCD Advocacy Strategies in Support of Accessible Transportation." In *Making Equality: History of Advocacy and Persons with Disabilities in Canada*, ed. Deborah Stienstra and Aileen Wight-Felske with Colleen Watters. Concord, ON.: Captus Press, 2003.

Dolmage, Jay, and Cynthia Lewiecki-Wilson. "Refiguring Rhetorica: Linking Feminist Rhetoric and Disability Studies." In *Rhetorica in Motion: Feminist Rhetorical Methods & Methodologies*, ed. Eileen Schell and K.J. Rawson. Pittsburgh: University of Pittsburgh Press, 2010.

Hirsch, Karen. "From Colonization to Civil Rights: People with Disabilities and Gainful Employment." In *Employment, Disability, and the Americans with Disabilities Act: Issues in Law, Public Policy and Research*, ed. Peter Blanck. Evanston, IL: Northwestern University Press, 2000.

Hosek, Jennifer. "The Canadian National Security War on Queers and the Left." In *New World Coming: The Sixties and the Shaping of Global Consciousness*, ed. Karen Dubinsky. Toronto: Between the Lines, 2009.

Longmore, Paul. "Conspicuous Contribution and American Cultural Dilemmas: Telethon Rituals of Cleansing and Renewal." In *Rethinking Normalcy: A Disability Studies Reader*, ed. Tanya Titchkosky and Rod Michalko. Toronto: Canadian Scholars' Press, 2009.

Longmore, Paul, and Lauri Umansky. "Disability History: From the Margins to the Mainstream." In *The New Disability History: American Perspectives*, ed. Paul Longmore and Lauri Umansky. New York: New York University Press, 2001.

Morris, Ian. "Technology and Disabled People: A Global View." In *The Future of Work for Disabled People: Employment and the New Technology*, ed. American Foundation for the Blind. Washington, DC: President's Committee on Employment of the Handicapped,1986.

Morton, Desmond. "Supporting Soldiers' Families: Separation Allowance, Assigned Pay, and the Unexpected." In *Canada and the First World War: Essays in Honour of Robert Craig Brown*, ed. David Mackenzie. Toronto: University of Toronto Press, 2005.

Neufeldt, Aldred. "Growth and Evolution of Disability Advocacy in Canada." In *Making Equality: History of Advocacy and Persons with Disabilities in Canada*, ed. Deborah Stienstra and Aileen Wight-Felske with Colleen Watters. Concord, ON: Captus Press, 2003.

Oliver, Michael. "The Social Model in Context." In *Rethinking Normalcy: A Disability Studies Reader*, ed. Tanya Titchkosky and Rod Michalko. Toronto: Canadian Scholars' Press, 2009.

Overboe, Frank. "'Difference in Itself': Validating Disabled People's Lived Experience." In *Rethinking Normalcy: A Disability Studies Reader*, ed. Tanya Titchkosky and Rod Michalko. Toronto: Canadian Scholars' Press, 2009.

Peters, Susan. "From Charity to Equality: Canadians with Disabilities Take Their Rightful Place in Canada's Constitution." In *Making Equality: History of Advocacy and Persons with Disabilities in Canada*, ed. Deborah Stienstra and Aileen Wight-Felske with Colleen Watters. Concord, ON: Captus Press, 2003.

Peters, Susan. "The Politics of Disability Identity." In *Disability and Society: Emerging Issues and Insights*, ed. Len Barton. New York: Longman, 1996.

Prince, Michael. "Designing Disability Policy in Canada." In *Federalism, Democracy and Disability Policy in Canada*, ed. Alan Puttee. Montreal: Institute of Intergovernmental Relations, 2002.

Rayside, David, and Fraser Valentine. "Broadening the Labour Movement's Disability Agenda." In *Equity, Diversity, and Canadian Labour*, ed. Gerald Hunt and David Rayside. Toronto: University of Toronto Press, 2007.

Reaume, Geoffrey. "No Profits, Just a Pittance: Work, Compensation, and People Defined as Mentally Disabled in Ontario, 1964-1990." In *Mental Retardation in America*, ed. S. Noll and J. Trent. New York: New York University Press, 2004.

Reaume, Geoffrey. "Patients at Work: Insane Asylum Inmates' Labour in Ontario, 1841–1900." In *Rethinking Normalcy: A Disability Studies Reader*, ed. Tanya Titchkosky and Rod Michalko. Toronto: Canadian Scholars' Press, 2009.

Rioux, Marcia, and Michael Prince. "The Canadian Political Landscape of Disability: Policy Perspectives, Social Status, Interest Groups and the Rights

Movement." In *Federalism, Democracy and Disability Policy in Canada*, ed. Allan Puttee. Montreal: McGill-Queen's University Press, 2002.

Rioux, Marcia, and Fraser Valentine. "Does Theory Matter: Exploring the Nexus Between Disability, Human Rights, and Public Policy." In *Critical Disability Theory: Essays in Philosophy, Politics, Policy and Law*, ed. Diane Pothier and Robert Devlin. Vancouver: UBC Press, 2006.

Roulstone, Alan. "Employment Barriers and Inclusive Futures?" In *Disabling Barriers, Enabling Environments*, ed. John Swain, Sally French, Colin Barnes, and Carol Thomas. 2nd ed. London: Sage, 2004.

Snyder, Sharon, and David Mitchell. "Body Genres: An Anatomy of Disability in Film." In *The Problem Body: Projecting Disability on Film*, ed. Sally Chivers and Nicole Markotic. Columbus: Ohio State University Press, 2010.

Struthers, James. "Welfare to Workfare: Poverty and the 'Dependency Debate' in Post-Second World War Ontario." In *Ontario Since Confederation: A Reader*, ed. Edgar-Andre Montigny and Lori Chambers. Toronto: University of Toronto Press, 2000.

Tompa, Emile, et al. "Precarious Employment and People with Disabilities." In *Precarious Employment: Understanding Labour Market Insecurity in Canada*, ed. Leah Vosko. Montreal: McGill-Queen's University Press, 2006.

Tremblay, Mary. "Going Back to Main Street: The Development and Impact of Casualty Rehabilitation for Veterans with Disabilities, 1945–1948." In *The Veterans Charter and Post-World War II Canada*, ed. Peter Neary and J.L. Granatstein. Montreal: McGill-Queen's University Press, 1998.

Trudeau, Pierre Elliott. "The Values of a Just Society." In *Towards A Just Society: The Trudeau Years*, ed. Pierre Elliott Trudeau and Lloyd Axworthy. Toronto: Penguin, 1990.

White, Lynda. "The Private Sector and Disability." In *In Pursuit of Equal Participation: Canada and Disability at Home and Abroad*, ed. Aldred Neufeldt and Henry Enns. Concord, ON: Captus Press, 2003.

Wilton, Robert. "Working at the Margins: Disabled People in Precarious Employment." In *Critical Disability Theory*, ed. Robert Devlin and Diane Pothier. Vancouver: UBC Press, 2005.

Dissertations and Theses

Clarke, Nic. "Unwanted Warriors: The Rejected Volunteers of the Canadian Expeditionary Force." PhD diss., University of Ottawa, 2009.

Feigan, Mark. "The Victorian Office of the Public Advocate: A First History, 1986–2007." PhD diss., La Trobe University, 2001.

Garland-Thomson, Rosemarie. "Aberrant Bodies: Making the Corporeal Other in Nineteenth- and Twentieth-Century American Cultural Representations." PhD diss., Brandeis University, 1993.

Grimm, Robert. "Working with Handicaps: Americans with Disabilities, Goodwill Industries and Employment, 1920s–1970s." PhD diss., Indiana University, 2002.

Ignagni, Esther. "Disabled Young People, Support and the Dialogical Work of Accomplishing Citizenship." PhD diss., University of Toronto, 2011.

Joachim, M. Kaye. "Conflicts between the Accommodation of Disabled Workers and Seniority Rights." MA thesis, University of Toronto, 1997.

Lawrie, Paul. "'To Make the Negro Anew:' The African American Worker in the Progressive Imagination, 1896–1928." PhD diss., University of Toronto, 2011.

Migliore, Alberto. "Sheltered Workshops and Individual Employment: Perspectives of Consumers, Families, and Staff Members." PhD diss., Indiana University, 2006.

Milligan, Ian. "Rebel Youth: Young Workers, New Leftists, and Labour in English Canada, 1964–1973." PhD diss., York University, 2011.

Morris, Janalee. "Working for Equity: Issues of Employment for Youth with Disabilities." MA thesis, University of Manitoba, 2000.

Reaume, Geoffrey. "999 Queen Street West: Patient Life at the Toronto Hospital for the Insane, 1870–1940." PhD diss., University of Toronto, 1997.

Rose, Sarah. "No Right to Be Idle: The Invention of Disability, 1850–1930." PhD diss., University of Illinois at Chicago, 2008.

Sandys, Judith. "'It Does My Heart Good': The Perceptions of Employers Who Have Hired People with Intellectual Disabilities Through Supported Employment Programs." PhD diss., University of Toronto, 1993.

Weinkauf, Tim. "Employer Attitudes and the Employment of People with Disabilities: An Exploratory Study Using the Ambivalence Amplification Theory." PhD diss., University of Alberta, 2010.

Williams-Searle, John. "Broken Brothers and Soldiers of Capital: Disability, Manliness, and Safety on the Rails, 1863–1908." PhD diss., University of Iowa, 2004.

Wright, Paul. "The Status of Disabled Persons in Canada: A Historical Analysis of the Evolution of Social Policy to Develop Effective Change Strategies Directed toward Achieving Equality." MA thesis, Carleton University, 1990.

Index

Illustrations and Appendix table indicated by page numbers in italics.

Milton Keynes UK
Ingram Content Group UK Ltd.
UKHW011931190424
441406UK00002B/230